3/00
77E

Cyprus

WORLD BIBLIOGRAPHICAL SERIES

General Editors:
Robert L. Collison (Editor-in-chief)
Sheila R. Herstein
Louis J. Reith
Hans H. Wellisch

VOLUMES IN THE SERIES

1. *Yugoslavia*, John J. Horton
2. *Lebanon*, Shereen Khairallah
3. *Lesotho*, Shelagh M. Willet and David Ambrose
4. *Rhodesia/Zimbabwe*, Oliver B. Pollack and Karen Pollack
5. *Saudi Arabia*, Frank A. Clements
6. *USSR*, Anthony Thompson
7. *South Africa*, Reuben Musiker
8. *Malawi*, Robert B. Boeder
9. *Guatemala*, Woodman B. Franklin
11. *Uganda*, Robert L. Collison
12. *Malaysia*, Lim Huck Tee and Wong Sook Jean
13. *France*, Frances Chambers
14. *Panama*, Eleanor Langstaff
15. *Hungary*, Thomas Kabdebo
16. *USA*, Sheila R. Herstein and Naomi Robbins
17. *Greece*, Richard Clogg and Mary Jo Clogg
18. *New Zealand*, R. F. Grover
19. *Algeria*, Richard I. Lawless
21. *Belize*, Ralph Lee Woodward, Jr.
23. *Luxembourg*, Carlo Hury and Jul Christophory
24. *Swaziland*, Balam Nyeko
25. *Kenya*, Robert L. Collison
26. *India*, Brijen Gupta and Datta Kharbas
27. *Turkey*, Meral Güçlü
28. *Cyprus*, P. M. Kitromilides and M. L. Evriviades
29. *Oman*, Frank A. Clements
30. *Italy*, Emiliana P. Noether
31. *Finland*, J. E. O. Screen
32. *Poland*, Richard C. Lewanski
33. *Tunisia*, Richard I. Lawless, Allan M. Findlay and Anne M. Findlay
34. *Scotland*, Eric G. Grant
35. *China*, Peter Cheng

VOLUME 28

Cyprus

Paschalis M. Kitromilides
Marios L. Evriviades
Compilers

CLIO PRESS
OXFORD, ENGLAND · SANTA BARBARA, CALIFORNIA

© Copyright 1982 by Clio Press Ltd.

All rights reserved. No part of this publication may be reproduced, stored in any retrieval system, or transmitted in any form or by any means, electronic, mechanical, photocopying or otherwise, without the prior permission in writing of the publishers.

British Library Cataloguing in Publication Data
Kitromilides, Paschalis M.
Cyprus. – (World bibliographical series; 28)
1. Cyprus – Bibliography
I. Title II. Evriviades, Marios L.
III. Series
016.95645   Z2854.C/

ISBN 0-903450-40-2

Clio Press Ltd.,
Woodside House, Hinksey Hill,
Oxford OX1 5BE, England.
Providing the services of the European
Bibliographical Center

American Bibliographical Center-Clio Press,
Riviera Campus, 2040 Alameda Padre Serra,
Santa Barbara, Ca. 93103, U.S.A.

Designed by Bernard Crossland
Typeset by Berkshire Publishing Services
Printed in Great Britain
by the Camelot Press, Southampton

THE WORLD BIBLIOGRAPHICAL SERIES

This series will eventually cover every country in the world, each in a separate volume comprising annotated entries on works dealing with its history, geography, economy and politics; and with its people, their culture, customs, religion and social organization. Attention will also be paid to current living conditions — housing, education, newspapers, clothing, etc. — that all are too often ignored in standard bibliographies; and to those particular aspects relevant to individual countries. Each volume seeks to achieve, by use of careful selectivity and critical assessment of the literature, an expression of the country and an appreciation of its nature and national aspirations, to guide the reader towards an understanding of its importance. The keynote of the series is to provide, in a uniform format, an interpretation of each country that will express its culture, its place in the world, and the qualities and background that make it unique.

SERIES EDITORS

Robert L. Collison (Editor-in-chief) is Professor Emeritus, Library and Information Studies, University of California, Los Angeles, and is currently the President of the Society of Indexers. Following the war, he served as Reference Librarian for the City of Westminster and later became Librarian to the BBC. During his fifty years as a professional librarian in England and the USA, he has written more than twenty works on bibliography, librarianship, indexing and related subjects.

Sheila R. Herstein is Reference Librarian and Library Instruction Coordinator at the City College of the City University of New York. She has extensive bibliographic experience and recently described her innovations in the field of bibliographic instruction in 'Team teaching and bibliographic instruction', *The Bookmark*, Autumn 1979. In addition, Doctor Herstein co-authored a basic annotated bibliography in history for Funk & Wagnalls *New encyclopedia*, and for several years reviewed books for *Library Journal*.

Louis J. Reith is librarian with the Franciscan Institute, St. Bonaventure University, New York. He received his PhD from Stanford University, California, and later studied at Eberhard-Karls-Universität, Tübingen. In addition to his activities as a librarian, Dr. Reith is a specialist on 16th century German history and the Reformation and has published many articles and papers in both German and English. He was also editor of the *American Society for Reformation Research Newsletter*.

Hans H. Wellisch is Associate Professor at the College of Library and Information Services, University of Maryland, and a member of the American Society of Indexers and the International Federation for Documentation. He is the author of numerous articles and several books on indexing and abstracting, and has most recently published *Indexing and abstracting: an international bibliography*. He also contributes frequently to *Journal of the American Society for Information Science*, *Library Quarterly*, and *The Indexer*.

v

Contents

INTRODUCTION ix

THE COUNTRY AND ITS PEOPLE 1

GEOGRAPHY 5
    General 5   Maps 9
    Political 7

TRAVEL AND TOURISM 10
    Travellers' accounts 10   Tourism 13

FLORA AND FAUNA 17
    Flora 17   Fauna 18

PREHISTORY AND ARCHAEOLOGY 20

HISTORY 32
    General 32   Ottoman rule, 1571-1878 46
    Ancient Cyprus 35   British rule, 1878-1960 48
    Byzantine period 38   Cyprus Question, 1945-60 53
    Frankish and Venetian   Cyprus Republic 64
      periods 40

FOREIGN RELATIONS 70
    General 70   Cyprus Question, 1974- 78
    United Nations and   Congressional and
      Cyprus 74   parliamentary publications 86

ETHNIC GROUPS AND ETHNIC RELATIONS 93

LANGUAGES AND DIALECTS 99

RELIGION 101

Contents

SOCIAL CONDITIONS 105
    Labour 105   Social problems 106
    Welfare 105

SOCIETY AND SOCIAL CHANGE 108

LAW AND CONSTITUTION 112

ECONOMICS 117

TRADE AND INDUSTRY 120
    General 120   Cyprus and the EEC 122

AGRICULTURE 124

STATISTICS 127

EDUCATION 128

LITERATURE 131

THE ARTS 134
    General 134   Folklore 138
    Byzantine period 135

NUMISMATICS, PHILATELY AND HERALDRY 141

MUSEUM GUIDES 144

MASS MEDIA 146
    Dailies 146   Turkish Cypriot press 149
    Weeklies 147   Periodicals 150

DIRECTORIES 154

BIBLIOGRAPHIES 155
    General 155   Specialist 156

INDEX OF AUTHORS, TITLES AND SUBJECTS 159

MAP OF CYPRUS 195

Introduction

This volume presents a portrait of Cyprus through a survey of what has been written about the island. It has been compiled within the guidelines of the general series of which it forms a part. Briefly put, this bibliographical guide comprises primarily works in the English language, giving preference to recent editions and easily accessible sources that potential readers might wish to use after consulting the annotations of our volume. This is not an exhaustive research bibliography, but an orientation to available resources for an initial but substantial acquaintance with Cyprus.

An effort has been made, nevertheless, to make the structure and scope of the selections to some extent reflective of the range of scholarly research and the varieties of writing about Cyprus. Thus occasionally it has been judged relevant to include items which might appear esoteric to the nonspecialist but which are important milestones in mapping the terrain of Cypriot studies. In short the purpose of this bibliography is twofold: 1. to draw a profile of useful and readily available resources for everyone interested in an informed familiarization with Cyprus; 2. to provide a point of departure for scholars who would like to proceed from the material presented in the following pages to more specialized research projects in particular sectors of Cypriot studies. The aspiration of the volume is to make a modest contribution toward an international infrastructure of Cypriot studies.

Given both the editorial guidelines of the series and the state of research in different disciplines, some fields are inevitably more adequately covered than others. Archaeology, for instance, is represented by a broad range of entries since this area of Cypriot studies has witnessed in the past several decades a unique flowering using mostly English as its medium of expression. Literature, on the other hand, is represented by very few entries, suggesting how much still needs to be done in terms of translations, criticism and literary history before a better knowledge of the literature of Cyprus can be achieved by the international public. The same is true of a number of other sectors of

Introduction

the life and culture of the island. Thus the internal discrepancies of this volume in a way constitute a topography of research needs in the study of the civilization of Cyprus.

In introducing this collection a few words about Cypriot studies and Cypriot bibliography are in order. The foundation of systematic research concerned with the civilization of Cyprus owes its existence to the contribution of three distinct traditions of national scholarship. Each of these national schools of research and writing can be primarily differentiated from the rest by its language but also by its research priorities and interpretative emphases. These traditions of national scholarship are the Greek, the British and the French, all dating from the 19th century. The emergence and development of these traditions of learning contributed to the foundation of systematic research that brought the orientations of mainstream 19th century scholarship to bear on the exploration of Cyprus's life and civilization. At its inception, research on Cypriot topics was influenced by two major currents of 19th century scholarship. The first was that of historical positivism which aspired to the 'objective' reconstruction of the past through the critical edition of the sources. The most prominent representatives of this outlook were Ranke and his school in Germany, and the Ecole de Chartres in France. A distinguished member of the latter school, Louis de Mas Latrie, brought the spirit and methods of historical positivism to bear on the study of Cyprus's mediaeval past through his wide-ranging researches on the crusader kingdom of the Lusignans. He thus became the founder of analytical Cypriot historiography by means of his monumental publications of documentary collections and chronographical sources. He did not, however, proceed beyond historical criticism to the tasks of synthesis. Indeed, his attempt at a synthesis of the history of mediaeval Cyprus remained incomplete.

The second intellectual current that influenced the foundation of Cypriot studies was 19th century philological romanticism. This tradition had been initiated by the Grimm brothers, Schlegel, and Herder in Germany, while Madame de Staël, Raynouard, Fauriel and Thierry contributed in their diverse ways to its inauguration in France. For political and cultural reasons, romantic philology exercised a profound impact on the formative stages of Greek scholarship in the 19th century. It was thence transmitted to the study of Cypriot subjects by Athanasios Sakellarios, a mainland Greek scholar who served as a schoolmaster in Larnaca in the 1850s and became the founder of research on the Cypriot dialect and folklore. He placed his philological researches in the broader context of the study of the geography, history and social institutions of Cyprus. Methodologically he inaugurated the comparative treatment of

Introduction

ancient and modern linguistic and folklore materials in Cypriot studies. The attempt to connect modern culture with ancient tradition was an integral part of the intellectual temper of Greek romantic nationalism. Sakellarios's research priorities and methods were inherited by his Cypriot disciples, most notably by Georgios Louka who contributed a remarkable treatise in comparative philology tracing ancient Greek cultural survivals in modern Cypriot folklore. At the turn of the century Simos Menardos, a leading Greek linguist, incorporated the study of the Cypriot dialect into the mainstream of modern Greek linguistics. In his programme the comparative method, which traced similarities and stressed survivals from ancient Greek, also remained paramount.

In this manner the foundations of Cypriot studies in the major fields of the human sciences were laid while Cyprus was still under Ottoman rule. The one field that still lagged behind was archaeology. Up to the British occupation of 1878 archaeological research had been undertaken by amateurs like R. Hamilton Lang and most notably the Cesnola brothers in whose case profiteering was a major motive — with all the consequences for the integrity of Cyprus's archaeological heritage. The British occupation brought measures for the protection of the island's archaeological treasures and this created the preconditions of scientific archaeology. Cypriot archaeology was essentially founded in the 1880s by the German scholar Max Ohnefalsch-Richter who, in cooperation with John L. Myres, organized the first Cyprus Museum. These two scholars can be considered as the founding fathers of the scientific investigation of Cyprus's archaeological wealth. The pioneering phase which they inaugurated came to a close in 1927 with the arrival of the Swedish Cyprus Expedition. This was a major turning point which marked the beginning of modern Cypriot archaeology. Over the following decades the field was destined to become the most distinguished branch of Cypriot studies. A succession of Swedish scholars writing in English were joined by Cypriots and scholars of other nationalities in arousing international interest in the civilization of ancient Cyprus, especially by unearthing the splendour of the Cypriot Bronze Age.

The strides in archaeology left behind the other branches of learning which had emerged previously as serious sectors of research in Cypriot studies. While Cypriot archaeology became a genuinely international field and transcended the confines of particular national schools, the other sectors of Cypriot studies remained objects of research within the clearly delimited traditions of national scholarship. The development of each of these scholarly traditions was inextricably interwoven with the involvement of those nations concerned with the island's political fate. The Greek school, which was inaugurated as an integral part of Greek

Introduction

19th century historicism and folklorism, concentrated its attention on the Hellenic character of Cyprus's heritage. These intellectual orientations were motivated by the political aspirations of Greek nationalism which sought 'scientific' supports for its claims. Nationalism as a cultural system remained a potent force in the subsequent development of Greek writing on Cyprus. The focus of the French contribution on the crusader kingdom of Cyprus underlined the introduction of the institutions and culture of mediaeval French feudalism into the eastern Mediterranean island. An outgrowth of the national self-consciousness of 19th century French scholarship, these projects were clearly boosted by the aspirations of the Second Empire in the Near East.

The British occupation of Cyprus in 1878 inaugurated the most comprehensive tradition of research and writing. An outpouring of books describing life in the new possession and its significance to the British Empire followed immediately upon the occupation. Through these sources one can glean a valuable picture of the island at the threshold of its first prolonged exposure to the influence of Western civilization. Not least of these influences was the introduction of printing in the year of the British occupation. The bibliographical significance of this development does not need to be underlined: the Cypriots as a people were given the medium to express themselves about their homeland and their problems. Moreover printing was used quite effectively from the outset in discharging the tasks of government. The administration's needs and British empiricism combined in producing valuable information in every field. The British first of all produced a priceless corpus of official sources, ranging from the introduction of decennial censuses beginning in 1881 to repeated codifications of the island's laws, statistical reports in all sectors of economic activity, and collections of documents on the island's perennial political problems. Furthermore, the British administration gave rise to a remarkable generation of scholars who became the founding fathers of systematic research in a number of sectors of Cypriot studies.

Thus Claude Delaval Cobham's researches entitle him to be recognized as the father of Cypriot bibliography. Indeed he was the first scholar to systematically attempt to expand the range of sources pertinent to the island's mediaeval and modern history and to codify his findings in bibliographical compendia. Most notably, however, Cypriot studies owe to British scholarship the monumental reconstruction of the history of the Church of Cyprus, from the introduction of Christianity in AD 45 to the dawn of the 20th century, by the Anglican clergyman John Hackett. This work remains authoritative and unsurpassed to the present day.

Introduction

British scholarship has been responsible as well for the first attempt at a general synthesis of the history of Cyprus in the four-volume work of the numismatist and director of the British Museum, Sir George Hill. At the close of half a century of British rule and at a time when the political future of Cyprus appeared to be entering a phase of intense contestation, Hill's history attempted to present a general characterization of the historical destinies of the island, drawing on the evidence of a century of Cypriot studies. Although the biases of the work in tone, emphasis and interpretation are too obvious to conceal its political motives, its value as a general history of Cyprus cannot be underestimated. Its sections on ancient Cyprus, especially Cypriot prehistory, have long been outdated by the advances in archaeological research, while its treatment of the Byzantine, Ottoman and British periods is apparently inadequate. In addition it ignores the social and cultural traditions, and shows scant appreciation for the indigenous civilization of the island. It does utilize, however, all evidence available at the time of writing, and where the evidence was nearly complete, as in the case of the mediaeval kingdom of Cyprus, its treatment has stood the test of time. Its value can most be appreciated in view of the disorganized state of knowledge concerning other regions of the Mediterranean world for which similar historical syntheses are lacking. By comparison, Hill's contribution to Cypriot studies provides a responsible chart of the terrain of a whole field of research and thus helps identify future priorities. As such it is a fine product of British empiricism, and sets the standard of all attempts in Cypriot historiography.

By its very nature, structure and editorial constraints, this volume gives special prominence to the British tradition. In order to avoid becoming trapped in some of the in-built biases of this school, especially in such controversial fields as history and politics where the British had their own interests and outlook to project and defend, the annotations, besides appraising the distinct contribution of each item to knowledge, attempt to bring a critical perspective to bear on this literature. The critical presentation of course does not intend to diminish the value of this tradition or of particular contributions within it. It is conceived, however, as a corrective on British attitudes toward what they perceived as another colonial culture — a bias which would otherwise colour the tone of this volume.

British rule has had a powerful impact on Cypriot bibliography in yet another aspect. The heritage of close ties with British culture and the massive pursuit of higher education by Cypriots in Britain and other English-speaking countries has put its imprint on the wide use of English as a written language in Cyprus. This aspect of Cypriot culture is reflected

Introduction

ted in the great number of books written by Cypriots, and published locally or abroad, in English. Cypriot bibliography thus enjoys a significant benefit in that such material provides an outlet, readily accessible to a wide international public, for the articulation of the Cypriots' own views on issues concerning their homeland. The English-language literature of Cypriot origin therefore can be seen as a balance to the problem of in-built biases which has been noted in connection with the British school of Cypriot bibliography. For this reason in the present collection a special effort has been made to represent as much as possible of the locally published English-language material.

It must be stressed, nevertheless, that the seminal contribution of Greek writing is indispensable for the understanding of the collective personality of Cyprus. The reader should be warned that no serious research into the civilization and history of Cyprus can ignore the writing of scholars in this tradition over several generations. The tradition provides a medium for an empathetic understanding of a whole civilization and of the ways through which a people and a culture have developed their modes of self-conception. A few outstanding sources from this tradition, especially in cases lacking a comparable contribution in English, have been included here.

The spirit of the Greek scholarly tradition has found expression in collective efforts to create an institutional structure for the systematic cultivation of research on Cyprus. The most remarkable among the pioneering initiatives in this direction was the publication of the journal *Kypriaka Chronika* (Cypriot Annals) by a group of Cypriot scholars based in Larnaca in the years 1922-37. The volumes of this journal contain a wealth of primary sources on the history and folklore tradition of the island. In this context as well are found the beginnings of research on the life of Cyprus under Ottoman rule, a period which had been overlooked in Mas Latrie's investigations. The study of this period posed to the Cypriot historical mind the question of the survival of Hellenism in the island under the tribulations of Ottoman rule. In considering this problem, Cypriot historians came to appreciate the significance of the intellectual basis of the phenomenon of ethnological continuity. Thus were produced in 1930, under the aegis of a competition sponsored by the Church of Cyprus, the two remarkable histories of the tradition of Greek letters in Cyprus under Ottoman rule by Loizos Philippou and Ieronymos Peristianis.

A firmer and better organized basis for the continuation of this tradition of research was created with the establishment of the Society of Cypriot Studies in 1937. Since that year the society has been annually producing *Kypriakai Spoudai* (Cypriot Studies), a volume of

Introduction

authoritative scholarly papers on all aspects of the civilization of Cyprus, from antiquity to the 20th century, with emphasis in the areas of history, language and folklore. *Kypriakai Spoudai* now forms an imposing series of over forty volumes which include many contributions in English. In addition to its scholarly bulletin the Society of Cypriot Studies has sponsored a series of independent scholarly publications dealing with different aspects of Cypriot history and folk culture. The society has also instituted the periodical convocation of the International Congress of Cypriot Studies, of which the first was held in 1969. This initiative has created an international forum for the promotion of Cypriot studies in all fields of knowledge.

With the establishment of the Cyprus Research Centre under the republic, the tradition of indigenous research has been placed on a new organizational and methodological basis. With its monumental annual volumes of major research papers and bibliographical documentation appearing as its *Epeteris* (Annual) since 1967 and with the imposing volumes of its two series of publications, *Texts and Studies of the History of Cyprus* and *Publications of the Cyprus Research Centre,* this institution has attained a level of scholarship equal in quality to that of the leading international organizations of its kind. The English-language publications of the centre are included here, but an acquaintance with its work as a whole is a necessary point of departure for any research project concerned with mediaeval or modern Cyprus that aspires to be authoritative.

A weaker strain of Turkish writing has been belatedly added to the other schools of national writing in the mid-20th century. Its significance lies in its attempts to argue the Turkish case on the Cyprus Question. It cannot be claimed, however, that this latter-day tradition has made a contribution to our knowledge comparable to those of the British, French or Greek schools. A few works in Western languages from this tradition will be found in the following pages as specimens of the articulation of the Turkish point of view.

A few specifics concerning the selection and organization of the material in this volume must be given at the outset. After the presentation of the standard general sources about Cyprus and its people (including many beautiful picture-books) in the opening section, a general survey of the natural environment brings together sources dealing with the geology, geography, climate, vegetation and fauna of the island. A selection of available maps has been included in this section. It is hoped to provide in this way a general idea of the natural conditions of human life in an island where, according to Fernand Braudel, geography has weighed decisively in shaping collective destinies.

Introduction

One of the greatest challenges encountered in compiling the bibliography was presented by the field of archaeology. Material is so rich and extensive that a number of choices had to be made. First all periodical articles had to be excluded to reduce the available material to manageable proportions. It was assumed that the general reader is unlikely to be interested in the specialized nature of this material, while the specialist would know where to look. Furthermore, periodical literature is adequately represented in the bibliographies of the books included in our selections. In covering the field of archaeology, therefore, two objectives were set in selecting the material: first, an attempt was made to give an idea of the history of the field by citing some pioneering older sources from the pre-1927 period; secondly, the development and state of the discipline through to 1980 has been outlined by means of a comprehensive presentation of selected major publications, giving preference to more general books rather than highly specialized monographs.

In presenting the field of history we have followed the well-established periodization in broad historical epochs broken down by reference to the foreign conquests of the island. History is conceived in its broadest sense, as the history of civilization. Accordingly, each subdivision includes not only sources on political history but also on the economy and social structure, art and intellectual life of the pertinent period. Thus it is hoped to present a global picture of the life and civilization of Cyprus as they were affected by changing political fortunes.

Cyprus's contemporary history is broken down into the two broad phases which mark the unfolding of the Cyprus Question and which flank the political history of the Cyprus Republic in the years 1960-74. Politics during Cyprus's unitary statehood were essentially an intervening phase of the Cyprus Question and therefore material pertaining to its political evolution in that period is included in the history section. The first phase of the Cyprus Question (1945-60) was marked by the internationalization of the Cypriots' demand for self-determination that prepared the way for independence. This period has a unity of its own in that it historically might be described as the very last phase of the erstwhile Eastern Question. The international and domestic problems that the 1959 settlement bequeathed to the Cyprus Republic constituted the roots of subsequent developments that have recast the Cyprus Question into an issue of contemporary power politics and have turned it into a regional manifestation of the world-wide confrontation of imperial systems. The accession of Cyprus to political independence was an event of major historical significance. It marked essentially the first time since antiquity that the Cypriots themselves assumed respon-

Introduction

sibility for handling their destiny. The major turning point in this pattern of political evolution has been the tragedy of 1974 which, besides opening a new explosive phase of the Cyprus Question, represents a drastic break in the history of Cypriot civilization, due to the Turkish invasion and occupation of northern Cyprus, the violent uprooting of one third of the population from their age-old hearths, and the attempted destruction of the cultural and historical character of the region.

The fundamentally political nature of a significant part of Cypriot bibliography has made this project particularly appealing to the political scientist. The ubiquity of the political is strikingly evident in one field after another, offering many hints for further explorations in the sociology of knowledge and in the study of ideology. Moreover, since the compilers are both political scientists by training, special attention has been paid to the presentation, in the relevant sections of the volume, of a professionally useful guide to research directions and resources on the Cyprus Question. This aspect of Cypriot bibliography is one of those most likely to interest a broad international public. It calls therefore for responsible critical presentation in order to sift out the voluminous ephemeral writing that has appeared on the subject and to retain books and important scholarly articles which have a substantial contribution to make to our knowledge of the problem.

Another issue that has to be noted in connection with the structure of the bibliography concerns the sections covering aspects of the collective life of Cypriot society in which the presence of the government as a producer of source material has been particularly pronounced. As must be obvious, far more is available than is presented here. English has long been established as the language of the government and civil service and, though not an official language under the republic after 1960, it has retained its role as the medium of communication between the two communities of Cyprus. Thus most publications of the different ministries and government departments have continued to appear in English. In the different sectors of economic life, in statistics, agriculture, geology, forestry, law and justice, health and labour the agencies of the Cyprus government have been producing information of outstanding quality in English. In surveying the pertinent material for the purposes of this volume our concern has been not with the collection of adequate material but with the exercise of the proper choices in listing titles that are both essential and representative of the broad range of available sources. The delimitation of these fields has been largely dictated by the necessity to avoid turning this bibliography into a compendium of government publications.

Introduction

In conclusion, a word is called for about Cypriot bibliography. Apart from a few specialized bibliographies, our section on bibliography includes only three items of a general nature. This number exhausts available material and is indicative of how much still needs to be done in order to construct the essential bibliographical infrastructure of Cypriot studies with even elementary adequacy. From the three available sources of bibliographical documentation, Cobham's pioneering compilation (sixth definitive edition, 1929) is valuable as a point of departure and particularly interesting for alerting the researcher to little-known sources including the writings of many mediaeval and modern travellers. Cobham's and later Jeffrey's specifications and additions make this a bibliographically reliable source, but it remains quite incomplete in that it ignores most of the Greek sources, especially material pertaining to the cultural tradition of Cyprus. The reverse is the case with the bibliography of N. Kyriazis (1935). Although it came close to being a complete record of works published up to that time and replaces Cobham's simple alphabetical listing of authors with a basic thematic classification, it is scarcely a methodical bibliography. In the technical presentation of the items it suffers from many imperfections and inaccuracies. It does remedy, however, the basic defect of the Cobham-Jeffrey bibliography in covering comprehensively the Greek sources.

The thirty years following the publication of the Kyriazis compilation represent a period of an enormous expansion in Cypriot bibliography. This output registered to a significant degree the escalation of the Cyprus Question and the beginnings of the process of social and economic change. All this material has remained entirely unrecorded and uncodified. From 1967 onwards, however, the Cyprus Research Centre (CRC) has been compiling its own systematically organized bibliographical compendia which record Cypriot bibliography on an annual basis beginning with the year 1965. Although foreign publications often escape the attention of the CRC bibliographers, their coverage is practically complete as far as works published in Cyprus are concerned. Indeed one occasionally has the impression that more discriminating judgement might be desirable in recording items from the daily press or in citing books with one or just a few entries concerning Cyprus in their index. In any event, all this suggests that the range of the CRC bibliographies is quite comprehensive and almost exhaustive. What is even more important, their bibliographical data is complete and reliable. It appears therefore that with the publication of the CRC compendia Cypriot bibliography has finally been placed on a systematic basis of recording and codification. It remains to work retrospectively in order to produce first a systematic and comprehensive bibliography

Introduction

of the thirty critical years 1935-64 and secondly to update, correct and complete the bibliographical work that has been done for the years prior to 1935. The first of these projects is the most urgent. It will surely be an arduous task but it can begin safely with a perusal of the records of the British Library which, as the copyright library of the British Empire, is the only repository of all publications produced in Cyprus in the eighty years of British rule. It also houses almost complete collections of other Cyprus-oriented materials.

In the context of the foregoing desiderata of Cypriot bibliography the contribution of this volume might be modest but, hopefully, useful. Regarding the pre-1935 material, it does provide the technically acceptable bibliographical documentation that is wanting in the older sources. In connection with the thirty-year gap, our collection constitutes a first kernel of the material (even if primarily in only one of the major languages of Cypriot bibliography) that is necessary to close this gap. It is to be hoped that the future bibliographer of this period will find in our material a starting point. Our collection forms, as it were, a bridge between the older bibliographies and the massive documentation of the CRC bibliography. With reference to the latter we might note that the two projects fulfill complementary roles: whereas the CRC bibliographies purport to be exhaustive by codifying indiscriminately all available raw material in order to place it at the disposal of the scholar of Cypriot topics, ours attempts to be critical and thus to provide a structured guide — rather than mere raw material — to the aspiring student of Cyprus.

Acknowledgements

The major part of the research for this volume has been carried out in Widener Library, Harvard University, at the Gennadeion Library in Athens, the Cyprus Museum library and the Public Information Office library in Nicosia. The resources of the Library of Congress have been useful throughout in identifying and verifying material. It is to be regretted that the specialized collection on Cyprus of the Phaneromeni Library in Nicosia, a veritable mine of valuable material, remains to this day inaccessible to the researcher due to its transfer to safety outside the city following the Turkish invasion.

The compilation of even a select bibliography like this one has proved a more arduous task than initially anticipated. In carrying it out, therefore, the compiler originally charged by the publisher with the task has had to rely on the assistance and kindness of many people. The primary debt of course is owed to the fellow compiler Marios L. Evriviades who brought his broad knowledge of Cyprus's political problems to the

Introduction

composition of the volume. Many other good people, especially in Cyprus, have helped with the collection and verification of the material presented in the following pages. Among them I would like to single out Eleni Dimitriou and Andreas Sophocleous for their substantial help. Miltos C. Mildiadou in Washington has also been helpful with the research for the volume. Finally, as it has always been the case with my scholarly ventures, Magda Kitromilides has been untiring in rendering her assistance.

Paschalis M. Kitromilides

The Country and Its People

1 **Cyprus: a portrait and an appreciation.**
Harry Luke. London: George G. Harrap, 1957. Reprinted, 1965. 190p.
A sympathetic appraisal of the life, history and cultural tradition of Cyprus by a British scholar and colonial administrator intimately familiar with the Middle East. However, the concluding chapter, which deals with the national aspirations of the Cypriots, betrays a total lack of will to concede to the subject people the sacred rights cherished in the liberal culture of the metropolis.

2 **Cyprus: then and now.**
Gordon Home, preface by Lord Harding of Petherton. London: J. M. Dent & Sons, 1960. xii + 243p. bibliog. illus. gloss.
A readable and compact volume published on the eve of Cyprus's independence, it surveys Cyprus's history and elaborates on points of interest (towns, monasteries, etc.). Its descriptive accounts are illustrated by seventy superb line drawings by the author. Chapter 14 dealing with the EOKA revolt (1955-59) is written by Viola Bayley. It includes a glossary and chronology.

3 **Cyprus: the country and its people.**
Celia Henderson. London: Queen Anne Press, 1968. 105p. map. illus. (The World Today).
A well-written and handy little book for the tourist and traveller, but dated with regard to recent political developments.

4 **Greece, Cyprus, Mount Athos.**
New York: Greystone Press, 1964. 216p. maps. illus. (The World and Its People).
Cyprus is covered on p. 195-216. An illustrated survey intended for the general reader, it contains descriptions of the island's physical, human, and economic geography as well as brief historical essays on the cultural and sociological history of the islanders. An introductory essay describes the political and constitutional institutions of the republic set up after Cyprus's independence from Great Britain.

The Country and Its People

5 **Cyprus.**
 H. D. Purcell. New York: Frederick A. Praeger, 1969. 402p. maps. bibliog. illus. (Nations of the Modern World).

The greater part of this work, written by a former British intelligence officer familiar with Cyprus, is devoted to the country's long history. The material on the post-independence period can be useful to the researcher. Of particular interest is the information on the internal politics of the Turkish Cypriots during the 1960s. A general introductory chapter offers an acquaintance with modern Cyprus.

6 **Chypre d'aujourd'hui.** (Today's Cyprus.)
 Marina Sacopoulo. Paris: Maisonneuve et Larose, 1966. 406p. 2 maps. 22 plates.

A guide to contemporary Cyprus in historical perspective. It provides a survey of the cities, villages, mountains, forests and plains of Cyprus, with frequent digressions into the past which is ever present in the author's sense of Cypriot reality.

7 **Cyprus: a handbook on the island's past and present.**
 Nicosia: Greek Communal Chamber, 1964. rev. ed. 307p. illus.

An illustrated handbook comprehensively surveying various aspects of the history, modern life and culture of Cyprus, stressing the prevailing Hellenic character of the island. Originally published under the title *The Greek heritage of Cyprus* (Nicosia, 1963).

8 **Cyprus: a country study.**
 Edited and introduced by Frederica M. Bunge. Washington, DC: US Government Printing Office, 1980. 3rd ed. xxi + 306p. maps. bibliog. tables. illus. gloss. (Foreign Area Studies. American University/Department of the Army, Area Handbook Program).

Designed primarily for the use of US officials — diplomats, army personnel and others — this work disclaims that its contents represent the official view of the United States. However, sufficient caution is exercised, especially in the terminology employed, not to contradict or criticize that view. Its five chapters are by different contributors: 1. 'Historical setting', by Eugene K. Keefe; 2. 'The society and its environment', by J. Jeffrey Hoover; 3. 'The economy', by Donald P. Whitaker; 4. 'Government and politics', by Margarita Dokert; 5. 'National security', by James D. Rudolf. This work supersedes the two earlier editions by Eugene K. Keefe and others (1971) and T. W. Adams and others (1964). For comparative purposes the interested reader may wish to consult all three.

9 **Portrait of Cyprus.**
 Reno Wideson, introduction by Lawrence Durrell. The Hague: Deppo Holland [n.d.]. illus.

The Country and Its People

10 Cyprus in pictures.
Reno Wideson, introduction by Andrew Wright. London: McGibbon & Kee, 1953. 180p. illus.

The black-and-white photography in this and the preceding item captures superbly the people, land and beauty of Cyprus.

11 Picture book of Cyprus.
Arranged and edited by K. Rustem, introduction by Hugh Foot. Nicosia: K. Rustem & Brother, 1959. illus.

Contains 185 black-and-white photographs of rural and urban Cyprus on the eve of independence.

12 Cyprus: island of Aphrodite.
George Lanitis, foreword by Dilys Powell, introduction by A. Christophides. Nicosia, 1965. 128p. illus.

Acquaints the reader with Cyprus through the eyes of a leading native master of the art of photography. It illustrates the place, the people and the cultural tradition of the island through the beautiful photographs.

13 Cyprus the sweet land.
Patroclos Stavrou, artistic supervision by A. Tassos. Nicosia: Achilles Ghinis Publications [n.d.]. 159p. illus.

A lavishly illustrated introduction to the charms of Cyprus. It surveys in pictures the historical heritage and artistic treasures of the island, from neolithic to Byzantine times, its tourist attractions and folk art.

14 Nicosia: capital of Cyprus then and now.
Kevork K. Keshishian. Nicosia, 1978. 262p. illus.

A richly illustrated guidebook on the city's past and present, full of many useful and interesting details. The presentation of the material is a little unsystematic, but the reader will enjoy the many rare pictures and other illustrations.

15 Kyrenia: a historical study.
Rina Katselli. Kyrenia, Cyprus: Kyrenia Flower Show Edition, 1974. 140p. bibliog. illus.

An illustrated overview of human life and history in Kyrenia from ancient times to the Second World War.

The Country and Its People

16 **Paphos.**
Loizos Philippou. Nicosia: Zavallis Press, 1948. 2nd ed. 92p. bibliog. app.

Originally published in 1936 and intended as a tourist guide to 'the most attractive district of Cyprus', this is in fact a historical topography of the city of Paphos (Ktima) and the district of which it is the capital. The work of one of the foremost scholars of 20th century Cyprus, it contains reliable information on the ancient and mediaeval monuments of the area, the major points of interest and the monasteries of the district. It includes an appendix listing the district's 135 villages.

17 **Karavas.**
Edited by Andreas Stylianou, Kalliope Harmanta. Karavas, Cyprus: Athletic Union of Karavas, 1969. 229p. folding map. illus.

A bilingual (Greek and English) illustrated edition surveying the life, history, artistic heritage and natural surroundings of the two charming communities of Lapithos and Karavas on the northern coast of Cyprus. The section on 'The treasures of Lambousa' by A. and J. Stylianou (p. 45-111) is available in a separate reprint.

18 **Invitation.**
John Aristides, Athanasios Papadopoulos. Kakopetria, Cyprus, 1977. 80p. folding map. illus.

A richly illustrated description of the historical heritage, topography and traditional ways of life in one of Cyprus's most beautiful and best-preserved villages. It includes chapters on the development of Kakopetria into a leading tourist centre and on the important old painted churches of the region. An indispensable companion to every visitor of the area.

Geography

General

19   **A synopsis of the stratigraphy and geological history of Cyprus.**
  F. R. S. Henson, R. V. Browne, J. McGinty. *Quarterly Journal of the Geological Society of London,* vol. 105 (19 Nov. 1949), p. 1-49. bibliog.
This is the basic source on the geological past of Cyprus.

20   **The seismic history of Cyprus.**
  N. N. Ambrazeys. London [1967?]. 26p.
A brief survey of the history of earthquakes in Cyprus, beginning in 1500 BC and focusing on the period 180 BC to AD 1900 on the basis of the evidence of historical sources.

21   **An outline of the geology and geomorphology of Cyprus.**
  Th. M. Pantazis. *Geographical Chronicles,* vol. 1, no. 1 (Jan. 1971), p. 5-20.
An account of the geological evolution and geomorphological characteristics of the three major geological regions of Cyprus — the Troodos mountain range, the Kyrenia mountain range and the Mesaoria plain — over 100 million years of geological time.

22   **Some relationships between geology and topography in Cyprus.**
  David J. Burdon. Nicosia: Geographical Association of Cyprus, 1951. 15p. bibliog.
A concise examination of the impact of geological factors on the topography of Cyprus.

23   **Rocks and scenery in the Kyrenia region.**
  William Dreghorn. Nicosia, 1971. 99p. illus.
Examines the Kyrenia coastline, the geology of the region of terraces between the coast and the mountains, the Kyrenia mountain range, and the Panagra gorge, and points out the geological curiosities of the region. Illustrated with drawings.

Geography. General

24 The geology of the Bellapais-Kythrea area of the central Kyrenia range.
Charles Ducloz. Nicosia: Ministry of Agriculture and Natural Resources, Geological Department, 1972. 75p. folding map. bibliog. illus.

A total area of about thirty-seven square miles in the Kyrenia range in northern Cyprus is described in great geological detail. An excellent bibliography on the geology of Cyprus is included.

25 A geographical approach to the Krasokhoria.
Pierre-Yves Péchoux. *Geographical Chronicles,* vol. 4, no. 7-8 (Jan.-Dec. 1975), p. 88-94.

A brief but useful consideration of the natural and human geography of the cluster of wine-producing villages in the highland regions of Limassol district.

26 Morphology and relief of Kissonerga village area of Paphos district, Cyprus.
A. Cl. Sophocleous. *Geographical Chronicles,* vol. 8, no. 13 (Jan.-June 1978), p. 48-62.

An account of the physical characteristics of the area of Kissonerga north of Paphos on the western coast of Cyprus.

27 A geographical study of Lapithos area, Cyprus.
Panayiotis Argyrides. *Geographical Chronicles,* vol. 9-10, no. 16-17 (July 1979-June 1980), p. 3-37.

A global study of the geology and physical, human and economic geography of the Lapithos region on the northern coast of Cyprus.

28 Geographical aspects of development of tourism in Cyprus.
Günter Heinritz. *Geographical Chronicles,* vol. 2, no. 4 (Jan. 1973), p. 69-75.

Discusses the geographical factors in the development of the tourist industry in Cyprus.

29 Survey of groundwater and mineral resources: Cyprus.
United Nations Development Program. New York: United Nations, 1970. iii + 19p. tables, figs. charts. (DP/SF/UN/50).

Geography. Political

30 **Survey of groundwater and mineral resources: Cyprus.**
United Nations Development Program. New York: United
Nations, 1970. iii + 229p. maps. bibliog. plates. tables.
(DP/SF/UN/50 — Technical Report).

In 1962 the government of Cyprus requested the United Nations Special Fund, now the United Nations Development Program, to undertake a survey of groundwater and mineral resources in Cyprus. The project was completed in 1969. The first of the works cited (see the preceding entry) reports on the project results, conclusions and recommendations. The second is a comprehensive technical report that assesses the mineral reserves and groundwater resources and pinpoints the areas with the best potential while also dispelling the belief, prevalent in Cyprus for so long, that there were large reservoirs of water beneath the Mesaoria plain. In addition to the statistical data and relevant figures, the technical report includes a complete bibliography of reference works and monographs used during the undertaking, which are available at the library of the Cyprus Geological Survey Department at Nicosia.

31 **The rainfall of Cyprus.**
Nicos Christou. Nicosia: Department of Water Development, 1967.
167p. illus.

This illustrated study of the levels of rainfall touches upon one of the central problems of the island's agricultural economy.

Political

32 **The geographical distribution of communities in Cyprus.**
Alexander Melamid. *Geographical Review,* vol. 46, no. 3
(July 1956), p. 355-74. maps. illus.

The various geographic areas/districts of Cyprus are described in terms of land geography, resources and the percentage distribution of the Greek and Turkish communities to be found there. The work is illustrated with maps and photographs. Short notes on land use and the political geography of Cyprus by the same author are to be found in vol. 48, no. 1 (Jan. 1958), p. 112-14; vol. 50, no. 4 (Oct. 1960), p. 588-90; vol. 51, no. 2 (April 1961), p. 307-08.

Geography. Political

33 Political geography and the Cyprus conflict: 1963-1971.
Richard A. Patrick, edited by J. H. Bater, R. Preston. Waterloo, Canada: University of Waterloo, 1976. xx + 481p. bibliog. apps. (Department of Geography Publication Series, no. 4).

A study of the geographical dimension of the ethnic conflict in Cyprus, focusing on the confrontation of the mid-1960s. The work emphasizes the locational aspects of each incident and the locational consequences of conflict as reflected in the evacuation of villages and refugee movements, and their economic impact on agriculture, land tenure and industrial labour. The relevance of the case of Cyprus for unified field theory in political geography is underlined. The study includes useful appendices and a rich bibliography. Six shorter studies dealing with Cyprus in the framework of political geography are also included.

34 Proceedings – International Symposium on Political Geography.
Nicosia: Theopress, 1976. vii + 169p. maps. diags. illus.

In the aftermath of the 1974 crisis, the geographic demography of Cyprus was forcefully altered. In this symposium, sponsored by the Cyprus Geographical Association and held in Nicosia in February 1976, various experts from Cyprus and overseas examine the courses and effects on the island of those events, and offer suggestions and ideas as to how a viable solution can be found based on geographic and other criteria. Originally published as vol. 5, no. 9-10 of *Geographical Chronicles* (Jan.-Dec. 1976).

35 Guerre civile et mutations du paysage urbain. (Civil war and changes in the urban landscape.)
Pierre-Yves Péchoux. *Revue Française d'Etudes Politiques Mediterranéennes*, no. 18-19 (June-July 1976), p. 44-62.

A consideration of the impact of ethnic confrontation and war on the patterns of urban settlement in Cyprus.

36 Proposals for a solution of the Cyprus problem.
George Karouzis. Nicosia: Cosmos Press, 1976. 208p. maps. bibliog. tables.

In the aftermath of the 1974 crisis, a Cypriot geographer proposes an alternative solution to the Cyprus problem based on the consolidation of the scattered land ownerships and settlements of Turkish Cypriots into homogeneous areas. The book is useful for its statistical data on Greek and Turkish homogeneous and mixed villages (population, land ownership, etc.).

Maps

37 A trigonometrical survey of the island of Cyprus.
H. H. Kitchener. London: E. Stanford, 1885. 13 maps.
The first scientific cartographical survey of Cyprus.

38 [Topographical maps.]
Nicosia: Department of Lands and Surveys.
A series of lithographed maps published by the Department of Lands and Surveys of the Republic of Cyprus. Besides a number of more specialized maps, the series includes the following island-wide maps: 'Cyprus: general use map', 1:500,000 (1976); 'Cyprus: administration and road map', 1:250,000 (1979); 'Cyprus: distribution of population by ethnic group 1960 and positions of the invading Turkish forces', 1:250,000 (1976); 'Cyprus: Troodos and hill resorts', 1:250,000 (1969); 'Cyprus: state forests map', 1:250,000 (1978); 'Cyprus: geological map', 1:250,000 (1979); 'Cyprus: hydrogeological map', 1:250,000 (1970); 'Cyprus: average annual precipitation map 1941-70', 1:250,000 (1972); 'Cyprus: general soil map', 1:200,000 (1970).

39 Cyprus touring map.
Nicosia: Department of Lands and Surveys, 1981.
An excellent touring map of the island, indicating the latest extent of the road network, all places of interest and other useful information for the traveller. An indispensable companion to the foreign visitor, and also to Cypriots desiring to explore the diverse charms of their island.

40 [Street names maps.]
Nicosia: Department of Lands and Surveys.
A series of detailed maps indicating street names in the major towns of Cyprus. It includes maps of Nicosia (east, west and town within the walls), Limassol, Famagusta (north and south), Larnaca and Scala, Paphos, Kyrenia, Morphou, Dhali.

41 [Cadastral plans.]
Nicosia: Department of Lands and Surveys.
These specialized maps include plans of land holdings and distribution for each village, town and district in Cyprus.

Travel and Tourism

Travellers' accounts

42 **Through Cyprus with the camera in the autumn of 1878.**
    John Thomson. London: Sampson Low, Maston, Searle & Rivington, 1879. 2 vols. Reprinted, Nicosia, 1978. 54p. 60 plates.

A profile of the landscape and the human face of Cyprus in the first year of British rule. The sixty beautiful photographs illustrate the physical and social conditions of the island at the point of its first exposure to Western civilization.

43 **Cyprus as I saw it in 1879.**
    Samuel White Baker. London: Macmillan, 1879. xx + 501p.

One of the best accounts of Cyprus at the time of the British occupation, by a perceptive author of serious travel books about different parts of the British Empire. Sir Samuel Baker arrived in Cyprus in January 1879 and spent the following spring and summer travelling all over the island. He recorded his impressions 'as an independent traveller, unprejudiced by political considerations and unfettered by the responsible position of an official'. In the context of many acute observations on the condition of the island and remarks on the task ahead for the newly established British administration, he touched on some important aspects of the life of Cyprus. Of special interest are his remarks on religious life as he observed it at the lovely monastery of Trooditissa, on the problems of land ownership and taxation, and his concluding political reflections on the island's strategic significance for Britain.

44 **In an enchanted island or a winter's retreat in Cyprus.**
    W. H. Mallock. London: Bentley, 1889. 298p.

This is a charming account of a winter's residence in Cyprus which gave the author the occasion to appraise the quality of life there in the second decade of British rule. The author shows great sensitivity to the beauty of the landscape and also to the sense of the past that survived in the monuments of the island. The combination of these two elements nurtured the spell cast over the author by Cyprus. The narrative provides many anecdotal observations on local politics.

Travel and Tourism. Travellers' accounts

45   **Our home in Cyprus.**
   Esmé Scott Stevenson. London, 1890. xxvii + 332p. folding maps.
   8 plates. app.

This is an account of her residence in Cyprus by Mrs. Scott Stevenson, wife of the then British district commissioner of Kyrenia. Like all other British officials the Stevensons travelled extensively throughout the island, and Mrs. Scott Stevenson recorded her impressions meticulously. In addition to the general descriptions of the country and the people, her personal sensitivity allowed her to capture many details and to offer glimpses into aspects of life which often escaped the attention of other writers. She records many details about domestic life, personal relations, daily affairs and concerns, decorations, food, and life styles in Cyprus at the beginning of British rule. Of special interest are her observations of Cypriot women and her comments on British attitudes toward Greek and Turkish Cypriots. She also grasped the intricacies of Cypriot politics and recorded the existence of strong Greek national feeling and the influence exercised by the clergy. In the appendix she classifies some general information about the island.

46   **Through Cyprus.**
   Agnes Smith. London: Hurst & Blackett, 1887. ix + 351p. map.
   illus. app.

A descriptive travel account of the whole of the island, with observations on the people and their culture.

47   **A lady's impressions of Cyprus in 1893.**
   Elizabeth A. M. Lewis. London: Remington & Co., 1894. viii +
   346p. map. illus.

Besides giving a sympathetic portrait of life in Cyprus and describing the island's landscape toward the close of the 19th century, this book is an important source on Cypriot folk art and crafts. Mrs. Lewis has recorded with perceptiveness and precision many details on the domestic crafts practised especially by Cypriot women (weaving, dyeing, embroidery, pottery) which make her book much more than a mere account of travels in the Cypriot countryside. It is in fact an essential source on the history of Cypriot crafts.

48   **My experiences in Cyprus.**
   Basil Stewart. London: Routledge; New York: Dutton, 1908.
   xii + 268p. 48 plates.

This book records the author's impressions from two periods of residence in Cyprus during the first decade of the 20th century. His purpose was to convey a picture of a country which he found still unspoilt and which could give 'some idea of how the people of the era before Christ lived'. He describes the soil and climate of Cyprus, the native people and some of their customs, the island's past and antiquities, but devotes most of the book to an account of his travels throughout the island and of his visits to its major cities. The narrative is beautifully illustrated by many contemporary photographs of sites and people. The book concludes with a sane plea for a recognition of the needs of the people of Cyprus by their British masters.

Travel and Tourism. Travellers' accounts

49 **Unspoiled Cyprus.**

Maynard Owen Williams. *National Geographic Magazine,* vol. 54, no. 1 (July 1928), p. 1-55. illus.

In this descriptive account of a journey through Cyprus, illustrated with sixty-six captioned photographs, some of them in colour, the beauty of the island and its people and of a bygone milieu are underscored.

50 **Across Cyprus.**

Olive Murray Chapman. London: John Lane, Bodley Head, 1943. 254p. map.

Originally published in 1937, this is the record of the journeys through Cyprus of an experienced writer of travel books. Illustrated with beautiful contemporary photographs, the book describes the landscape, the monuments, life and tradition of the island just prior to the irruption of rapid socio-economic change. It captures the spell that Cyprus has always exercised on the visitor.

51 **The orphaned realm: journeys in Cyprus.**

John Patrick Douglas Balfour Kinross, photographs by Dimitri. London: Percival Marshall, 1951. 221p. map. bibliog. illus.

An account of journeys in Cyprus in the late 1940s by the future biographer of Ataturk. He gives an enchanting picture of the landscape and monuments of the past and records his impressions of modern politics, focusing in particular on village elections, the struggles of communist and anti-communist forces in municipal politics and the church-led campaign for union with Greece. The book emphasizes the achievements of the British administration in improving living conditions in the island, and hints at the possibility of an Anglo-Greek understanding on Cyprus.

52 **Bitter lemons.**

Lawrence Durrell. London: Faber & Faber, 1957. 256p.

This book brings together the recollections of the author's residence in Cyprus in 1953-56. It contains exquisite descriptions of the landscape of the island, especially of the northern coastal region, and sympathetic portraits of the author's local friends. It also offers the author's personal interpretation 'of the moods and atmospheres of Cyprus during the troubled years' of the outbreak of the anti-colonial revolt. It is an impressionistic but classic account which has been reprinted many times since it was first published.

53 **Rendezvous in Cyprus.**

Barbara Toy. London: Cox & Wyman, 1970. 147p. map. illus.

A personal account of travel around the island, focusing on the experiences and interests of the author.

54 **Journey into Cyprus.**
Colin Thubron. London: William Heinemann, 1975. xi + 256p.
bibliog. illus.

Personal impressions of travels around Cyprus with evocations of the history of the island.

Tourism

55 **The island of Cyprus: an illustrated guide and handbook.**
Compiled and edited by L. Mangoian, H. A. Mangoian. Bristol, England: Vandyck Printers, 1947. 246p. maps. bibliog. tables. illus.

This is the first comprehensive guidebook published on Cyprus catering for the general public and not for special interests and/or antiquarians. Although a lot of its information is dated the guidebook is nonetheless unique. It contains thirty-one brief commentaries on subjects ranging from history, the various communities and religious denominations, to folk music, birds and flora. Written by scholars and/or prominent religious or public figures, these commentaries are of great value to researchers. The book's 205 photogravures provide a fascinating photo-essay on the life, scenery and folk art of Cyprus before the Second World War.

56 **Everybody's guide to romantic Cyprus.**
Kevork Keshishian. Nicosia, 1980. 15th rev. ed. 320p. 9 folding maps.

A richly illustrated guidebook containing reliable information on all aspects of life in Cyprus. Besides many useful tips for both the foreign visitor and the native traveller desiring to explore the charms of Cyprus, it contains information on weather and rainfall, the historical heritage and religious tradition of Cyprus, the major cities and their curiosities, archaeological sites, monasteries, mountain resorts and mountain castles. It also carries concise reports on the press, philately, mining, labour and social insurance, agriculture, forests, flora and fauna. It reprints with the author's permission the collection of Cypriot folklore entitled *The inner life of Cyprus* (q.v.) by Demetrios Stylianou.

57 **The traveler's guide to Cyprus.**
Hazel Thurston, photographs by Guy Gravett. Indianapolis, Indiana; New York: Bobbs-Merrill; London: Jonathan Cape, 1971. rev. ed. 286p. maps. charts. illus.

This is a well conceived and prepared travel book, with excellent street guide and distance charts that will guarantee the traveller no time lost in reaching his destinations. Concise descriptions and background material on all points of interest (archaeological sites, monasteries, etc.) is another of its attractions. Also available in a German edition, *Cypern* (Stuttgart, GFR: Hans Gunther Verlag, 1972).

Travel and Tourism. Tourism

58 **Aphrodite's realm.**
   Robin Parker. Nicosia, 1968. 328p. illus.

An illustrated guide and handbook to Cyprus by district, pointing out places of interest to the visitor as well as facilities available. It provides useful basic information on life on the island.

59 **Cyprus invitation.**
   William Forwood. London: Garnstone Press, 1971. 169p. maps. bibliog. illus.

This is largely a present-day descriptive account of Cyprus, done by district and subregion and illustrated with black-and-white photographs.

60 **Cyprus.**
   Prepared under the direction of Roger Milliex, English version by H. S. B. Harrison. New York: McGraw Hill, 1964. 2nd ed. 159p. maps. plans. (Nagel Travel Guide Series).

A pocket-book travel guide with maps, descriptive accounts of places of interest throughout the island, a vocabulary of useful expressions, and relevant tourist information.

61 **Cyprus.**
   Michael Lee, Hanka Lee. Newton Abbot, England: David & Charles, 1973. 208p. maps. bibliog. illus. (The Islands Series).

A publication for the layman and the tourist who may have some leisure time while visiting to read about the island's history, culture and contemporary developments.

62 **Cyprus.**
   David Ford. London: New English Library, 1973. 106p. map. illus.

A short, readable guidebook with tips on what to see, eat and do while visiting.

63 **Cyprus.**
   Introduction by G. B. Pusey. Nicosia: K. Rustem & Brother, 1960. 112p. folding map. illus.

A short guide to the island's towns, villages, historical places and resorts. It is illustrated throughout with black-and-white photographs.

64 **Cyprus: the island of Aphrodite.**
   Achilleas Lymbourides. Nicosia: Cosmos Press, 1963. 2nd ed. 100p. maps. charts. illus.

An illustrated guidebook, with short accounts of the island's archaeology, history, mythology, art, literature and other useful information for the traveller.

Travel and Tourism. Tourism

65 **Your guide to Cyprus.**
Alan Ryalis, foreword by Nicos Demetriou. London: Alvin Redman, 1969. 202p. maps. bibliog. plans. tables. illus.

Descriptive account of the historic and tourist attractions throughout the island, including photographs, maps, city plans, tables and other details of concern to tourists and casual visitors.

66 **Touring Cyprus.**
Philip Ward. Stoughton, Wisconsin: Oleander Press, 1972. xxii + 143p. illus.

A tourist guide with useful information on points of interest, communications, transportation and tourist-related services.

67 **Cyprus in your pocket: a practical illustrated guide book.**
Yam Tihony. Tel-Aviv, Israel: Ben-Dor Israel Publishing, 1960. 119p. maps. illus.

A practical guidebook by an Israeli author, written for the increasing number of Israeli tourists who were discovering the beauties of their neighbouring island in the early 1960s.

68 **Paphos: a tourist guide.**
Andreas K. Phylactou. Nicosia: Zavallis Press, 1978. 148p. maps. bibliog.

Illustrated with colour and black-and-white photographs and with maps, this is a tourist guide that delves into the past and discusses the cultural personality of the most attractive district of Cyprus. It offers much more than what is expected from a usual tourist guide.

69 **Your way around Paphos.**
Ch. G. Christodoulides. Paphos, Cyprus, 1980. 48p. bibliog.

An illustrated tourist guide to the antiquities and other places of interest in one of the most charming areas of Cyprus.

70 **A comprehensive up to date Cyprus guide.**
Nicosia [n.d.]. 198p.

A general guide including an A-to-Z atlas of Nicosia and suburbs with an index to street names.

71 **Kopiaste: a book on Cyprus customs and cuisine.**
Amaranth Sitas. Limassol, Cyprus, 1968. Reprinted, 1974. 110p.

A lucidly written cookery book which, besides surveying the whole range of Cypriot cooking, attempts to connect it with the social customs of everyday family life. It stresses the element of Cypriot hospitality and the role of cooking in the fabric of social relations in Cypriot life.

Travel and Tourism. Tourism

72 **The Cypriots at table.**
    Marios Mourdjis. Nicosia [n.d.] . 220p.

A richly illustrated collection of recipes revealing the delights of Cypriot cuisine. It contains suggestions and hints for all occasions in the social life of the household.

73 **Cyprus: Time Out.**
    Edited by Ellada Sophocleous. Nicosia: Centre of Communication Arts, 1978- . monthly.

This is a monthly shopping and entertainment guide that commenced publication in April 1978. Like all publications of its kind it is inundated with advertisements, but tourists and businessmen will find it extremely useful. In addition to the monthly calendar of happenings, it contains standard information on accommodation, food, entertainment, travel and shopping, as well as time schedules for travel to and from Cyprus.

Flora and Fauna

Flora

74 **Flora of Cyprus.**
    R. D. Meikle. London: Bentham Moxom Trust, Royal Botanic Gardens, 1977. xii + 832p. map. 52 plates. apps.

This whole work, volume 1 and the forthcoming volume 2, provides a comprehensive and up-to-date descriptive account of Cyprus's plants which supersedes the two other works on the subject, Holmboe's *Studies in the vegetation of Cyprus* (Bergen, Norway, 1914) and Esther F. Chapman's *Cyprus trees and shrubs* (q.v.).

75 **Cyprus trees and shrubs.**
    Esther F. Chapman. Nicosia: Government Printing Office, 1949. 88p. diags. gloss.

A botanical reference book containing systematic descriptions of families and species of the Cyprus trees, shrubs and woody plants. It includes a glossary of botanical terms, diagrams, natural and artificial keys, and indexes to species and to Greek names.

76 **Lilies of the field: a book of Cyprus wild flowers.**
    Ann Matthews. Limassol, Cyprus, 1968. 54p. map. illus. gloss.

A descriptive record of the wild flowers of Cyprus. It gives basic botanical data on fifty-four flowers (including their Greek vernacular names). Each of the flowers is illustrated by a colour photograph. It includes a map, glossary, index of Greek names and chart of flower seasons.

77 **Wild flowers of Cyprus.**
    R. Desmond Meikle, photographs by Electra Megaw. London; Chichester, England: Phillimore & Co., 1973. 18p. 40 plates.

An attractive volume on Cyprus's wild flowers. The text is by the leading contemporary scholar of Cyprus botany, who makes the secrets of his science accessible to the layman, and the superb photographs are by Electra Megaw.

Flora and Fauna. Fauna

78 **The Cyprus fungi.**
John Ph. Zyngas. Nicosia: Ministry of Agriculture and Natural Resources, Department of Agriculture, 1973. 55p.

This pamphlet amalgamates the information on the fungi recorded in Cyprus from 1931-70. The work is primarily intended for specialists and researchers in the areas of tree and field crop diseases.

Fauna

79 **A guide to the sea shells of Cyprus.**
G. A. Stavrinos. Famagusta, Cyprus, 1974. 78p. illus.

A listing, illustrated with drawings, of the sea shells found on the coasts of Cyprus.

80 **The insects and mites of Cyprus with emphasis on species of economic importance to agriculture, forestry, man and domestic animals.**
George P. Georghiou. Athens: Benaki Phytopathological Institute, 1977. 347p. bibliog.

A systematic compilation of information on the insects and mites of Cyprus. Since most of the species injurious to agriculture had been studied before, this work devotes special attention to insect orders or families which had not previously been adequately covered. The monograph contains records of 2,884 species of Insecta and 67 species of Acarida.

81 **Birds of Cyprus.**
David A. Bannerman, W. Mary Bannerman. Edinburgh, London: Oliver & Boyd, 1958. 384p. illus.

A complete and profusely illustrated record of the birds of Cyprus, classified in a systematic list of families and species. It also includes a history of Cyprus ornithology, a list of bird recorders 1336-1958, prominent personalities in Cyprus ornithology, birds ringed and recovered in Cyprus, and basic data on temperature, humidity and rainfall. The authors' *Handbook of birds of Cyprus and migrants of the Middle East* (Edinburgh: Oliver & Boyd, 1971, 237p.) is a subsequent edition of the same material.

82 **Common birds of Cyprus: a concise, simple and fully illustrated guide.**
J. M. E. Took, illustrated by Robin Reckitt. Nicosia, 1973. 86p. illus. (Distributed by the Moufflon Book and Art Centre, Nicosia).

A record of eighty-six birds commonly found in Cyprus, providing a descriptive identification for each bird and data on its status, habitat, voice, breeding and sighting time.

Flora and Fauna. Fauna

83 **Check-list of the birds of Cyprus, 1972.**
Nicosia: Cyprus Ornithological Society, 1972. 14p.

A comprehensive check-list containing all species recorded in Cyprus up to January 1972. It also contains descriptions of three Cypriot species not described in *A field guide to the birds of Britain and Europe* by Roger Peterson (London: Collins).

84 **Bird Reports.**
Nicosia: Cyprus Ornithological Society, 1970- . annual.

An annual record of the ornithological resources of Cyprus, including reports on bird sightings in the island, ringing reports, and weather summaries of interest to ornithologists. It is a valuable source for the professional ornithologist as well as for anyone interested in the birds of Cyprus. Between 1971-79 six reports were published for the years 1970-75.

Prehistory and Archaeology

85 **Cyprus: its ancient cities, tombs and temples.**
Louis (Luigi) Palma di Cesnola. London: J. Murray, 1877. 448p.
2 maps. illus.

Illustrated with maps and prints of several of the ancient objects found by the author in Cyprus, this is a record of the author's archaeological surveys and excavations as well as of his service as the American consul in Cyprus from 1865-76. The book is an important source both as an account of the beginnings of archaeological research in Cyprus and as a description of life and politics in the island during the last decade of Ottoman rule.

86 **Salaminia (Cyprus): the history, treasures and antiquities of Salamis in the island of Cyprus.**
Alexander Palma di Cesnola. London: Whiting & Co., 1884.
2nd ed. 276p.

Previously vice-consul for the USA at Paphos (1873-76), the author, following the example of his brother Luigi Palma di Cesnola, carried out excavations in the region of ancient Salamis from 1876-79. He provides a detailed record of his findings and thus his book can be considered the foundation of archaeological research on Salamis. The 14,000 objects yielded by his excavations composed the Cesnola Collection of Cypriot antiquities (see *Handbook of the Cesnola Collection of antiquities from Cyprus*, q.v.).

87 **Ancient places of worship in Kypros.**
Max Ohnefalsch-Richter. Berlin: H. S. Hermann, 1891.
x + 51p. 18 plates.

A translation of the author's doctoral dissertation at the University of Leipzig. A pioneering contribution to scientific archaeological research, it is based on the author's surveys and excavations of sites of worship in ancient Cyprus during the 1880s. The material is drawn from sites all over Cyprus. The introduction offers a survey of the state of Cypriot archaeology up to the time of writing, and appraises earlier contributions.

Prehistory and Archaeology

88 **Devia Cypria: notes of an archeological journey in Cyprus in 1888.**
G. D. Hogarth. London: H. Frowde, 1889. vii + 124p. illus.

A pioneering and fascinating contribution to the exploration of ancient Cyprus, focusing on the two most isolated regions of the island at the time of Hogarth's visit, Paphos and the Karpass peninsula. The author recorded his archaeological observations, including the transcription of many inscriptions, during a trip from May to October 1888. His field observations were supplemented by evidence from published sources. The book is illustrated with very good photographs of ancient and Christian monuments.

89 **A catalogue of the Cyprus Museum.**
John L. Myres, Max Ohnefalsch-Richter. Oxford, England: Clarendon Press, 1899. 224p. 8 plates.

This is the best record of the state of Cypriot archaeology at the close of the 19th century. It includes a brief chronicle of excavations since the British occupation, and a survey of Cypriot prehistory and archaeology to the Hellenistic age. The main body of the book comprises a detailed catalogue of the items composing the first government collection of antiquities, which formed the nucleus of the Cyprus Museum. The book closes with comprehensive indexes.

90 **A description of the historic monuments of Cyprus: studies in the archæology and architecture of the island with illustrations from measured drawings and photographs.**
George Jeffery. Nicosia: Government Printing Office, 1918.
x + 469p. bibliog. illus.

The best available topography of Cyprus in English. A systematic survey of the physical, social and historical geography of Cyprus, paying particular attention to the archaeological heritage and the ancient and mediaeval monuments surviving in the island. The book is a very useful guide to the towns and villages of Cyprus as they existed in the opening decades of British rule.

91 **Studies on prehistoric Cyprus.**
E. Gjerstad. Uppsala, Sweden, 1926. viii + 342p.

This is the doctoral dissertation of the father of 20th century scientific archaeological research on Cyprus. It records the author's initial researches on Cypriot prehistory by offering a survey of the topography, architecture, tombs, pottery and other archaeological finds. It also considers the relative and absolute chronology and the external relations of prehistoric Cyprus. In the approach to archaeological research employed in this volume, one sees the methodological outlines of the monumental project directed later by Einar Gjerstad and embodied in the several volumes of *The Swedish Cyprus Expedition* (see the following items).

Prehistory and Archaeology

92 **The Swedish Cyprus Expedition. Finds and results of the excavations in Cyprus 1927-1931.**
Einar Gjerstad, John Lindros, Erik Sjoqvist, Alfred Westholm.
Stockholm: Swedish Cyprus Expedition, 1934-37. 3 vols.

Volume 1: *An account of excavations at Petra tou Limniti, Lapithos, Kythrea, Ajios Iakovos, Nikovlita, Paleoskoutella, Kountoura, Trachonia, Trachonas, Enkomi,* (578p.); volume 2: *An account of archeological research at Amathus, Stylli, Marion, Idalion, Ajia Irini* (861p.); volume 3: *Archaeological researches at Kition, Vouni, Mersinaki, Soli, Arsos* (675p.). Each volume is accompanied by a separate volume of plates.

93 **The Swedish Cyprus Expedition: vol. 4, part 1A. The Stone Age and the early Bronze Age in Cyprus.**
P. Dikaios, James R. Stewart. Lund, Sweden: Swedish Cyprus Expedition, 1962. 401p. 156 plates.

A study by P. Dikaios of the archaeology of the Stone Age in Cyprus, focusing on the sites of Khirokitia, Troulli, Sotira, Kalavassos, Erimi, Ambelikou-Ayios Georghios, Philia and Kyra, and of the archaeology of the early Cypriot Bronze Age by James Stewart. The absolute chronology of the periods covered ranges from about 5800-1750 BC.

94 **The Swedish Cyprus Expedition: vol. 4, part 1B. The middle Cypriote Bronze Age.**
Paul Åström. Lund, Sweden: Swedish Cyprus Expedition, 1972. 307p. 40 plates.

A study of the archaeology of the middle Bronze Age in Cyprus, employing the basic method established by the Swedish Cyprus Expedition. It covers the period from about 1800-1600 BC.

95 **The Swedish Cyprus Expedition: vol. 4, parts 1C-1D. The late Cypriote Bronze Age.**
Paul Åström, Lena Åström, M. R. Popham, V. E. G. Kenna.
Lund, Sweden: Swedish Cyprus Expedition, 1972. 854p. bibliog. 86 plates.

The archaeology of Cyprus in the late Bronze Age from 1600-1050 BC. This was the great age of Cypriot prehistoric civilization during which Mycenaean influence predominated in art and Greek colonization introduced the Arcado-Cypriote language into the island.

Prehistory and Archaeology

96 The Swedish Cyprus Expedition: vol. 4, part 2. The Cyprogeometric, Cypro-archaic and Cypro-classical periods.
Einar Gjerstad. Stockholm: Swedish Cyprus Expedition, 1948.
543 p. 71 plates.

A study of the architecture, pottery, sculpture, arts and crafts, relative and absolute chronology and foreign relations of Cyprus in the geometric, archaic and classical periods. It covers the years from 1050-325 BC.

97 The Swedish Cyprus Expedition: vol. 4, part 3. The Hellenistic and Roman periods in Cyprus.
Olof Vessberg, Alfred Westholm. Stockholm: Swedish Cyprus Expedition, 1956. 246p.

A study of the architecture, pottery, sculpture, arts and crafts of Hellenistic and Roman Cyprus, concluded by a historical survey of the period from the closing decades of the 4th century BC to the early Christian and Byzantine periods and the eve of the Arab onslaught in the 7th century AD.

98 Khirokitia: final report on the excavation of a neolithic settlement in Cyprus on behalf of the Department of Antiquities 1936-1946.
Porphyrios Dikaios. London: Oxford University Press, 1953.
xxii + 447p. 152 plates.

A monumental study of the archaeological evidence yielded by ten years of excavations in one of the major neolithic sites of Cyprus, tentatively dated at the period 3700-3400 BC.

99 Sotira.
Porphyrios Dikaios (and others). Philadelphia: University Museum, University of Pennsylvania, 1961. 252p. bibliog.
122 plates. (Museum Monographs).

A description of the site, excavations and finds of the neolithic settlement at Sotira, Cyprus. The importance of the Sotira settlement lies in the fact that it fills the gap in the knowledge of prehistoric Cyprus between the earlier neolithic cultural stage of Khirokitia and the chalcolithic stage of Erimi.

100 Enkomi: excavations 1948-1958.
Porphyrios Dikaios. Mainz am Rhein, GFR: Verlag Philipp von Zabern, 1969-71. 4 vols. bibliog.

A monumental account of ten years of excavations in a major prehistoric site of Cyprus. Volume 1: *The architectural remains. The tombs* (xvi + 438p.) discusses architectural remains, areas III and I, the finds, stratified pottery of Mycenaean and derivative styles, tombs and their contents; volume 2: *Chronology, summary and conclusions* (p. xvi, 439-942) provides a relative and absolute chronology, historical conclusions, and a catalogue of finds from the stratified deposit; volume 3a: plates 1-239; volume 3b: plates 240-95.

Prehistory and Archaeology

101 Cyprus in the neolithic and chalcolithic periods.
H. W. Catling. In: *The Cambridge ancient history*. Edited by
I. E. S. Edwards. Cambridge, England: Cambridge University
Press, 1970. 3rd ed. vol. 1, pt. 1, p. 539-56.

102 Cyprus in the early Bronze Age.
H. W. Catling. In: *The Cambridge ancient history*. Edited by
I. E. S. Edwards. Cambridge, England: Cambridge University
Press, 1971. 3rd ed. vol. 1, pt. 2, p. 808-23.

103 Cyprus in the middle Bronze Age.
H. W. Catling. In: *The Cambridge ancient history*. Edited by
I. E. S. Edwards. Cambridge, England: Cambridge University
Press, 1975. 3rd ed. vol. 2, pt. 1, p. 165-75.

104 Cyprus in the late Bronze Age.
H. W. Catling. In: *The Cambridge ancient history*. Edited by
I. E. S. Edwards. Cambridge, England: Cambridge University
Press, 1975. 3rd ed. vol. 2, pt. 2, p. 188-216.

This item and the three preceding it are authoritative surveys of the development of the civilization of ancient Cyprus to the eve of the historical era. The main problems are discussed in the light of the new archaeological research, and Cyprus is placed in the context of Mediterranean and Near Eastern civilizations. The main bibliography is included in the pertinent sections of the general bibliography that closes each volume.

105 Cypriot bronzework in the Mycenean world.
H. W. Catling. Oxford, England: Clarendon Press, 1964.
335p. bibliog. 54 plates. figs.

One of the leading sources on the material civilization of Bronze Age Cyprus and on the colonization of the island by the Mycenaean Greeks. It examines the evidence concerning the metal crafts of the Bronze Age in connection with the establishment of Mycenaean settlers in the coastal cities of Cyprus from the 13th century BC onward and the gradual extension of their control over the most important economic network of the island, the copper industry.

106 The civilization of prehistoric Cyprus.
Vassos Karageorghis. Athens: Ekdotike Athenon, 1976.
230p. map. bibliog. illus.

A lavishly produced volume with 191 colour illustrations and photographs spanning thousands of years of Cypriot prehistory from the Stone Age to the Bronze and the Mycenaean period (5800-1050 BC). This is the only volume comprehensively surveying Cyprus's prehistoric civilization. A Greek edition was also published.

Prehistory and Archaeology

107 Prehistoric Greece and Cyprus: an archeological handbook.
Hans-Gunter Buchholz, Vassos Karageorghis, translated by Francisca Gavrie. London: Phaidon, 1973. 514p. bibliog.

The section on ancient Cyprus surveys the periods of Cypriot prehistory from the Stone Age to the late Bronze Age, and provides lists of excavated sites, tombs and artefacts.

108 Cyprus.
Vassos Karageorghis. Geneva: Nagel, 1968. 259p. bibliog. illus.

With 181 colour and black-and-white illustrations, this volume is a comprehensive survey of the ancient civilization of Cyprus to the Roman period. In addition to the useful chronology and bibliography there is a listing of the main excavations up to 1960 together with the sites, their locations, and the relevant academic publication that resulted. Also published as *The ancient civilization of Cyprus* (New York: Cowles Education Corporation. Archaeologia Mundi Series).

109 Treasures in the Cyprus Museum.
Vassos Karageorghis. Nicosia: Department of Antiquities, 1962. v + 29p. bibliog. 48 plates. (Picture Book Series, 1).

The first in a series of picture-books published by the Cyprus Department of Antiquities, designed to convey a vivid impression of the range and wealth of the island's archaeological heritage. This volume contains a brief introduction to the archaeology of Cyprus and a select bibliography, and focuses on a description of the main artistic treasures of the Cyprus Museum which are depicted in the plates.

110 Mycenean art from Cyprus.
Vassos Karageorghis. Nicosia: Department of Antiquities, 1967. 48p. bibliog. 44 plates. (Picture Book Series, 3).

A picture-book presenting a selection of the best examples of Cypriot Mycenaean art.

111 Ancient monuments of Cyprus.
Kyriacos Nicolaou. Nicosia: Department of Antiquities, 1968. 33p. bibliog. 48 plates. (Picture Book Series, 4).

The fourth in the picture-book series of the Cyprus Department of Antiquities, this volume includes representative plates, preceded by detailed description, of the leading archaeological sites of Cyprus.

112 Jewelry in the Cyprus Museum.
Angeliki Pierides. Nicosia: Department of Antiquities, 1971. v + 59p. bibliog. 40 plates. (Picture Book Series, 5).

The fifth of the picture-books of the Cyprus Department of Antiquities, this volume offers a historical introduction to the fine craft of jewellery in ancient Cyprus and a detailed description of objects in the Cyprus Museum which are reproduced in the plates.

Prehistory and Archaeology

113 Cypriot inscribed stones.
Ino Nicolaou. Nicosia: Department of Antiquities, 1971. 37p. bibliog. 25 plates. (Picture Book Series, 6).

A picture-book of representative items of ancient Cypriot epigraphy.

114 Salamis in Cyprus Homeric, Hellenistic, and Roman.
Vassos Karageorghis. London: Thames & Hudson, 1969. 212p. bibliog. illus.

A survey of the archaeology of Salamis from the end of the Bronze Age to its final abandonment in the 13th century AD. Richly illustrated and drawing on all earlier research, this is a lucid reconstruction of the archaeological profile of a major ancient site. The diversity, extraordinary interest and great monumentality of the ancient remains which make Salamis one of the most important ancient sites in the Mediterranean are here presented with great skill. Special emphasis is given to the 'age of exuberance' by surveying the necropolis in the 8th and 7th centuries BC. The cenotaph of King Nicocreon, last king of Salamis (311 BC) before its fall to the Ptolemies, and a survey of the art and architecture of the ancient city are also included.

115 Excavations in the necropolis of Salamis.
Vassos Karageorghis. Nicosia: Department of Antiquities, 1967-78. 4 vols. bibliog. plates.

Description of the monumental tombs excavated in the necropolis of Salamis, ranging chronologically from the 8th century BC to the early Byzantine period, and of their contents. The excavations have unearthed evidence of unique funerary customs which is of great importance to the study of Aegean and Near Eastern archaeology. Five separate volumes of plans and plates supplement the illustrations in the four main volumes.

116 Sculptures from Salamis I.
Vassos Karageorghis. Nicosia: Department of Antiquities, 1964. 56p. 54 plates.

117 Sculptures from Salamis II.
Vassos Karageorghis, C. C. Vermeule. Nicosia: Department of Antiquities, 1966. 41p. bibliog. 20 plates.

The first of the above two volumes covers sculptures recovered for the most part in the gymnasium and theatre of ancient Salamis during excavations between 1952-61. The second volume publishes additional sculptures from Salamis discovered by a variety of archaeological missions and now scattered in different museums of the world.

Prehistory and Archaeology

118 **Kition: Mycenean and Phoenician discoveries in Cyprus.**
Vassos Karogeorghis. London: Thames & Hudson, 1976. 184p. bibliog. illus.

A richly illustrated volume presenting a new view of the late Bronze Age in the site of Kition after recent archaeological discoveries. Fourteen years of research and excavations have revolutionized knowledge about the prehistoric past of Kition. The new discoveries document the settlement of Achaean colonists prior to the coming of the Phoenicians, and the finds throw light on the burial customs and religious life of ancient Kition. The rich discoveries have sustained the evidence of traditional records concerning the fame of Kition among Near Eastern peoples. Also published as *View from the Bronze Age: Mycenean and Phoenician discoveries at Kition* (New York: Dutton, 1976).

119 **The historical topography of Kition.**
Kyriakos Nicolaou. Göteborg, Sweden: Paul Åströms Förlag, 1976. xxxiv + 373p. bibliog. 37 plates. (Studies in Mediterranean Archaeology, vol. 42).

A detailed survey of the topography of Kition, examining the city wall, harbour, acropolis, sanctuaries, gymnasium theatre, stadium and hippodrome, aqueduct and necropolis of the ancient city. In addition, the sculpture, pottery, coins and inscriptions yielded by recent excavations are discussed. The historical summary that concludes the volume reconstructs our knowledge of ancient Kition on the basis of the discoveries of new archaeological research which has placed Kition's history on a new basis.

120 **American Expedition to Idalion, Cyprus: first preliminary reports. Seasons of 1971 and 1972.**
Lawrence E. Stager, Anita Walker, G. Ernest Wright. Cambridge, Massachusetts: American School of Oriental Research, 1974. xxx + 178p.

The first report of an excavation of a hitherto undug major ancient site. The archaeological research presented here is particularly interesting on account of its concentration on the investigation of metal exploitation in antiquity and on the presentation of working hypotheses to test theories of cultural diffusion, innovation and adaptation.

Prehistory and Archaeology

121 **Acts of the International Archeological Symposium: the Mycenaeans in the eastern Mediterranean.**
Nicosia: Department of Antiquities, 1973. xiv + 410p. 25 plates.

A volume of important contributions by the foremost authorities on ancient Cyprus discussing the question of the arrival of the Achaean Greek settlers in Cyprus. The symposium included papers presenting the findings of archaeological research concerning the settlement of the Mycenaeans in Cyprus, as well as discussions of historical and literary sources. The arrival of the Greek colonists was debated by the participants with two views emerging as to its chronology and character: it took either the form of gradual penetration in the course of the 14th and 13th centuries BC, or as a refugee wave in the 12th century.

122 **Acts of the International Archeological Symposium: the relations between Cyprus and Crete, ca. 2000-500 BC.**
Nicosia: Department of Antiquities, 1979. 327p. 61 plates.

The product of a conference held in Nicosia in April 1978, the volume contains research reports by some of the leading scholars on ancient Crete and Cyprus. They document the contacts and exchanges between the two leading eastern Mediterranean islands over one and a half millenia.

123 **The Greek and Latin inscriptions from Salamis.**
T. B. Mitford, I. Nicolaou. Nicosia: Department of Antiquities, 1974. xvi + 211p. bibliog. 20 plates.

The authors have deciphered and transcribed 136 Greek and Latin inscriptions found in the various sites of ancient Salamis during the archaeological researches of the 1950s. The inscriptions are primarily Greek, and date from the Hellenistic, Roman and later empire periods. The epigraphical evidence attests to the survival of Salamis as a Greek city that preserved into Roman times its lively Greek cultural tradition.

124 **The inscriptions of Kourion.**
T. B. Mitford. Philadelphia: American Philosophical Society, 1971. xvi + 422p. 4 maps. bibliog. (Memoirs, vol. 83).

A compendium of inscriptions found at Kourion, ranging chronologically from the archaic to the early Byzantine periods (7th century BC-6th century AD).

125 **Les inscriptions chypriotes syllabiques: recueil critique et commenté.** (The Cypriot syllabic inscriptions: a critical annotated collection.)
Olivier Masson. Paris: Editions de Boccard, 1961. 452p. bibliog. 72 plates. (Ecole Française d'Athènes, Etudes Chypriotes, 1).

A monumental study of the ancient Cypriot syllabic writing in use in the island down to the 3rd century BC. After a substantial historical introduction on the problems of the Cypriot syllabary, the surviving inscriptions are published. The inscriptions are categorized according to place of provenance, both within and outside Cyprus (especially from Egypt and Nubia).

Prehistory and Archaeology

126 **Resurrecting the oldest known Greek ship.**
Michael L. Katzer, photographs by Bates Littlehales.
National Geographic, vol. 137, no. 6 (June 1970), p. 841-57.
illus.

Ninety feet off the Cyprus northern coast a local sponge diver discovered what turned out to be a Greek merchantman of the 4th century BC and until now the oldest ship to be found. This is the story of how an American archaeological expedition salvaged and restored the wreck, with superb undersea photographs and artist's renditions of the ancient Greek traders. Named after the nearby town, the Kyrenia ship is preserved in Kyrenia castle.

127 **Manuel de céramique chypriote: 1. Problèmes historiques, vocabulaire, méthode.** (A manual of Cypriot ceramics:
1. Historical problems, vocabulary, method.)
Maguerite Yon. Lyons, France: Institut Courby, 1976.
vii + 250p. bibliog.

This is a thorough guide to the techniques, forms and decorative themes of ancient Cypriot pottery which is considered in the perspective of age-old techniques of folk pottery production still practised in Cyprus. A classic work of its kind, it is an indispensable work for all students of ancient Cypriot ceramics.

128 **The archeology of Cyprus: recent developments.**
Edited by Noel Robertson. Park Ridge, New Jersey: Noyes Press, 1975. 232p. illus.

An illustrated collection of papers on the archaeology of Cyprus surveying recent research in the field. They were originally presented at the first International Colloquium on Ancient Cyprus held at Brock University, Ontario, in 1971. Besides a number of specialized reports, the volume includes introductory surveys of Cypriot archaeology by the editor and V. Karageorghis, and an essay on the main problems and interpretations of ancient Cypriot history by Robert S. Merrillees.

129 **Studies presented in memory of Porphyrios Dikaios.**
Nicosia: Lions Club, 1979. 218p. 33 plates.

A collection of papers by leading scholars of the archaeology of Cyprus, presenting research on all periods of the ancient heritage of the island.

Prehistory and Archaeology

130 The art of Cyprus.
Tony Spiteris, translated from the French by Thomas Burton. New York: Reynal & Co., 1970. 215p. map. bibliog. illus. tables. (Forms and Colors Series Books).

A richly illustrated survey of six millenia of ancient Cypriot art from neolithic to Roman times. The book examines the dawn of Cypriot civilization in the neolithic and chalcolithic periods, the great flowering of Cypriot art in the Bronze Age (2300-1050 BC), and the accomplishments of the geometric and archaic periods. It stresses the originality of Cypriot art deriving from the interplay of Eastern and Western influences on that crossroad of civilizations. The survey concludes by looking at the loss of originality and the decline of Cypriot art due to the uniformity brought by incorporation into the great empires of the Hellenistic and Roman worlds. Comparative tables that relate events in Cyprus to those of Greece and the Middle East are included.

131 Cyprus BC: 7000 years of history.
Edited by Veronica Tatton-Brown, with contributions by V. Karageorghis, E. J. Peltenburg, S. Swiny. London: British Museum Publications, 1979. 117p. bibliog. illus.

The illustrated catalogue of a splendid exhibition of ancient Cypriot art at the British Museum. Composed of the best specimens from the museums of Cyprus, the exhibition and its catalogue demonstrated in its fullness the richness of Cyprus's ancient heritage.

132 Treasures of Cyprus: an exhibition of Cypriot art.
Vassos Karageorghis. Washington, DC: Smithsonian Institution, 1976. 78p. bibliog. illus.

The illustrated catalogue of an exhibition of ancient Cypriot art organized on the occasion of the bicentennial celebrations of American independence.

133 Greek and Roman Cyprus: art from classical through late antique times.
Cornelius Vermeule. Boston, Massachusetts: Museum of Fine Arts, 1976. 134p. illus.

A survey and appreciation of the artistic production of ancient Cyprus from the classical age (5th century BC) through the early Byzantine period to the 5th century AD. The art of Cyprus is discussed in terms of the interplay between imported styles and the insular traditions, whose blend gave it its characteristic vitality. Each chapter is followed by notes with bibliographical references, and the work is richly illustrated.

Prehistory and Archaeology

134 **Who's who in Cypriote archeology: bibliographical and biographical notes.**
Paul Åström. Göteborg, Sweden, 1971. vi + 88p. (Studies in Mediterranean Archeology, vol. 23).

A useful compendium of biographical and bibliographical information on Cypriot archaeological research. It provides an effective introduction to Cypriot archaeology.

History

General

135 **A history of Cyprus.**
George Hill. Cambridge, England: Cambridge University Press, 1940-52. 4 vols. maps. bibliogs. plates. illus.
Volume 1: *To the conquest of Richard Lion Heart* (xviii + 352p.); volumes 2 and 3: *The Frankish period* (p. xi + 1-496; vi + 497-1198); volume 4: *The Ottoman province, the British colony 1571-1948,* edited by Harry Luke (xxxi + 640p.).
A monumental historical synthesis, bringing together available evidence from all periods of history in a lucid reconstruction of the fortunes of Cyprus through eight millenia. Some parts of the work, especially in the first and fourth volume, have been superseded by subsequent research, while some of the author's interpretative positions, mostly found in the same volumes, are obviously obscured by biases towards official British attitudes. Volumes 2 and 3 utilize effectively the researches of Mas Latrie and others on the Latin kingdom and remain an authoritative and still unsuperseded account. With its footnote documentation and bibliographies in several languages, the work constitutes one of the most comprehensive and judicious bibliographical guides to Cyprus studies.

136 **Excerpta Cypria: materials for a history of Cyprus.**
Translated and transcribed by Claude Delaval Cobham. New York: Kraus Reprint, 1969. 523p. bibliog.
A monumental collection of extracts selected and translated from a great variety of sources dealing with Cyprus, ranging in time from AD 23 to 1866. There are works in twelve languages by eighty different writers. It includes Cobham's *An attempt at a bibliography of Cyprus.* It attempts to register the 'title of all books treating of Cyprus, its peoples, history, numismatics, epigraphy and language, of which I have found any trace'. Included also are lists of local newspapers, of maps of the island, of consular reports and parliamentary papers, and references to the Cesnola controversy. Reprinted from the 1908 Cambridge University Press edition.

History. General

137 Supplementary excerpts on Cyprus or further materials for a history of Cyprus.
Theophilus A. H. Mogabgab. Nicosia: Pusey Press, 1941. vol. 1; Zavallis Press, 1943-45. vols. 2-3.

An attempt to supplement Cobham's series of excerpts on Cyprus (see above). Each of the forty selections is briefly introduced and commented upon. The items range from classical Greek authors to 16th century accounts, including both Western and Near Eastern sources.

138 Cyprus in history: a survey of 5,000 years.
Doros Alastos. London: Zeno, 1976. xvi + 426p.

A general survey of the history of Cyprus, more concise than that of Hill's *A history of Cyprus* (q.v.) to which it was meant to be a response. It sets against Hill's British colonial perspective the view of a Cypriot who, though remarkably detached, follows the Hellenic theme in the history of the Cypriot people from the earliest times to the eve of Cyprus's liberation struggle. Reprint of the 1955 edition.

139 A short history of Cyprus.
Philip Newman, foreword by Franklin Lushington. London, New York, Toronto: Longmans, Green & Co., 1953. 2nd ed. viii + 235p. maps. illus.

A concise yet comprehensive survey of Cypriot history from the earliest geological period, through the successive occupations, down to the British times. Special reference is made to those events in the history of the surrounding civilizations which left their mark on Cyprus.

140 A brief history of Cyprus.
Constantinos Spyridakis. Nicosia: Zavallis Press, 1974. 236p. bibliog.

A survey of the history of Cyprus from earliest times to the achievement of independence, stressing the Hellenic character of the island's heritage and traditions. It is important as an ideological statement of the historical theory of Greek Cypriot nationalism.

141 Cyprus: from earliest time to the present day.
Franz George Maier, translated from the German by Peter George. London: Elek Books, 1968. 174p. maps. bibliog. illus.

This is a concise and comprehensive work starting with the prehistory and early cultures of the island. But for a brief essay on the republican experiment, the story concludes with the British period and the Cyprus Question. Its bibliography and notes for every chapter make this work a useful introduction for the layman and a basic text for the serious student.

History. General

142   **Praktika tou Protou Diethnous Kyproloyikou Synedriou.**
(Proceedings of the First International Congress of Cypriot Studies.)
Nicosia: Society of Cypriot Studies, 1972-73. 4 vols.

The proceedings of the first International Congress of Cypriot Studies, held in Nicosia, 14-19 April 1969. It includes many papers in English. Volume 1 comprises the proceedings of the ancient section, volume 2 those of the mediaeval section, the first part of the third volume modern history and geography, and the second part of the third volume modern philology, literature and folklore.

143   **Historic Cyprus: a guide to its towns and villages, monasteries and castles.**
Rupert Gunnis. London: Methuen, 1936. xiii + 495p. folding maps. bibliog. 4 plates. 7 plans.

This is one of the most useful works on Cyprus. Handy and lucidly written, it is a first-rate historical geography of an island where the memories of history have remained alive in its towns, villages, monasteries and castles. The book includes a chapter on icons and the Greek Church by D. Talbot Rice, a brief survey of the history of Cyprus, and a description of the internal arrangement of an Orthodox church. The main body of the book comprises a chapter on each of Cyprus's six leading towns and an alphabetical listing of villages, monasteries and castles with a historical description of each. A bibliography, a chronology and an index close the book.

144   **The history of the cartography of Cyprus.**
Andreas Stylianou, Judith A. Stylianou. Nicosia: Cyprus Research Centre, 1980. xx + 449p. bibliog. illus. (Publications, no. 8).

The product of thirty years of research, this cartographic history of Cyprus traces the development of the mapping of the island from 500 BC to the construction of the first scientific map by Kitchener and Graves in 1878-82. The work identifies, describes and illustrates 228 items. A must for the scholar and the collector alike.

145   **An historical toponymy of Cyprus.**
Jack C. Goodwin. Nicosia, 1978. rev. ed. 1150p. (mimeo.)

A monumental research project that indexes place-names, past and present, in the Republic of Cyprus. Basic information about each place, the names and spellings used over the years and significant historical information are provided. It includes 17,443 entries with information on 8,282 places in Cyprus.

History. Ancient Cyprus

146 **Location and development of the town of Leucosia (Nicosia), Cyprus.**
F. S. Maratheftis. Nicosia: Nicosia Municipality, 1977.
iv + 159p. illus. (mimeo.)

A study of the historical topography of Nicosia from the earliest traces of human settlement in the area in the chalcolithic and Bronze Ages, through the period of the ancient city-kingdom of Ledra, the Hellenistic and Roman periods, the Middle Ages and the era of the foreign conquerors (Lusignan, Venetian and Ottoman), down to the British occupation of 1878. Of special interest are the sections dealing with the topography of Lusignan and Turkish Nicosia and its struggles with the port cities of Famagusta and Larnaca.

Ancient Cyprus

147 **Ancient Cyprus: its art and archeology.**
Stanley Casson. London: Methuen, 1937. Reprinted, Westport, Connecticut: Greenwood Press, 1970; Chicago: Obol International, 1977. xii + 214p.

An introduction to the history and art of ancient Cyprus by a distinguished classicist. It brings together the sources and research available at the time of its composition, and stresses the distinctly Cypriot nature of the culture of ancient Cyprus that managed to transform and integrate the many outside influences. It pays special attention to the problems of Cypriot script and the character of ancient Cypriot art.

148 **Voices of stone: the history of ancient Cyprus.**
Wilson E. Strand. Nicosia: Zavallis Press, 1974. viii + 166p.

A concise history of ancient Cyprus from prehistoric times to the death of Nicocreon of Salamis in 311 BC and the subjugation of Cyprus to the Ptolemies. A rather impressionistic account.

149 **Evagoras I. von Salamis.** (Evagoras I of Salamis.)
Konstantin Spyridakis. Stuttgart, Germany: Verlag W. Kohlhammer, 1935. 123p. bibliog.

This is the standard biography of the most illustrious king of the leading state of ancient Cyprus. It stresses Evagoras's policies which made Salamis a major centre of Hellenic culture during his reign (411-374 BC), and his resistance to Persian encroachments on the independence of Cyprus. A Greek version was published by the Society of Cypriot Studies (Nicosia, 1945).

History. Ancient Cyprus

150 **Le peuplement de Chypre dans l'antiquité.** (The population of Cyprus in antiquity.)
Robert P. Charles. Paris: Editions de Boccard, 1962. 81p. bibliog. (Ecole Française d'Athènes, Etudes Chypriotes, 2).

A study of anthropological types in the ancient population of Cyprus from the 6th millenium BC to the end of the Roman Empire. On the basis of evidence furnished by 283 subjects, the study traces the evolution of the Cypriot populations in antiquity from the presence of Balkan types prior to the 4th millenium BC to the gradual extension of colonization moves from northern and central Greece to Cyprus. By the 15th century BC Cyprus had important Minoan elements in her population, and from the 16th century BC the increasing Mycenaean presence led to the full Hellenization of the population of Cyprus by the end of antiquity. Although geographically an extension of the Asian continent, demographically Cyprus appears to have been 'a bastion of Europe and of the Hellenic world'.

151 **Stasinus and the Cypria.**
Hugh Lloyd Jones. *Stasinos*, vol. 4 (1968-72), p. 115-22.

A prominent classicist appraises the ancient Cypriot epic known as the *Cypria*, and examines the question of its authorship.

152 **The religion of ancient Cyprus.**
Kyriacos Nicolaou. *Stasinos*, vol. 2 (1964-65), p. 11-21.

A survey of the cults and places of worship of the Olympian deities in ancient Cyprus. The cults of Aphrodite and Apollo, both of whom bore the epithet 'Cypriot' in their local cults, were the most widely practised.

153 **Syncrétisme religieux à Slamine de Chypre?** (Religious syncretism in Salamis, Cyprus?)
Jean Pouilloux. In: *Les syncrétismes dans les religions de l'antiquité.* Edited by Fr. Dunard, P. Levêque. Leiden, the Netherlands: Brill, 1975, p. 76-86.

An examination of indications of religious syncretism in ancient Salamis on the basis of available archaeological evidence. It is concluded that, in the absence of literary or epigraphical evidence, the existing archaeological finds cannot be conclusively considered as evidence of religious syncretism, although many indications appear to point in that direction.

History. Ancient Cyprus

154 **La rencontre de l'hellénisme et de l'Orient à Chypre entre 1200 et 300 av. J.C.** (The encounter of Hellenism with the East in Cyprus between 1200 and 300 B.C.)
Jean Pouilloux. In: *Assimilation et résistance à la culture greco-romaine dans le monde ancien*. Edited by D. M. Pippidi. Bucharest: Editura Academiei; Paris: Société d'Editions 'Les Belle Lettres', 1976, p. 233-40.

An examination of the relations of Cyprus with the Middle Eastern monarchies and cultures during the millenium of the island's Hellenization. Our knowledge of this pattern has become much more precise as recent archaeological research has illuminated the interplay of influences which shaped the character of ancient Cypriot Hellenism. Oriental influences remained strong through the 8th and 7th centuries BC, but ties with the Hellenic West proved decisive in the subsequent periods.

155 **Recherches sur les Phéniciens à Chypre.** (Researches concerning the Phoenicians in Cyprus.)
O. Masson, M. Sznycer. Paris, Geneva: Droz, 1972.
149p. 22 plates.

Comprises studies on the Phoenician inscriptions found in different locations in Cyprus and now exhibited in museums in the island and several other countries. This epigraphical evidence allows a more precise appraisal of the controversial issues of the extent and depth of Phoenician presence in ancient Cyprus.

156 **Salamine de Chypre: histoire et archéologie, état des recherches.** (Salamis in Cyprus: history and archaeology, the state of research.)
Paris: Editions du CNRS, 1980. 400p.

Contains the papers presented at an international colloquium held in Lyons in March 1978 and dealing with all aspects of the archaeology and history of Salamis from the origins of the city to the early Byzantine city of Constantia.

157 **Literary, epigraphic and numismatic evidence on Nicocles king of Paphos.**
Ino Michaelidou-Nicolaou. *Kypriakai Spoudai*, vol. 40 (1976), p. 15-28.

A collection and commentary on all sources pertaining to the late 4th century BC King Nicocles of Paphos.

158 **Prosopography of Ptolemaic Cyprus.**
Ino Michaelidou-Nicolaou. Göteborg, Sweden: Paul Åströms Förlag, 1976. 172p. bibliog. (Studies in Mediterranean Archaeology, vol. 44).

Drawing primarily on epigraphical evidence, this volume offers a record of all persons, native or foreign, important or humble, who lived and worked in Cyprus from 295/4-58 BC and from 48/7-30 BC.

History. Byzantine period

159 **I archaia Kypros eis tas ellinikas pigas.** (Ancient Cyprus in the Greek sources.)
Kyriacos Hadjioannou. Nicosia: Holy Archdiocese of Cyprus, 1971-1980. 5 vols.

This monumental series assembles all the Greek literary references to Cyprus covering the period from the earliest sources to AD 395.

Byzantine period

160 **Cyprus between Byzantium and Islam, A.D. 688-965.**
R. J. H. Jenkins. In: *Studies presented to David Moore Robinson.* Edited by George Mylonas, Doris Raymond. Saint Louis, Missouri: Washington University, 1953. vol. 2, p. 1,006-14.

A consideration of the political status of Cyprus between the Byzantine-Arab treaty of 688 and the final recovery of the island by Nicephorus II in 965. On the evidence of the sources, it is concluded that during this period the island did not belong to either Byzantium or the Arabs, except for Basil I's attempt to annex it. This work was reprinted as study no. 22 of the author's *Studies on the Byzantine history of the 9th and 10th centuries* (London: Variorum Reprints, 1970).

161 **The political status of Cyprus AD 648-965.**
A. I. Dikigoropoulos. In: *Report of the Department of Antiquities 1940-1948,* Nicosia, 1958, p. 94-114.

An attempt to trace the changing political fortunes of Cyprus in the three centuries of Byzantine-Arab confrontation in the eastern Mediterranean. Based on an examination of available literary evidence, the study concludes that the Cypriots were prepared to accept a status of neutrality for their island between Byzantium and the Arabs only when an Arab garrison was stationed in Cyprus to enforce it. Otherwise they were eager to accept Byzantine rule, especially when Orthodox emperors assumed the crown during the iconoclastic controversy. It was only reluctance to accept the authority of iconoclastic emperors that made the Cypriots acquiesce to a neutral status.

162 **Agrarian conditions and the demography of Cyprus during the period of the Arab wars AD 648-965.**
A. I. Dikigoropoulos. *Geographical Chronicles,* vol. 8, no. 13 (Jan.-June 1978), p. 3-14.

Based on an archaeological survey of settlement patterns in the early Byzantine period and on toponymic evidence. It is suggested that the depopulation and inland movement of settlement from the mid-8th century onward was primarily due to the devastating effects of plague and famine, rather than to the Arab raids of the same period.

History. Byzantine period

163   Slavs in Cyprus?
      D. Georgagas. *Kypriakai Spoudai*, vol. 14 (1950), p. 1-32.

The author argues that there is no authentic historical evidence concerning the settlement of Slavs in Cyprus during the 7th century AD or later.

164   A forgotten Byzantine conquest of Kypros.
      R. H. Dolley. *Bulletin de l'Académie Royale de Belgique (Classe des Lettres)*, 5th series, vol. 34 (1948), p. 209-24.

Cyprus was captured by a Byzantine fleet about 906, and was only lost in the aftermath of the reign of Leon VI.

165   Chypre: frontière ethnique et socio-culturelle du monde byzantin: rapports et co-rapports, XV Congrès International d'Etudes Byzantines V. (Cyprus: ethnic and sociocultural frontier of the Byzantine world: relations and connections, 14th International Congress of Byzantine Studies, 5.)
      Th. Papadopoullos. Athens: International Congress of Byzantine Studies, 1976. 51p.

An attempt to develop a general perspective on the history of Cyprus in the Byzantine period, emphasizing its role as the outpost marking Byzantium's ethnic and cultural frontiers in the south-east and the point of confrontation with alien civilizations.

166   L'empereur Isaac de Chypre et sa fille (1155-1207). (The emperor Isaac of Cyprus and his daughter.)
      W. H. Rudt de Collenberg. *Byzantion*, vol. 38, no. 1 (1968), p. 123-79.

In this long article the author discusses the controversial figure of Isaac Comnenus, who usurped the rule of Cyprus from his rightful Byzantine sovereign and proclaimed himself emperor of the island, just a few years before the long centuries of Cyprus's foreign occupations. It is argued that Isaac's life and career provide an important example of 12th century cosmopolitanism, which resulted from interlocking Western and Eastern interests in the eastern Mediterranean at the time. The author draws extensively on the pertinent sources, demonstrating his thesis by following the fortunes of Isaac and his daughter, 'Damsel of Cyprus'. He makes, however, some controversial claims concerning Isaac's relations with Cypriot monasticism.

History. Frankish and Venetian periods

Frankish and Venetian periods

167   **The kingdom of Cyprus, 1191-1291.**
Elizabeth Chapin Fuber. In: *A history of the crusades. The later crusades, 1189-1311.* Edited by Robert Lee Wolff, Harry W. Hazard. Madison, Wisconsin: University of Wisconsin Press, 1969, p. 599-629.

168   **The kingdom of Cyprus, 1291-1369.**
Harry Luke. In: *A history of the crusades. The fourteenth and fifteenth centuries.* Edited by Harry W. Hazard. Madison, Wisconsin: University of Wisconsin Press, 1975, p. 340-60.

169   **The kingdom of Cyprus, 1369-1489.**
Harry Luke. In: *A history of the crusades. The fourteenth and fifteenth centuries.* Edited by Harry W. Hazard. Madison, Wisconsin: University of Wisconsin Press, 1975, p. 361-95.
This and the two preceding items are authoritative and concise surveys of the three centuries of Lusignan rule, synthesizing the available evidence.

170   **Cyprus under an English king in the twelfth century.**
George H. Jeffery. London: Zeno, 1973. viii + 185p.
An account of the adventures of Richard the Lionheart and the crowning of his queen Berengaria in Cyprus in 1191. This story of mediaeval chivalry provides an insight into the life of the island at the stormy point of transition from Byzantine to Latin rule. It supplies information on the mediaeval cities and the condition of the countryside, the attitudes of the natives toward foreign intrusions, the presence of foreign commercial colonies, the peasant rising against Anglo-Norman rule at the end of 1191, the transactions which led to the sale of the island to the Lusignan dynasty, and the introduction of the institutions of European feudalism into this east Mediterranean territory. Reprinted from the 1926 edition.

171   **Richard the Lionheart**
John Gillingham. New York: Times Books, 1978. viii + 318p. maps. bibliog. illus.
Chapter 8 (p. 143-68) entitled 'Sicily and Cyprus 1190-1191' covers Richard the Lionheart's travels and adventures in the two Mediterranean islands. The part on Cyprus recounts the capture of Cyprus by Richard the Lionheart and his wedding to Berengaria. 'Richard and Berengaria were married in the chapel of St. George at Limassol and then Berengaria was crowned Queen by John, Bishop of Evreux. So in a Cypriot town a Queen of England was married by a bishop of a Norman see.'

History. Frankish and Venetian periods

172   **The Knights of St. John in Jerusalem and Cyprus c. 1050-1310.**
Jonathan Riley-Smith. London: Macmillan, 1967. xv + 553p.
12 maps. 8 plates.
A study of the privileges, organization, ecclesiastical practices and economic assets and activities of the Knights of St. John, whose adventures in the crusaders' East included involvement in the affairs of the Latin kingdom of Cyprus in 1291-1310.

173   **The feudal nobility and the kingdom of Jerusalem 1174-1277.**
Jonathan Riley-Smith. London: Macmillan; Hamden, Connecticut: Archon Books, 1973. xiv + 351p. bibliog.
A study of the implantation of European feudal nobility in the Middle East during the crusades from where it expanded to Cyprus. Many references to the feudal régime of Cyprus and the adoption of its laws and customs from the feudal kingdom of Jerusalem.

174   **The medieval kingdoms of Cyprus and Armenia.**
Williams Stubbs. Oxford, 1879. 54p.
A lucid survey of the history of the mediaeval kingdom of Cyprus by one of the leading mediaevalists of his time. As the author notes, this is simply a general presentation of a subject whose knowledge had just been greatly enhanced through the 'thorough and exhaustive' labours of French scholars, notably Mas Latrie.

175   **Recital concerning the sweet land of Cyprus entitled 'Chronicle'.**
Leontios Makhairas, edited with a translation and notes by
R. M. Dawkins. Oxford, England: Clarendon Press, 1932.
Reprinted, New York: AMS Press [n.d.] ; Famagusta, Cyprus: Editions l'Oiseau [n.d.] . 2 vols. map. gloss. genealogical table.
The most important mediaeval chronicle of Cyprus, written in Cypriot Greek by Leontios Makhairas in the 15th century and first published in 1873. After an introductory survey of the Christian background and vicissitudes of Cyprus, the author concentrates on the events of his time, describing the reigns of the Lusignan kings Peter I (1359-69), Peter II (1369-82), James I (1382-98), Janus (1398-1432), and John II (1432-58). The Greek text and the translation are given on facing pages.

176   **The chronicle of George Boustronios 1456-1489.**
George Boustronios, translated by R. M. Dawkins. Melbourne, Australia: University of Melbourne Cyprus Expedition, 1964.
xiii + 84p. folding map. 4 plates. (Publications, no. 2).
An English version of the chronicle which continues the narrative of Leontios Makhairas (see the preceding item) covering the last thirty years of Lusignan rule down to the cession of Cyprus to Venice by the last queen, Catherine Cornaro. George Boustronios recorded events of which he was an eye-witness and wrote, like his predecessor Makhairas, in the local Cypriot Greek dialect.

History. Frankish and Venetian periods

177 Histoire de l'île de Chypre sous le règne des princes de la maison de Lusignan. (A history of the island of Cyprus under the reign of the princes of the house of Lusignan.)
Louis de Mas Latrie. Paris: Imprimérie Imperiale, 1852-1861.
3 vols. Reprinted, Famagusta, Cyprus: Editions l'Oiseau, 1970.
5 vols.

The first volume of this monumental work attempts a historical synthesis of the first century of Lusignan rule in Cyprus (1192-1291), based primarily on the documentary evidence published previously in the other two volumes. The detailed narrative deals with the conquest of Cyprus by Richard the Lionheart and the successive sales of the island to the Knights Templar and to Guy de Lusignan, and surveys the geography and ancient history of Cyprus, the period of Byzantine rule and the establishment of Latin rule in 1192. It then considers the history of the reign of the first seven Lusignan kings and the changed international circumstances of the kingdom of Cyprus following the termination of the crusades at the end of the 13th century. Due attention is paid to the role of Cyprus in the commerce of the Levant in this period. The second volume comprises a rich collection of documents of the Lusignan kings of Cyprus, drawn mostly from French and Italian archives and ranging over the three centuries of Lusignan rule. The extensive preface presents an appraisal of the state of historical knowledge on Cyprus and a description of Mas Latrie's own researches. The third volume includes additional documents on the remaining reigns to the end of Lusignan rule and supplements to the documentary collections published in volume 2. In addition, documents pertaining to the Venetian and Ottoman periods up to the late 17th century are included so as to illuminate subsequent European interest in the destinies of Cyprus. The series was supplemented by two subsequent collections, appearing as *Nouvelles preuves* . . . and *Documents nouveaux* . . . in 1873-74 and 1882 respectively and forming volume 4, parts 1 and 2, of the 1970 reprint.

178 Description de toute l'isle de Chypre et des roys, princes, et seigneurs, tant payens que chrétiens qui ont commandé en icelle. (Description of the entire island of Cyprus and of the kings, princes and lords, both pagan and Christian, who have held sway in her.)
Etienne de Lusignan. Paris: Guillaume Chaudière, 1580.
Reprinted, Famagusta, Cyprus: Editions l'Oiseau, 1968. 292p.

A French translation of *Chorografia e breve historia universale dell' isola di Cipro*, Bologna, 1573. Although the narrative of the older phases of the history of Cyprus from the Deluge onwards contains many fantastic and improbable happenings, this is a valuable source on the periods of the Lusignan kingdom and Venetian rule. It provides vivid first-hand details on the war of Cyprus in 1570-71 and on the Ottoman conquest. Of special importance is the topography of the island at the close of the Venetian occupation and the other details of the social geography of Cyprus. These aspects of the book furnished valuable material to the 18th century historian Archimandrite Kyprianos, who was otherwise sceptical of the reliability of the historical information supplied by Lusignan and critical of his emphasis on Western Latin rule.

History. Frankish and Venetian periods

179 **Chronique de l'île de Chypre.** (Chronicle of the island of Cyprus.)
Florio Bustron, edited by René de Mas Latrie. Paris: Impremèrie Nationale, 1884. 531p.

The work of a 16th century Cypriot intellectual nobleman who fell fighting the Turks during the seige of Nicosia in 1570. This chronicle, written in Italian, begins with a description of the natural, human and historical geography of Cyprus, and goes on to recount the history of the mediaeval Latin kingdom drawing freely on the chronicle of Makhairas (q.v.). It brings the story down to the cession of Cyprus to Venice and the establishment and organization of Venetian rule. It thus forms a complete chronographical source on the fates of Cyprus under the Lusignans. The volume is completed with some additional fragments by Florio Bustron which have survived in two of the existing manuscripts.

180 **France de Chypre.** (France of Cyprus.)
Nicolas Iorga. Paris: Societé d'Editions 'Les Belles Lettres', 1966. 2nd ed. 215p. (Collection de l'Institute Néo-hellénique, no. 10.)

A charming reconstruction, first published in 1931, of the history and life of the mediaeval feudal kingdom of Cyprus under the French Lusignan dynasty. The work of a great historian, it pays particular attention to the institutions and social structure, mores, religion, and culture of Cyprus in the age of chivalry. It concludes by noting the survival and advent of the Greek element and its culture in the historical life of the island.

181 **Chypre sous les Lusignans: documents chypriotes des archives du Vatican (XIVe et XVe siècles).** (Cyprus under the Lusignans: Cypriot documents from the Vatican archives, 14th and 15th centuries.)
Edited by Jean Richard. Paris: Guethner, 1962. 179p. 2 maps.

Continuing a venerable tradition of French mediaevalist research on the Latin kingdom of Cyprus, Jean Richard brings together in this volume a collection of documents from the Vatican's *Archivio Segreto* which had been inaccessible to his 19th century predecessors. The collection includes documents in Latin, French and Greek written in Latin characters, on the history of the Latin church of Cyprus in the 14th century as well as a series of royal decrees of the years 1432-57. This documentary evidence throws considerable light on the historical geography of 14th and 15th century Cyprus.

182 **Orient et Occident au Moyen Age: contacts et relations (XIIe-XVe s.).** (East and West in the Middle Ages: contacts and relations, 12th-15th centuries.)
Jean Richard. London: Variorum Reprints, 1976.

The third section of this collection brings together six studies on the mediaeval kingdom of Cyprus, dealing with political and ecclesiastical history.

History. Frankish and Venetian periods

183 **Les relations entre l'Orient et l'Occident au Moyen Age: études et documents.** (Relations between East and West in the Middle Ages: studies and documents.)
Jean Richard. London: Variorum Reprints, 1977.

Studies 4, 5 and 6 in this collection consider various aspects of the social and cultural history of the mediaeval Latin kingdom of Cyprus. They are accompanied by the presentation of unpublished texts and documents on the rural and ecclesiastical life of Lusignan Cyprus. The rest of the book brings together many other studies by this leading student of mediaeval Cyprus, dealing with the crusades and the larger international context of the period. Many of these studies are of direct interest to the student of the mediaeval life of Cyprus. Study 12, 'Chypre du protectorat à la domination venitienne' (Cyprus from protectorate to Venetian domination), considers the stages of Venetian penetration until the eventual annexation of Cyprus.

184 **Une économie coloniale? Chypre et ses ressources agricoles au Moyen Age.** (A colonial economy? Cyprus and its agricultural resources in the Middle Ages).
Jean Richard. *Byzantinische Forschungen,* vol. 5 (1977), p. 331-52.

A study of the economic history of Cyprus in the late Middle Ages, utilizing the evidence accumulated by a century of mediaevalist research. It focuses on the agricultural resources of the island economy and on the structure of rural society, and concludes that under the Lusignans the Cypriot rural economy was balanced as a productive unit. Agriculture and local industry using domestic agricultural raw materials supplied an important export trade, and, although the profits benefited primarily the aristocracy and the mercantile class, the needs of the population at large appear from the sources to have been fulfilled. This balanced economy was destroyed by the Venetians who, after 1489, redirected the production of Cyprus to suit the requirements of their metropolitan economy, thus reducing the Cypriot economy to colonial status.

185 **Catherine Cornaro, reine de Chypre.** (Catherine Cornaro, queen of Cyprus.)
Marcel Brion. Paris: Editions Albin Michel, 1945. 289p.

A biography of the last queen of Cyprus. It narrates the history of Catherine Cornaro's reign (1474-89), during which Venetian infiltration gradually replaced formal Lusignan rule in Cyprus.

186 **L'art gothique et la Renaissance en Chypre.** (Gothic art and the Renaissance in Cyprus.)
Camille Enlart. Paris: E. Leroux, 1899. Reprinted, Famagusta, Cyprus: Editions l'Oiseau, 1966. 2 vols. bibliog. 34 plates.

A detailed study, illustrated by drawings, of mediaeval Gothic architecture in Cyprus. It surveys the buildings and remains of Gothic churches throughout Cyprus, mostly of the Lusignan period, as well as the monuments of civil and military architecture of the Lusignan and Venetian periods.

History. Frankish and Venetian periods

187   **Villes mortes du Moyen Age. (Dead cities of the Middle Ages).**
Camille Enlart. Paris: Editions de Boccard, 1920. 162p. bibliog. illus.

A section of this book (p. 111-62) is devoted to the 'dead cities of the Kingdom of Cyprus', surveying the mediaeval remains of Paphos and Famagusta. Illustrated with photographs and drawings of the monuments.

188   **Lacrimae Nicossienses: recueil d'inscriptions funéraires la plupart françaises existant encore dans l'île de Chypre.**
(Nicosia's tears: a collection of funerary inscriptions, mostly French, still surviving in the island of Cyprus.)
Tankerville J. Chamberlayne. Paris: Librairies-Imprimeries Réunies, 1894. 172p. 29 plates.

A publication of the funerary inscriptions and monuments surviving at the close of the 19th century in the mediaeval Latin churches of Nicosia. Besides the rich archaeological and topographical evidence about mediaeval Nicosia, the publication of the epigraphical material and the editor's commentaries provide a perspective on the social life in the capital of the crusader kingdom of Cyprus.

189   **The arts of Cyprus: ecclesiastical art.**
T. S. R. Boase. In: *A history of the crusades. The art and architecture of the crusader states.* Edited by Harry W. Hazard. Madison, Wisconsin: University of Wisconsin Press, 1977, p. 165-95.

190   **The arts of Cyprus: military architecture.**
A. H. S. Megaw. In: *A history of the crusades. The art and architecture of the crusader states.* Edited by Harry W. Hazard. Madison, Wisconsin: University of Wisconsin Press, 1977, p. 196-207.

This and the preceding item are authoritative surveys drawing on all previous research on the monuments left behind by the crusader kingdom of Cyprus.

191   **An Italo-Byzantine series of wall-paintings in the church of St. John Lampadhistis, Kalopanayiotis, Cyprus.**
Andreas Stylianou. In: *Akten des XI Internationales Byzantinisten Kongresses Munchen 1958.* Edited by Franz Dolger, Hans Georg Beck. Munich, GFR: C. H. Beck'sche Verlagsbuchhandlung, 1960, p. 595-98.

A presentation and discussion of early Italian Renaissance influences on the wall-paintings of one of the foremost monuments of post-Byzantine art in Cyprus.

History. Ottoman rule, 1571-1878

Addendum

191a The Mediterranean and the Mediterranean world in the age of Philip II.
Fernand Braudel, translated by Siân Reynolds. New York: Harper & Row, 1972. 3 vols. bibliog.

This masterpiece of 20th century historiography contains valuable insights into the history of Cyprus in the 16th century. Besides considering the place of the island in the context of the collective destinies of the Mediterranean world in the period, it pays attention to the determinants of the social history of Cyprus under Venetian rule and to its role in 16th century international relations. The war of the Ottoman Empire with Venice over Cyprus in 1570-71 and its immediate result, the great battle of Lepanto, receive due attention.

Ottoman rule, 1571-1878

192 Cyprus under the Turks: 1571-1878.
Harry Luke. Oxford, England: Clarendon Press, 1921.
Reprinted, London: C. Hurst & Co., 1969. 218p. folding map. bibliog.

This is a classic record of Ottoman rule in Cyprus, based on the archives of the English consulate originally founded by the Levant Company in 1626. The book offers an account of Turkish rule from 1571 to 1788 (reprinting Cobham's translation of *Archimandrite Kyprianos*) and of the activities of the Levant Company in Cyprus, 1626-1825, and sifts through the British consular archives from 1710-1878 in order to glean characteristic details on life and government in Ottoman Cyprus in the 18th and 19th centuries.

193 The main problems concerning the history of Cyprus.
H. Inalcik. *Cultura Turcica*, vol. 1 no. 1 (1964), p. 44-51.

This is a very brief and not particularly suggestive overview of the history of Ottoman rule in Cyprus and its main themes and problems. It is nevertheless interesting as an appraisal of what is significant in this period from the point of view of the leading Turkish historian of the Ottoman Empire.

194 Social and historical data on population, 1570-1881.
Theodoros Ch. Papadopoullos. Nicosia: Cyprus Research Centre, 1965. xl + 248p.

This is the most important study available on the historical demography of modern Cyprus. On the basis of surviving census data and the information of foreign visitors to the island, it attempts to reconstruct the evolution of the Cypriot population during the critical period of Ottoman rule. It concludes with a consideration of the first British census of 1881 which recorded the demographic profile of Cyprus as it had evolved by the end of the Ottoman occupation.

History. Ottoman rule, 1571-1878

195 Considérations sur le peuplement moderne de Chypre et ses origines. (Considerations on the modern population of Cyprus and its origins.)
Robert P. Charles. *Kypriakai Spoudai,* vol. 29 (1965), p. 3-26.

On the basis of anthropological evidence, the author concludes that the community derived from the Turkish conquerors of Cyprus in the 16th century does not exceed 6.5 per cent, while another 6 per cent of the population is of Armenian origin. Therefore 87.5 per cent are considered to be of Greek origin.

196 The sieges of Nicosia and Famagusta with a sketch of the earlier history of Cyprus.
Edited by Claude D. Cobham. London: St. Vincent's Press, 1899. 57p.

An excerpt from Robert Midgley's 1687 English translation of Bishop Antonmaria Graziani's history of the war of Cyprus. Graziani was intimately involved in the diplomacy of the war of Cyprus as papal nuncio to the princes of Italy, and in this section he describes the military events of the sieges of the two leading cities of Venetian Cyprus in 1570-71 on the basis of contemporary accounts.

197 Travels in the island of Cyprus.
Giovanni Mariti, translated by Claude D. Cobham. London: Zeno, 1971. viii + 199p.

The Abbé Giovanni Mariti was an official of the Imperial and Tuscan consulates in Cyprus from 1760-67. He travelled extensively throughout the island visiting all major towns and many villages, even in the inaccessible mountainous regions of Cyprus. In his book he recorded his travels as well as an account of the 1764 rising, a description of the island's commerce and of the consular institutions. His work is the most important contemporary source on the condition of Cyprus in the third quarter of the 18th century. The book also includes the contemporary accounts of the sieges of Nicosia and Famagusta in 1570-71 by Gio. Pietro Contarini and Nestor Martinengo. Reprint of 1909 edition.

198 The communal character of the administration of church property in Cyprus under Ottoman rule.
C. P. Kyrris. *Balkan Studies,* vol. 12, no. 2 (1971), p. 463-78.

On the basis of evidence from 18th century archiepiscopal registers and of comparative observations concerning the experience of other sections of Ottoman Hellenism, it is suggested that the laity, organized on communal lines, participated in the management of church properties under Ottoman rule.

199 Cyprus and the War of Greek Independence 1821-1829.
John T. A. Koumoulides. London: Zeno, 1974. xiii + 117p. folding map. bibliog. plates.

After a general survey of the history of Cyprus from earliest times to 1800, this book examines Greco-Turkish relations in the island in the first two decades of the 19th century, the events of the tragic year 1821, and the fate of Cyprus during the period of the Greek War of Independence to 1829.

History. British rule, 1878-1960

200 **L'île de Chypre: sa situation présente et ses souvenirs du moyen age.** (The island of Cyprus: its present position and its recollections of the Middle Ages.)
Louis de Mas Latrie. Paris: Firmin-Didot, 1879. 432p. folding map.

This is a very interesting account of the natural, political and economic geography of Cyprus in the closing years of Ottoman rule by the foremost French specialist in the history of the island. The second section of the first part comprises the basic guidelines and data for the construction of a map of Cyprus. The second part of the book brings together some of Mas Latrie's findings on the mediaeval past of Cyprus concerning relations between the island and Asia Minor, the publication of 103 mediaeval inscriptions, and a list of fiefs and royal domains in the Frankish period.

British rule, 1878-1960

201 **Cyprus: its history, its present resources and future prospects.**
Robert Hamilton Lang. London: Macmillan, 1878. x + 370p. 4 maps.

The author was a consul in the island immediately prior to the British occupation, and gives a sympathetic portrait of Cyprus at that time. He gives a general account of the island's past, talks at length about its agricultural resources and problems, its mineral and salt deposits, and its antiquities. The author describes lovingly the landscapes and good-hearted people of Cyprus whom he met on his trips and on his farm. He appraises the Turkish administration and hails the British occupation as the dawn of a new age that will bring 'the diffusion of the blessings of civilization and the elements of an enlightened progress' to Cyprus.

202 **British Cyprus.**
W. Hepworth Dixon. London: Chapman & Hall, 1879. xi + 368p.

This book is interesting as a description of Cyprus, whose major cities and countryside the author came to know well in the first year of British rule. It offers many interesting details and picturesque insights into the life of Cyprus at that time of transition, but in its attitude to the subject, this is a rather complacent and superficial source. It celebrates the coming of British rule and acclaims the 'British right' to Cyprus as dating back to the conquest of Richard the Lionheart.

History. British rule, 1878-1960

203   **Cyprus: historical and descriptive from the earliest times to the present day.**
      Franz von Löher, translated by A. Batson Joyner. New York: R. Worthington, 1878. 324p.

Besides a mass of meticulously collected information on Cyprus's past and present at the time of the British occupation, this source is very important as a pointer to German interest in the island. It attempts to trace the historical connections of Germany with Cyprus since the crusades, and stresses the strategic importance of Cyprus as a base of traffic for the contemplated Euphrates valley railway.

204   **Great Britain and Cyprus Convention policy of 1878.**
      Dwight E. Lee. Cambridge, Massachusetts: Harvard University Press, 1934. x + 230p. folding map. apps.

This is the definitive study of the inception and execution of British policy in the occupation of Cyprus in 1878. It provides a detailed diplomatic history of British moves from 1875-80 designed to secure imperial control over the eastern Mediterranean island which constituted an indispensable strategic link on the road to India.

205   **Memorandum concerning Cyprus, 1878.**
      Dwight E. Lee. *Journal of Modern History*, vol. 3, no. 2 (June 1931), p. 235-41. app.

The memorandum of 8 June 1878 on Cyprus, drawn up by Colonel Home of the War Office intelligence department, is analysed (and appended) in this brief article. It shows that it is on the basis of the recommendations of this memorandum, to which Lord Salisbury also contributed, that Prime Minister Disraeli (Lord Beaconsfield) decided to press for the British acquisition of Cyprus from the Sultan in 1878 at the Congress of Berlin.

206   **Disraeli and Cyprus.**
      Harold Temperley. *English Historical Review*, vol. 46, no. 182 (April 1931), p. 274-79.

A historical brief on Disraeli's concern with British strategic interests in the Mediterranean and the Middle East, his concern with Russian objectives in the region, and the overall strategic thinking that eventually led to Disraeli's 1878 decision to seek the acquisition of Cyprus from the Sultan as Britain's *place d'armes* in the Mediterranean.

207   **The Gladstone government and the Cyprus Convention, 1880-1885.**
      W. N. Medlicot. *Journal of Modern History*, vol. 12, no. 2 (June 1940), p. 186-208.

An analysis of the attitudes of the Liberal government of 1880 *vis-à-vis* the Cyprus Convention, which they had criticized when concluded by Disraeli in 1878. Despite their initial reservations the Liberals did nothing to change things.

History. British rule, 1878-1960

208 **Cyprus under British rule.**
George Chacalli. Nicosia, 1902. 177p.

A survey intended to familiarize Britons with the island, emphasizing its Greek cultural character. Interesting details on the character of the British administration are provided as well as requests for greater Cypriot participation in the internal administration of the island. Many of these requests are excerpted from the minutes of the Legislative Council.

209 **Cyprus under British rule.**
C. W. J. Orr. London: Zeno, 1972. 192p. folding map.

A survey of administrative practice and of political and economic problems in Cyprus during the first forty years of British rule. Written by a leading official of the British administration, the book gives a fair impression of what was accomplished but also of what was neglected by British rule in its early decades in Cyprus, and is therefore important for an understanding of the origins of the Cyprus Question. Reprint of 1918 edition.

210 **Churchill's 1907 visit to Cyprus: a political analysis.**
G. S. Georghallides. *Epetiris,* vol. 3 (1969-70), p. 167-220.

An account of Winston Churchill's visit to Cyprus in October 1907 and of his sympathetic reactions to the Cypriots' grievances and claims.

211 **A political and administrative history of Cyprus 1918-1926; with a survey of the foundations of British rule.**
G. S. Georghallides. Nicosia: Cyprus Research Centre, 1979. x + 471p. apps.

The first part of the book is a survey of the establishment of the British administration in Cyprus, the institutional changes it introduced, and the financial, political and national problems it faced in dealing with the Cypriots in the years 1878-1918. The second and major part of the book is an in-depth study of the political history of Cyprus in the years 1918-26, the attempts at administrative reform and their eventual failure which created the political and social impasse of the inter-war period in Cyprus's history. A particularly interesting section of the book appeared originally as an article entitled 'Turkish and British reactions to the emigration of the Cypriot Turks to Anatolia, 1924-1927' (*Balkan Studies,* vol. 18, no. 1 (1977), p. 43-52). The book includes useful appendixes and a prosopography of Greek Cypriot political figures composed by A. L. Coudounaris.

212 **The 1915 British offer of Cyprus to Greece in the light of the war in the Balkans.**
Christos Theodoulou. *Epetiris,* vol. 4 (1970-71), p. 417-30.

The diplomatic background of the October 1915 British offer of Cyprus to Greece, based on the evidence of Foreign Office documents.

History. British rule, 1878-1960

213   **Greek Cypriot manifestations of allegiance to Greece and British reactions (1915-1916).**
Christos Theodoulou. *Kypriakai Spoudai*, vol. 35 (1971), p. 165-89.

An account of the emotional responses precipitated among the Greek Cypriots by the British offer of the island to Greece in 1915.

214   **The unredeemed isles of Greece.**
Hamilton Fish Armstrong. *Foreign Affairs,* vol. 4, no. 1 (Oct. 1925), p. 154-57.

The Dodecanese and Cyprus are treated as the 'unredeemed isles' in this brief note that dwells on the historical and/or legal claims of Greece and of the islands. With regard to Cyprus, interestingly enough, objections for an eventual union with Greece are seen as coming from France, which was alarmed that Greek expansion in the eastern Mediterranean would threaten her interests in the Levant.

215   **Disturbances in Cyprus in October, 1931.**
Ronald Storrs. London: HM Stationery Office, 1932. 42p. (Cmnd. no. 4045).

The official colonial account and explanation of the 1931 Cypriot uprising against the policies and practices of the British administration. It is written by the then governor of Cyprus and is addressed to the secretary of state for the colonies. The account chronicles and interprets the events and contains documents and official exchanges between the colonial government and representatives of the Cypriots.

216   **Cyprus, the British Empire and Greece.**
Arnold J. Toynbee. In: *Survey of international affairs 1931.* Edited by Arnold J. Toynbee. London: Oxford University Press, 1932, p. 354-94.

A perceptive study of the background and character of the 1931 rebellion in Cyprus. It examines the politics and social problems of the first phase of British rule in Cyprus and explains the growth of Greek Cypriot nationalism. It remains one of the best sources on the politics of Cyprus in the early 20th century.

217   **Orientations.**
Ronald Storrs. London: Nicholson & Watson, 1945. 532p.

The memoirs of Sir Ronald Storrs's service to the British Empire in the Near East. Chapters 19-20 (p. 456-517) offer an account of Sir Ronald's governorship in Cyprus from 30 November 1926 to 9 June 1932. It provides an appraisal of the island's problems under British rule, especially in the inter-war years, Sir Ronald's attempted reforms, and the political agitation that culminated in the nationalist rising of October 1931. An American edition appeared as *The memoirs of Sir Ronald Storrs* (New York: Putnam, 1937).

History. British rule, 1878-1960

218 **The Cypriote Question, considered from the points of history and international law.**
Michael Dendias. Athens: Pyrsos, 1937. 255p.

This is a little-known English version of one of the most important sources on the Cyprus Question in the inter-war period. The work of public law professor at the University of Athens, it was published originally in French in 1934 in order to bring the Greek point of view on Cyprus to the attention of the international public. It is, however, much more than a propagandist work. It presents one of the best analyses of the character and psychological dynamics of Cypriot irredentism, besides surveying the issues arising from the international position of Cyprus. It constitutes the most serious rejoinder to the British line on Cyprus and remains to this date one of the indispensable sources on the history of the Cyprus Question. Originally published as *La question cypriote aux points de vue historique et de droit international* (Paris: Sirey, 1934).

219 **Cyprus: a brief survey of its history and development.**
W. H. Flinn. Nicosia: W. J. Archer, Government Printer, 1924. 93p. map. bibliog. illus.

Illustrated throughout with black-and-white photographs, this book briefly reviews significant events in Cypriot history and provides detailed descriptions of the agricultural, industrial and other natural resources of the island. A basic economic profile of the island in the inter-war years.

220 **The handbook of Cyprus.**
Ronald Storrs, Bryan Justin O'Brien. London: Christophers, 1930. 9th ed. 368p. bibliog. gloss.

An authoritative guide to Cyprus in the inter-war years, providing a general picture of the island as it had developed after fifty years of British rule. It offers information on the geography and history, peoples and religion, places of interest, communications and tourist attractions, government and government activities, geology, mineral resources, mining and industries, natural history and sport, as well as useful miscellaneous tips to the visitor and a glossary of basic terms.

221 **The story of the Cyprus government railway.**
B. S. Turner. London: Mechanical Engineering Publications, 1979. ix + 178p. maps. bibliog. charts. illus.

What! A railway in Cyprus? Yes indeed – some of the old-timers will tell you and will show you what is left of its tracks in the Famagusta-Nicosia-Morphou-Evrykhou route. For the first time the fascinating story of this picturesque little railway which operated from 1904-51 is modestly but lucidly chronicled by an enthusiast of the subject. Details of its planning, construction and operations as well as its final demise are now preserved in this work, recording yet another chapter of the island's colonial history. A chronology is included.

Cyprus Question, 1945-60

222 **Die Zypernfrage.** (The Cyprus problem.)
Ludwig Dischler. Frankfurt am Main; Berlin, GFR: Alfred
Metzner Verlag, 1960. 174p. bibliog. (Dokumente, vol. 33).

This monograph is divided in two parts. The first provides a brief but meticulously collected documentary record from the 1878 British acquisition to the 1958-59 Zurich-London compromise agreements. Included are invaluable historical details regarding the British attitude and proposals for internal self-government, the Cypriot reaction, and the evolution of the last phase of colonial rule that climaxed in the Cypriot anti-colonial rebellion. The second part is a collection of thirty-six official documents and statements. These range from the 5 May 1878 communication of Lord Beaconsfield (Disraeli) to Queen Victoria on the desirability of acquiring Cyprus and thus enhancing British power, to the statement of Aneurin Bevan of the opposition in the British Parliament eighty-one years later, endorsing the Zurich-London agreements but also criticizing the Conservative government for pursuing policies that made it impossible for agreement to be reached earlier. Almost all documents and statements are reproduced in English, the original language, with a few in French. As a collection, they are immensely convenient to the researcher.

223 **Le conflit de Chypre 1946-1959.** (The Cyprus conflict 1946-1959.)
François Crouzet. Brussels: Etablissements Emile Bruylant, 1973.
2 vols. folding map. bibliog. graphs.

A historical synthesis of the evolution of the Cyprus Question from 1946-59, which attempts to weave together all dimensions of the problem, domestic as well as international. It draws on all available evidence in presenting a masterful picture of the emergence, gradual escalation and eventual settlement of the conflict in 1959. An examination of the 'roots of the conflict' is followed by an in-depth account of its successive phases (1946-50, 1950-55, 1955-57, 1957-59).

224 **Cyprus challenge. A colonial island and its aspirations: reminiscences of a former editor of the** *Cyprus Post.*
Percy Arnold. London: Hogarth Press, 1956. 222p.

A description of life and politics in Cyprus during the Second World War by the editor of the island's English-language newspaper, the *Cyprus Post*. From 1942-45 the author witnessed closely the local political scene and in his book he discusses the national aspirations of the Cypriots as voiced by the church and the schools; British attitudes and administrative practices; local journalism; the labour movement and the communist party. He explains the national aspirations of the Cypriots as a desire to terminate the anachronism of colonialism in the modern world, and criticizes the repressive measures and the reluctance of the British to respond to Cypriot demands which he sees as the root of the violence of the 1950s.

History. Cyprus Question, 1945-60

225 **Cyprus past and ... future.**
Doros Alastos. London: Committee for Cyprus Affairs, 1943. 75p.

After surveying the basic problems of British rule in Cyprus (the tribute, poverty and official neglect, repression following the 1931 rising), the author voices the wartime aspirations of progressive opinion in the island.

226 **British policy on the question of enosis 1945-1946.**
George M. Alexander. *Kypriakai Spoudai,* vol. 43 (1979), p. 79-94.

A study of the Labour government's deliberations in 1945-46 concerning the possibility of a cession of Cyprus to Greece. It is followed by the relevant documents.

227 **Toward 'toil and moil' in Cyprus.**
Stephen G. Xydis. *Middle East Journal,* vol. 20, no. 1 (winter 1966), p. 1-19.

A study of Greek diplomatic initiatives in the Cyprus Question from the end of the Second World War to the outbreak of the EOKA revolt in 1955.

228 **Cyprus conflict and conciliation, 1954-1958.**
Stephen G. Xydis. Columbus, Ohio: Ohio State University Press for the Mershon Center for Education in National Security, 1967. xviii + 704p. bibliog.

One of the most important sources on the diplomacy of the Cyprus Question, this book discusses in great detail Greek policy from 1954-58, especially in connection with the United Nations deliberations over the fate of Cyprus in this period. The author has had privileged access to the personal papers of some of the leading Greek protagonists of the drama. The book illuminates the evolution of Greek policy from the unconditional demand of self-determination for Cyprus to the acceptance of independence.

229 **Cyprus: reluctant republic.**
Stephen G. Xydis. The Hague, Paris: Mouton, 1973. 553p. bibliog. app.

This is a minutely detailed diplomatic history of the quest for a settlement of the Cyprus Question from the beginning of 1958 to the proclamation of Cypriot independence in 1960. The author has had privileged access to the pertinent official Greek and Greek Cypriot records, and has consulted widely all other published sources. His narrative documents the conflicts and obstacles which surrounded the birth of the Republic of Cyprus as well as the constraints and compromises which conditioned its independence. This is a remarkably objective and factual record of the inception of the problems that have plagued the reluctant island republic ever since its independence. The book contains in appendix the draft agreement between Cyprus, Greece and Turkey on the application of the Treaty of Alliance not available elsewhere.

230 **The Cyprus Question.**
Leontios Ierodiakonou. Stockholm: Almqvist & Wiksell, 1971.
311p. maps. bibliog.

This is a study of the international aspects of the Cyprus Question from 1954-59. It reconstructs the diplomatic history of the problem and examines the policy initiatives of the parties involved. A substantial postscript surveys the politics of the Cyprus Republic up to 1969.

231 **La tragédie Chypriote.** (The Cypriot tragedy.)
Charalambos D. Marinos. Athens, 1964. 489p.

A detailed survey of the development of the Cyprus Question, year by year, focusing on the period from 1955-64, with special attention on 1955-59. Of special interest is the survey of the views held by other than the principal actors (chapter 12, p. 424-40).

232 **Legacy of strife: Cyprus from rebellion to civil war.**
Charles Foley. London: Penguin, 1964. rev. ed. 187p.

An account of the Cyprus revolt of 1955-59 through to the breakdown of ethnic relations in the 1963 constitutional crisis. The author, a leading journalist with intimate knowledge of local conditions in Cyprus, exemplifies an understanding of the temper and stakes of Cypriot politics which is rare among British commentators. This is a revised and expanded edition of the author's *Island in revolt* (London: Longman, 1962. 248p.).

233 **The struggle for Cyprus.**
Charles Foley, W. I. Scobie. Stanford, California: Hoover Institution Press, 1975. x + 193p. bibliog. illus.

The bulk of this work covers the years of 1955-60 and recounts the EOKA story. It is based on numerous interviews with almost all of the leading figures of the EOKA underground. Extremely valuable for understanding EOKA's internal politics and the feuds and quarrels that were carried over into the post-independence period.

234 **Enosis and its background: race and religion in Cyprus.**
Round Table, vol. 42, no. 186 (March 1957), p. 129-40.

With the outbreak of the Cypriot anti-colonial movement in 1955 and the demand for union with Greece, the need arose to educate much of the English public, and indeed many of the British policy-makers, with the island's long history and especially the historical and ideological forces that brought about the enosis campaign under the leadership of the Greek Orthodox Church of Cyprus. The attempt is made in this essay by an unidentified writer who, though well informed on history, often lapses into the defence of British policies and of British colonialism.

History. Cyprus Question, 1945-60

235 **The Cyprus revolt: an account of the struggle for union with Greece.**
Nancy Crawshaw. London: George Allen & Unwin, 1978.
448p. 3 maps. bibliog. apps.

This is a detailed study of the processes and conflicts leading to the outbreak of the EOKA revolt in Cyprus in 1955-59, of the actual course of the revolt, its international ramifications, its settlement and its aftermath to 1976. The author is a journalist with considerable experience in Cypriot affairs. She provides a detailed account of political events and a very useful history of the EOKA movement, but she shows little understanding of the underlying causes and broader issues in the conflict. The book contains useful appendixes and an important bibliography, including the official and documentary sources on the Cyprus Question up to 1976.

236 **The memoirs of General Grivas.**
George Grivas, edited by Charles Foley. New York; Washington, DC: Frederick A. Praeger, 1965. 226p. illus. apps.

This is an edited version of Grivas's memoirs originally published in Athens in 1961. They give the general's story on the organization and implementation of the EOKA campaign, on his disagreements with Archbishop Makarios and the Greek government, and the reasons for his opposition to the Zurich-London accords which for him were a betrayal of the EOKA struggle for union with Greece.

237 **General Grivas on guerilla warfare.**
George Grivas, translated by A. A. Pallis. New York; Washington, DC: Frederick A. Praeger, 1965. xi + 109p. apps.

General Grivas's own account of how he organized the Cypriot liberation campaign against the British. Includes details of his strategy and tactics, organization details and general conclusions on guerilla warfare.

238 **Terrorism in Cyprus: the captured documents.**
London: HM Stationery Office [n.d.] . 82p.

George Grivas, leader of the anti-colonial Cypriot underground, kept copious diaries from the autumn of 1954 through to the end of the Cypriot revolt. Part of these diaries were discovered by British intelligence along with other documents and photographs during the summer of 1956. This work contains extracts from the diaries, translated and issued by the Secretary of State for the Colonies. They record Grivas's candid opinions of his fellow fighters and of politicians in Greece and Cyprus including Archbishop Makarios, and also reveal details of the EOKA organization. The British used extracts from the captured diaries to prove their contention that a close working relationship existed between Grivas and Makarios. The evidence against the archbishop was also used as a justification for his exile. Although cast as propaganda, the historical importance of this publication cannot be disregarded.

History. Cyprus Question, 1945-60

239   **Grivas: portrait of a terrorist.**
Dudley Barker. New York: Harcourt, Brace & Co., 1959.
202p. illus. apps.

A highly personalized account of the Cyprus anti-British revolt, centering on the actions of EOKA's leader George Grivas, alias Dhighenis. It reflects British views and attitudes.

240   **Grivas and the story of EOKA.**
W. Byford-Jones. London: Robert Hale, 1959. 192p.

A biography of Grivas by an acquaintance since the events in Athens during the 1940s, in the context of a study of the organization and tactics of EOKA.

241   **Cyprus guerilla: Grivas, Makarios and the British.**
D. Alastos. London: Heinemann, 1960. 224p. map. illus. app.

A Cypriot historian chronicles the EOKA campaign against Britain detailing its various phases, military and political, while providing valuable insight into the thinking and personalities of two of its major protagonists: Grivas and Makarios.

242   **Challenge and response in internal conflict: the experience in Europe and the Middle East: vol. 2.**
D. M. Condit, Bert H. Cooper, Jr. (and others). Washington, DC: American University, Center for Research in Social Systems, 1967. xxv + 618p.

Chapter 12 of this work (p. 355-80, with a select bibliography) is entitled 'Cyprus 1954-1958' and is by Charilaos G. Lagoudakis. It deals with the EOKA insurgency, giving its background and identifying its major actors and the ideologies motivating them. EOKA's tactics and the British counter-insurgency response are also analysed.

243   **On revolt.**
J. Bowyer Bell. Cambridge, Massachusetts; London: Harvard University Press, 1976. xii + 265p.

In chapter 6 (p. 115-65), entitled 'Two classical confrontations: containment of EOKA in Cyprus and concession to NLF in South Arabia', an account of Britain's attempt to suppress the EOKA movement is given. Details of Britain's and EOKA's tactics and counter-tactics are provided. Considered a tactical success, the EOKA revolt is judged as failing to achieve its ultimate goal, i.e. enosis.

History. Cyprus Question, 1945-60

244 The problem of Cyprus.
Lord Radcliffe. *United Empire,* vol. 49, no. 1 (Jan.-Feb. 1958), p. 15-19, 24.

This was the first public statement on Cyprus by Lord Radcliffe since the publication of his 1956 *Constitutional proposals for Cyprus* (q.v.). It gives a brief background of the reasons that brought the British to the island, presents some of the arguments of the main antagonists, including Britain, and concludes that because of the lack of a 'sober political tradition' mere constitutional proposals do not carry 'very much weight with the Cypriots today'.

245 The Cyprus problem in relation to the Middle East.
Lord Harding of Petherton. *International Affairs,* vol. 34, no. 3 (July 1958), p. 291-96.

A significant article revealing the strategic and politico-military considerations (i.e. oil and anti-communism) that determined Britain's policy towards Cyprus during the late 1950s. The author served as military governor on the island in the early phase of the emergency period.

246 Harding of Petherton.
Michael Carver. London: Weidenfeld & Nicolson, 1978. ix + 239p. maps. bibliog. illus.

Field Marshal Lord Harding of Petherton was appointed military governor of Cyprus (1955-57) following the outbreak of the Cypriot anti-colonial revolt. Chapters 12 and 13 (p. 195-228) of this biography deal with the field marshal's Cyprus tenure. His goals and objectives and those of British policy in general are treated sympathetically. The book contains some anecdotal material on the period that should be of interest to researchers.

247 A start in freedom.
Hugh Foot. London: Hodder & Stoughton, 1964. 256p.

Chapter 9 (p. 143-87) records the author's recollections of his service in Cyprus in 1943-45 and again during the turbulent years of 1957-60, the tenure of the last British governor of the island.

248 Emergency exit.
Sylvia Foot. London: Chatto & Windus, 1960. 192p. illus.

Impressions and memories of the final two years of British rule, by the wife of the last governor of Cyprus, Sir Hugh Foot.

History. Cyprus Question, 1945-60

249 **Full circle.**
Anthony Eden. Boston, Massachusetts: Houghton Mifflin, 1960. 676p. illus.

Chapter 11 (p. 440-64) of Eden's memoirs relates his involvement with Cyprus, particularly from 1954-56, a determinative period in Cyprus's recent history, when Eden was Britain's chief policy-maker. Details of the evolving British policy towards the EOKA rebellion and other episodes of that time, e.g. Makarios's exile, are provided. Conspicuously absent are any references to the inter-relationship between Eden's Cyprus policies and those towards the Suez crisis, against whose background the initial and crucial British decision towards Cyprus were made.

250 **Tides of fortune, 1945-1955.**
Harold Macmillan. New York; Evanston, Illinois: Harper & Row, 1969. illus.

251 **Riding the storm, 1956-1959.**
Harold Macmillan. London: Macmillan, 1971.
ix + 786p. plates. illus.

As foreign minister and later prime minister, Macmillan made his mark on Cyprus's modern history. His role and that of many other British policy-makers during the Cyprus rebellion are recounted in the preceding item *Tides of fortune* (p. 661-78) and in *Riding the storm* (p. 222-31, 657-701). The latter memoir covers Macmillan's premiership from 1956-59, a period that witnessed the Zurich-London agreements and the emergence of Cyprus to independence. It is therefore of particular importance to students of Cypriot history.

252 **Quietly men 1957: Suez + Cyprus.**
Michael Foot, Mervyn Jones. New York: Rinehart & Co., 1957.
244p. illus.

The evolution of the Cyprus problem and the course of political developments following the 1955 EOKA rebellion are intricately entwined with the decline of the British imperial interests in the Middle East and cannot be understood unless seen in that context. This work indicts the men, policies and the Conservative political philosophy that sought to salvage British 'honour' and reassert, through force in Suez and Cyprus, British power and interests. Chapter 5 (p. 130-63), entitled 'Base for agression', chronicles the British policies in 1956 aimed at suppressing EOKA and concludes by stating that with the Suez attack Cyprus as a base had 'proved its value' for the Conservative hard-liners.

History. Cyprus Question, 1945-60

253 **Cyprus and Makarios.**
Stanley Mayes. London: Putnam, 1960. xii + 260p.

This is a journalistic history of the Cyprus conflict in the 1950s through a political biography of Archbishop Makarios up to his election to the presidency of the new Republic of Cyprus. The author is intimately familiar with the intricacies of the Cyprus Question, but he allows his personal dislike for the archbishop to colour his judgement beyond fair criticism. Thus even several of his well-taken criticisms and the thoroughness of his coverage of the archbishop's range of political activities are obscured by his bias.

254 **Makarios in exile.**
P. S. Le Geyt. Nicosia: Anagennisis Press, 1961. xxii + 192p. maps. illus. apps.

The first two parts of the book, written by the controller of the household of Makarios and the other Cypriot exiles in the Seychelles, are essentially the diaries the author and his wife kept during the period March 1956-April 1957 when they interacted with the exiles on a daily basis. Interesting and anecdotal. The third part of the book deals with the Seychelles.

255 **President Makarios of Cyprus.**
Panos Myrtiotis, translated by Robin Knight, Diana Markides, David Bailey, introduction by Chrysostomos Sofianos. Nicosia: Nicocles Press [n.d.] . 72p. illus.

An illustrated biography of Archbishop Makarios relating his life and struggles up to the creation of the republic. It is supplemented by quotations from the archbishop, official documents and other sources. In the introduction his last minister of education, writing shortly after Makarios's death, appraises the man and his contribution to Cyprus.

256 **The island of Cyprus and union with Greece.**
Zeno G. Rossides, edited by the Ethnarchy Council of Cyprus. Nicosia: Anagennisis Printing Works, 1954. 3rd ed. 26p. illus.

This pamphlet, originally published in 1953, argues the case for the Greek-Cypriot claim for self-determination and union with Greece. The author, a member of the Ethnarchy Council of Cyprus at the time and an activist for union with Greece, propounds through a brief historical survey the nationalist ideology that dominated Cypriot internal politics during the 1950s. His policy was sponsored, encouraged and financed by the church of Cyprus and had led to the EOKA rebellion (1955) against British colonial rule.

History. Cyprus Question, 1945-60

257 **Cyprus demands self-determination.**
Savas Loizides. Athens: National Committee for Self-Determination of Cyprus, 1956. 22p.

Written a year after the EOKA rebellion against British colonialism commenced, this pamphlet, after arguing the case for Cypriot self-determination, deals with selected developments during 1956: the first year of the guerilla war; the British reaction and the repressive measures instituted against the civilian population; the application of the Greek government against Great Britain before the European Commission of Human Rights of the Council of Europe concerning British violations of human rights in Cyprus; the ill-fated negotiations between the British governor Sir John Harding and Cypriot leader Archbishop Makarios; and the British decision to exile the Cypriot leader to the Seychelles. The tone and arguments of the author, nationalistic and critical of Britain, are characteristic of the period.

258 **The Cyprus Question: the British reply to the British.**
Spyros Kyprianou. Athens: National Committee for Self-Determination of Cyprus, 1956. 29p.

The case for Cyprus's self-determination made by a young political activist and future president of the Republic of Cyprus.

259 **The impartial knife: a doctor in Cyprus.**
Peter Paris. New York: David McKay Co., 1962. 215p.

This is the memoir of an Irish doctor who practised his profession in Cyprus during the years of the EOKA rebellion. Vivid descriptions of his hospital experiences in the midst of killings perpetrated by EOKA, the British forces and the Turks. A highly opinionated account at times, this work ends on a very pessimistic note on the prospects for a peaceful Cyprus − a prediction that was proven correct albeit not always for the reasons given.

260 **Below the tide.**
Penelope Tremayne. London: Hutchinson; Boston, Massachusetts: Little, Brown, 1958. 187p.

Observations concerning the impact of the events of the turbulent late 1950s on the life of civilians, especially in rural Cyprus.

261 **Cyprus: the dispute and the settlement.**
Royal Institute of International Affairs, Information Department. London: RIIA, 1964. 62 + xip. apps. (Chatham House Memoranda).

This background paper on the evolution of the enosis movement during the period of the British occupation was first published in 1955, and was revised and updated repeatedly as the Cyprus problem unfolded during the 1955-59 EOKA rebellion until the Zurich-London agreements were reached. It was finally reprinted in 1964. The account of the late 1950s draws primarily on the British press and the debates in the British Parliament. Two appendixes are included, one containing extracts from documents since 1878 and another describing the economy of Cyprus during the 1950s.

History. Cyprus Question, 1945-60

262 **The settlement of Cyprus – a complex and rigid constitution.**
Round Table, vol. 49 (1958-59), p. 256-65.
An account of the Zurich-London settlement of the Cyprus Question, focusing on the peculiarities and rigidities of the constitution of the new republic.

263 **The settlement in Cyprus.**
Eric Baker. *Political Quarterly,* vol. 30, no. 3 (July-Sept. 1959), p. 244-53.
This is a perceptive essay on the motivations that led Great Britain, Greece and Turkey to conclude the 1959 Zurich-London agreements. Also considered are the most important provisions of the Cyprus constitution, and the potentially divisive elements and issues are presciently identified.

264 **Cyprus: revolution and resolution.**
Roy P. Fairfield. *Middle East Journal,* vol. 13, no. 3 (summer 1959), p. 235-48.
An account of the 1959 settlement of the Cyprus conflict and an appraisal of the prospects of the new republic on the eve of its independence.

265 **Le conflit de Chypre et les Cypriotes Turcs.** (The Cyprus conflict and the Turkish Cypriots.)
A. Suat Bilge. Ankara: Ajans-Turk Matbaasi, 1961. 267p. (Publications de la Faculté des Sciences Politiques de l'Université d'Ankara).
After a historical introduction on the origins and social structure of the Turkish community the author surveys political developments in Cyprus from 1954-59 whilst articulating the position of Turkey and of the Turkish Cypriots.

266 **The Greco-Turkish feud revived.**
Panayotis Pipinelis. *Foreign Affairs,* vol. 37, no. 2 (Jan. 1959), p. 306-16.
In this essay reviewing Greco-Turkish relations the author, a Greek politician and diplomat, bemoans the revival of the Greco-Turkish feud (considered settled with the 1923 Treaty of Lausanne) as a result of the Cyprus issue. Writing on the eve of the Zurich-London accords, the author expresses cautious optimism that Greco-Turkish relations may weather the revived feud, enabling Greece and Turkey to play their role within the Western political and defence system.

267 **Cyprus and the United Nations: an appreciation of parliamentary diplomacy.**
Naomi Rosenbaum. *Canadian Journal of Economics and Political Science,* vol. 33 (1967), p. 218-31.
An appraisal of the handling of the Cyprus issue in the United Nations from the point of view of open diplomacy.

History. Cyprus Question, 1945-60

268 **Success in foreign policy: the British in Cyprus, 1878-1960.**
Naomi Rosenbaum. *Canadian Journal of Political Science,*
vol. 3, no. 4 (Dec. 1970), p. 605-27.

Much of this article is theoretical, and the Cyprus case is used as an example to validate the hypothesis that 'the more negative a foreign policy, the more likely it is to be successful'. It is the author's contention that British foreign policy was a 'success' because the 1959 Zurich-London accords were acceptable to Britain and 'were thoroughly compatible with Britain's goals on the island'. These goals were negative goals: preventing another power from controlling Cyprus (Soviet Union, Greece) and having the ability to effect this (Britain's bases). 'Success' is simply viewed from a British perspective without any reference to the internal situation. To the extent that Western security interests may be served by an internal and external deadlock, which neutralizes Cyprus strategically, Rosenbaum's thesis may be relevant to the post-1974 situation.

269 **The Tripartite Conference on the Eastern Mediterranean and Cyprus.**
London: HM Stationery Office, 1955. 46p. apps. (Cmnd. no. 9594, Miscellaneous no. 18).

The official text of the now famous 1955 Tripartite Conference called by the British government and in which Greece and Turkey but no Cypriots participated. It contains the official speeches of the British, Greek and Turkish foreign ministers, the official communiqué and other relevant material.

270 **Cyprus: correspondence exchanged between the governor and Archbishop Makarios.**
London: HM Stationery Office, 1956. 12p. (Cmnd. no. 9708).

The official texts of the correspondence exchanged between the British governor Sir John Harding and Archbishop Makarios are included together with a British statement of policy. The subject is the British offer for a development of constitutional self-government in Cyprus and the archbishop's counter-proposals on the matter. The exchanges had taken place in January-February 1956.

271 **Constitutional proposals for Cyprus.**
Lord Radcliffe. London: HM Stationery Office, 1956. 48p. app. (Cmnd. no. 42).

A comprehensive set of recommendations by Lord Radcliffe for a new constitution entailing self-government for Cyprus. The proposed departments and functions of the self-governing side are set out and explained in great detail in the appendix. The recommendations are based on the principles of liberal democracy while ensuring the rights of the various communities and religions and other racial groups. British sovereignty was to remain unaffected.

272 **Cyprus: statement of policy.**
London: HM Stationery Office, 1958. 3p. (Cmnd. no. 455).

The official British policy statement announcing the Macmillan Plan for the establishment of tripartite control (Britain, Greece, Turkey) over Cyprus.

History. Cyprus Question, 1945-60

273 **Discussion on Cyprus in the North Atlantic Treaty Organization.**
London: HM Stationery Office, 1958. 6p. (Cmnd. no. 566, Miscellaneous no. 14).

At about the same time as the announcement of the Macmillan Plan (June 1958) and the months following it, the NATO Council discussed Cyprus and its secretary general put forth some suggestions for a provisional solution modifying somewhat the Macmillan Plan which was unacceptable to the Greek side. Selected documents from that discussion are reproduced here.

274 **Conference on Cyprus: documents signed and initialled at Lancaster House on February 19, 1959.**
London: HM Stationery Office, 1959. 15p. (Cmnd. no. 679, Miscellaneous no. 4).

Included are the various documents (Zurich-London agreements) initiated or signed at Lancaster House and the pertinent declarations made by Great Britain, Greece, Turkey and the representatives of the Greek and Turkish Cypriot communities.

275 **Conference on Cyprus: final statements at the closing plenary session at Lancaster House on February 19, 1959.**
London: HM Stationery Office, 1959. 7p. (Cmnd. no. 680, Miscellaneous no. 5).

The official final statements of the British, Greek and Turkish prime ministers and of the representatives of the Greek and Turkish communities at the closing meeting of the Lancaster House conference called to obtain official acceptance of the Zurich-London agreements.

Cyprus Republic

276 **Cyprus a place of arms: power politics and ethnic conflict in the eastern Mediterranean.**
Robert Stephens. London: Pall Mall, 1966. 232p. maps. bibliog.

The work of a distinguished journalist with great experience in Middle Eastern affairs, this is one of the most illuminating accounts of the Cyprus Question. It considers the cause of Cyprus as an integral part of a broader complex formed by interlocking Greek, Turkish and British interests in the eastern Mediterranean, and traces the origins of the Cyprus problem through a survey of the historical fortunes of the region since the dawn of the 20th century. Local conflicts and aspirations are discussed with a perceptiveness unusual among commentators on Cyprus. It brings the story to the mid-1960s, and offers the most convincing appraisal of the misconceptions and policy failures that complicated the island's problems, apportioning the greatest blame to British policy.

History. Cyprus Republic

277 **Cyprus constitutionalism and crisis government.**
Stanley Kyriakides. Philadelphia, Pennsylvania: University of Pennsylvania Press, 1968. xii + 212p. bibliog. apps.

After a survey of the abortive attempts at constitutional change in the post-war period, this study concentrates on an analysis of the 1960 constitutional arrangements and the major constitutional 'tension areas'. In this context it examines the crisis that followed the attempt at constitutional revision initiated by President Makarios in 1963. As a study of the 1963-64 crisis in the Cyprus Question and as an analysis of the peculiarities of the constitution of the Republic of Cyprus, this is the most authoritative source available to date. In the appendixes it presents important documents and the only survey of Greek Cypriot political attitudes taken in the aftermath of the crisis.

278 **Chypre: histoire récente et perspectives d'avenir.** (Cyprus: recent history and future prospects.)
Georges Ténékidès. Paris: Nagel, 1964. 293p. bibliog.

A study of the 1963-64 crisis of the Cyprus Question in a broad perspective, enhanced by a lively sense of the factors at work in the island's history and the requirements of international justice and democratic constitutionalism. The author is accordingly able to articulate the antinomies of the Cyprus problem and to evaluate the various alternative solutions on the basis of their pertinence to human rights and the cultural possibilities of the island.

279 **Cyprus: the law and politics of civil strife.**
Linda Miller. Cambridge, Massachusetts: Center for International Affairs, Harvard University, 1968. viii + 97p. map. bibliog. apps.

This study focuses on the role of legal norms, international institutions and foreign governments in the evolution of the Cyprus conflict. It also includes a survey of the alternatives for a settlement proposed to the time of writing.

280 **Cyprus 1946-68.**
Hal Kosut. New York: Facts on File, 1970. 192p. map.

This book records international and domestic developments affecting Cyprus from 1946-68, adapted mostly from the reports appearing in *Facts on File*. It provides useful background to students and scholars unfamiliar with Cyprus who need a bird's-eye view up to the 1967 crisis.

History. Cyprus Republic

281 **The Cyprus dispute.**
Harry J. Psomiades. *Current History*, vol. 43, no. 285 (May 1965), p. 269-76, 305-06.

Most of this article is devoted to the politics between Greece, Turkey and Great Britain that brought about Cyprus's guaranteed independence in 1960 through the Zurich-London agreements. The salient elements of these agreements are also discussed, as are the friction points between the Greek and Turkish Cypriots which led to the partial collapse of the Zurich-London agreements and the outbreak of communal violence in 1963-64.

282 **The Cypriot labyrinth.**
James Hughes. *New Left Review*, no. 29 (Jan.-Feb. 1965), p. 41-52.

The outbreak of intercommunal violence in 1963-64 is placed into perspective by the author through an articulation of the politics of the main actors: Archbishop Makarios, General Grivas, Dr. Kutchuk, Rauf Denktash. The political realities of the post-independence period as these were shaped during the 1955-59 period are also addressed in the author's attempt to ascertain responsibility for the 1963-64 outbreak of violence. Constructive criticism of the leadership of both communities is made, while many of the myths about the innately hostile attitudes between the Greek and Turkish Cypriots are dismissed as historically unsubstantiated.

283 **Division over Cyprus.**
W. M. Dobell. *International Journal*, vol. 22, no. 2 (spring 1967), p. 278-92.

An overview of political developments in Cyprus from the outbreak of violence in 1963-64, prefaced with some historical background. Details of the 1964-66 mediation efforts, particularly those by the American Dean Acheson and by the United Nations, are provided.

284 **Our destiny.**
N. C. Lanitis. Nicosia: the author, 1963. 33p. app.

Based to a large extent on a series of articles that appeared in the English-language *Cyprus Mail*, 3-7 March 1963, this is a profound piece of work, ignored by those it was addressed to, viz. the leadership of the Greek Cypriot community. Written a few months before the outbreak of intercommunal conflict, it calls for unity between the Greek and Turkish Cypriots, who, the author maintains, have more things in common than they have differences. The destiny of all Cypriots lies within Cyprus, he argues, and not with the motherlands as nationalists in both communities would have it. Patriotism and economic development hold the key to a long-term solution and a prosperous Cyprus.

285 **The Republic of Cyprus and the events that have come to pass.**
Halil Fikret Alasya. Ankara: Ayyildiz Matbaasi, 1969. 18p.

The senior Turkish Cypriot historian considers the nature of ethnic conflict that plagued the republic's first decade.

History. Cyprus Republic

286 **The problem of Cyprus.**
Rauf R. Denktash. *Review of International Affairs* (Yugoslavia), vol. 22, no. 544 (5 Dec. 1972), p. 9-11.

The Turkish Cypriot perspective on Cyprus is articulated by the most prominent Turkish Cypriot leader. The emphasis is on the background to the problem and on the Turkish Cypriot desire for a constitutional solution ensuring self-government or autonomy for the Turkish Cypriots.

287 **Makarios: faith and power.**
P. N. Vanezis, introduction by James Cameron. London, New York, Toronto: Abelard-Schuman, 1971. 196p. map. bibliog. illus. app.

288 **Makarios: pragmatism v. idealism.**
P. N. Vanezis, foreword by Hugh Foot. London: Abelard-Schuman, 1974. 209p. bibliog.

289 **Makarios: life and leadership.**
P. N. Vanezis, foreword by Edward Kennedy. London: Abelard-Schuman, 1979. 177p. bibliog. illus. apps.

Post-Second World War Cypriot history is intricately entwined with the life and times of the late Archbishop Makarios III, first president of Cyprus (1960-77). In this trilogy (see the two preceding items) the author traces the archbishop's religious and political career and his struggle first against British colonialism and later, with the dissipation of the enosis dream, against external powers and internal forces seeking the demise of the Cypriot Republic. The works reflect the author's admiration for the archbishop-president, are non-critical, and by their nature often repetitive. They nonetheless constitute an important source on the archbishop and Cyprus.

290 **Makarios: a biography.**
Stanley Mayes. New York: St. Martin's Press; London: Macmillan, 1981. xi + 303p. bibliog. illus.

Unlike Mayes' earlier work *Cyprus and Makarios* (q.v.) the present one is surprisingly mellow and at times even sympathetic towards the late president. Overall it remains critical of the archbishop-president. His life is judged as a tragic failure and his policies on the Cyprus problem as lacking in statesmanship. This is the first full-length, albeit unofficial, biography of the ethnarch with some anecdotal material from his early life. Insights into Makarios's complex personality, his subtlety, sense of humour and his ambiguity, of which he has been acknowledged a master, are included.

History. Cyprus Republic

291 The rise and fall of the Cyprus Republic.
Kyriakos C. Markrides. New Haven, Connecticut; London: Yale University Press, 1977. xviii + 200p. map.

This is a study in the political sociology of the Cyprus Republic. It examines Cypriot social structure and political culture, through a study of the nature of Cypriot society before and after colonialism, the process of social change and the consequent emergence of nationalism and ethnic conflict. It includes an important, though not definitive, analysis of the role and sources of authority of Archbishop Makarios. Its most important contribution is the detailed sociological analysis of the 'disloyal opposition' which in collaboration with the Greek junta managed to overthrow the constitutional order in 1974 and to precipitate the Turkish invasion — and thus the 'fall' of the republic.

292 An unexplored case of political change: a research note on the electoral history of Cyprus.
Paschalis M. Kitromilides. *Epitheorisi Koinonikon Erevnon/ Greek Review of Social Research*, no. 38 (1980), p. 187-90.

A survey of forms of electoral participation in Cyprus under British rule and under the republic, pointing at the possibilities of political analysis in the study of the pertinent data.

293 The House of Representatives of the Republic of Cyprus.
Alecos Michaelides. *Parliamentarian*, vol. 60, no. 2 (April 1979), p. 67-71.

This is a descriptive account of the powers, functions and procedures of the Cypriot House of Representatives, authored by the then president of the House.

294 Communism in Cyprus.
T. W. Adams, Alvin J. Cottrell. *Problems of Communism*, vol. 15, no. 3 (May-June 1966), p. 22-30.

The authors trace the rise of the communist party of AKEL with some background on its sources of power and its strategy and tactics in the context of the Cyprus problem and the East-West rivalry. Written with the cold war perspective this work has been superseded by the authors' *Cyprus between East and West* (q.v.), and Adams's *AKEL: the communist party of Cyprus* (see below).

295 AKEL: the communist party of Cyprus.
T. W. Adams. Stanford, California: Hoover Institution Press, 1971. xxii + 284p. bibliog. apps.

This is a study of one of the most important factors in Cypriot politics, the history, organization and political role of the Working People's Uplifting Party (AKEL). Although the book, the only source on an important subject, contains much interesting information it is not free of inaccuracies and bias.

History. Cyprus Republic

296 **Report on west European communist parties.**
Foreign Affairs and National Defense Division, Congressional Research Service, Library of Congress. Washington, DC: US Government Printing Office, 1977. 326p.

As part of the above study, communism in Cyprus is covered by Stanley R. Sloan in 'The communist party of Cyprus' (p. 199-207). Brief details on the evolution, organization and leadership strength, and ideological outlook of the party are provided. The party's essentially moderate domestic strategy is seen as the major source of its strength.

297 **Cyprus: the ideological crucible.**
Kenneth Mackenzie, edited by Brian Crozier. London: Institute for the Study of Conflict, 1972. 15p. maps. charts. tables. (Conflict Studies, no. 26).

An essay on the conflict by a British journalist with extensive knowledge of the island. The motivations, tactics and goals of the major protagonists are analysed with interesting and insightful views on the confrontations between Makarios, Athens and Ankara and Makarios and Grivas. According to the author Britain and the US 'do not greatly care who runs Cyprus as long as (a) Britain can retain its bases, and (b) the island does not fall under communist control'. It is also his conviction that 'the root of the Cyprus problem is the Greek assumption of moral and cultural superiority; this rather than the fear of bullets and bombs is what enrages the Turkish Cypriots', and that 'the unchanging factor in Cyprus is the basic mistrust between the two main communities'.

298 **Cyprus under four flags: a struggle for unity.**
Kenneth MacLeish, photographs by Jonathan Blair. *National Geographic*, vol. 143, no. 3 (March 1973), p. 356-82. illus.

The four flags are those of Greece, Turkey, the United Nations and Cyprus, although in the same context a fifth one should be added — that of Great Britain. All fly over Cyprus, symbolizing the political conflict on the island and the involvement of outsiders in the island's affairs. In this essay, life and culture on the island are illustrated through pictures and intermingled references to the political antagonisms between the island's communities.

299 **Cyprus: the Makarios years.**
Ken Mackenzie. *Economist* (UK), vol. 252, no. 6830 (July 1974), 18p.

A special survey on Makarios's fourteen-year rule in Cyprus, written after the 15 July *putsch* but prior to the 20 July Turkish invasion. It provides a critical survey of Cyprus's post-independence political developments, with special articles on Makarios's style of leadership, the intercommunal talks, Grivas's politics, the role of the United Nations, and the economy and culture.

Foreign Relations

General

300 **International crises and the role of law: Cyprus 1958-1967.**
Thomas Ehrlich. London: Oxford University Press, 1974.
xii + 164p.

A study of the role of legal norms in decision-making at four major turning points in the evolution of the Cyprus Question: the British government's decision to relinquish sovereignty over Cyprus in 1958; the Cypriot government's decision in 1963 to propose revisions of the Cyprus constitution; the Turkish government's decision in 1964 to bomb Cyprus; the Greek government's decision in 1967 to withdraw the Greek troops from Cyprus. The major contribution of the book consists in the legal case it puts forward concerning the lack of any Turkish right to use military force against Cyprus.

301 **Cyprus between East and West.**
T. W. Adams, Alvin J. Cottrell, foreword by Robert E. Osgood.
Baltimore, Maryland: Johns Hopkins University Press, 1968.
xi + 92p. bibliog.

A short analysis of the Cyprus conflict in the cold war context. Emphasizes the regional and international aspects of the dispute, especially US policies and security concerns in the area. A chronology is included.

302 **The foreign policy of Cyprus.**
R. P. Barston. In: *The other powers: studies in the foreign policies of small states.* Edited by R. P. Barston. London: Allen & Unwin; New York: Harper & Row, 1973, p. 184-209.

One of the very few studies to deal with the foreign policy of Cyprus in a comprehensive way. Sections of the article deal with the background, setting, machinery and process of the Cypriot foreign policy. Two other sections discuss the Cyprus problem and how it was handled internationally, and the foreign economic policy of Cyprus. The last section deals with Cyprus and international cooperation, stressing the status of Cyprus as a non-aligned state. The author concludes that, 'by careful delineation of the limits of its power and international roles, Cyprus, on balance, has been successful in the management of its foreign policy'.

Foreign Relations. General

303 **Cyprus: the vulnerable republic.**
Dimitri S. Bitsios. Thessaloniki, Greece: Institute for Balkan Studies, 1975. 223p. annex.

A career Greek diplomat, who rose to the office of foreign minister, recollects his involvement in many critical phases of the diplomatic effort to deal with the Cyprus problem from the early 1950s to the mid-1970s.

304 **Le complot de Chypre.** (The Cyprus conspiracy.)
E. N. Dzelepy. Brussels: Editions Politiques, 1965. 317p.

Although this book may appear to be simply an example of the conspiracy theory of history, it still contains many bitter truths and valid statements concerning the manipulation of the Cypriots' aspirations and internal conflicts by outside powers desiring to use Cyprus for their own purposes. The book's focus is on the problems bequeathed to Cyprus by the Zurich-London settlement and on the crisis of the early 1960s. It underlines throughout the efforts of Archbishop Makarios on behalf of the freedom and independence of Cyprus.

305 **Facing the brink: an intimate study of crisis diplomacy.**
Edward Weintal, Charles Barlett. New York: Charles Scribner's Sons, 1967. vi + 248p. app.

In the context of this study chapter 2 (p. 16-36), entitled 'Aux armes citoyens!', is an account of the intervention and mediation role of the US, spearheaded by the then under-secretary of state George Ball and the former secretary of state Dean Acheson, in the 1964 Cyprus crisis. Essential for understanding the motivations behind the American decision to get involved actively and to espouse solutions like the partitionist Acheson Plan. In the appendix (p. 221), the letter of 28 August 1964 from Turkish foreign minister F. Erkin to US mediator Dean Acheson rejecting the Acheson Plan is reproduced.

306 **NATO and the Cyprus crisis.**
Philip Windsor. London: Institute for Strategic Studies, 1964. 19p. (Adelphi Papers, no. 14).

A lucid analysis of the Cyprus problem with special emphasis on Western security interests. The author points out the limits and questions the wisdom of NATO's involvement in the conflict. He suggests that Western interests can best be safeguarded in situations like the one in Cyprus through intervention by the UN. A chronology is included.

307 **Cyprus: the anatomy of the problem.**
Dean Acheson. *Chicago Bar Record,* vol. 46, no. 8 (May 1965), p. 349-56.

A revealing summary of the views of the author of the most controversial plan on the solution of the Cyprus problem.

Foreign Relations. General

308 **Cyprus: Britain's security role.**
Anthony Verrier. *The World Today* (UK), vol. 20, no. 3 (March 1964), p. 131-37.

In the aftermath of the December 1963 outbreak of hostilities in Cyprus this article examines, interchangeably, British security interests and Britain's security role in ensuring peace on the island. Such peace is deemed essential for British and Western security concerns.

309 **The Cyprus conflict and United States security interests.**
Dankwart A. Rustow. Santa Monica, California: Rand Corporation, 1967. 39p.

This is an unclassified version of a still-classified study on American security interests in Cyprus written for the Rand Corporation. The sanitized version gives a historical background to the conflict in the Cypriot republic and identifies the main actors and their security interests with special emphasis on those of the US and the Western alliance.

310 **The American concern in Cyprus.**
T. W. Adams. *Annals of the American Academy of Political and Social Science,* vol. 401 (May 1972), p. 95-105.

A fairly good account of the American (and Western) political and security interests in Cyprus emerges from this work despite its shortcomings both in content and analysis.

311 **President Johnson and Prime Minister Inonu.**
Middle East Journal, vol. 20, no. 3 (summer 1966), p. 386-93.

The historic letters exchanged between President Johnson and Prime Minister Inönü of Turkey in June 1964, as released by the White House on 15 January 1966, are reproduced here. The Johnson letter, drafted by the then under-secretary of state George Ball, is considered by many as having averted a Turkish invasion of Cyprus planned at the time and as causing Turkey to reassess its view of the NATO alliance.

312 **Foreign policy of Turkey at the United Nations: vol. 1.**
Compiled and edited by Yuksel Soylemez. Ankara: Ministry of Foreign Affairs, 1973. xxxiv + 827p.

This volume on political and legal questions contains selected public interventions, public documents and official communications in Turkey's foreign policy at the United Nations between the years 1966-72. The question of Cyprus is dealt with in chapter 12 (p. 141-301) which contains excerpts from official speeches in the various bodies of the United Nations.

Foreign Relations. General

313 **Turkey's foreign policy in transition 1950-1974.**
Kemal H. Karpat (and others). Leiden, the Netherlands:
E. J. Brill, 1975. 233p. bibliog.

Devoted to Turkey's foreign policy since 1950, this volume contains two articles on Cyprus: Suat Bilge's 'The Cyprus conflict and Turkey' (p. 135-85) and Kemal H. Karpat's 'War on Cyprus: the tragedy of enosis' (p. 186-205). Bilge's contribution is of particular importance since its author is well acquainted with Turkey's interests and concerns and, as an official in the Ministry of Foreign Affairs, he has been associated with the formulation of Turkey's Cyprus policy since the 1950s. Bilge's article, written in an essay form, is updated to 1972. Kemal H. Karpat's essay discusses events up to and including the 1974 crisis.

314 **The Cyprus conflict as a prisoner's dilemma game.**
Malvern Lumsden. *Journal of Conflict Resolution*, vol. 17, no. 1 (March 1973), p. 7-32.

An application of game theory to the analysis of the Cyprus conflict. It is concluded that the Cyprus conflict could be considered as a 'prisoner's dilemma' game where war is not seen as the worst possibility by either side and peace offers a Pareto optimal solution.

315 **The Cyprus dilemma: options for peace.**
New York: Institute for Mediterranean Affairs, 1967.
91p. bibliog. charts.

A collection of individual essays by independent scholars and authorities on the eastern Mediterranean (Thomas P. Trombetas, Kemal H. Karpat, Georges Mikes, S. Merlin). The essays offer guidelines for a peaceful solution to the Cyprus conflict from divergent points of view. S. Merlin's article is an attempt to reconcile the opposing views, and offers his suggestions for a solution. The volume includes a chronology.

316 **The Cyprus problem and its solution.**
Elie Kedourie, introduction by E. A. Bayne. Rome: Center for Mediterranean Studies, American Universities Field Staff, 1974.
iv + 26p. maps. app.

This is a report of a seminar held in Rome in November 1973 to discuss the Cyprus problem and explore the possibilities of its settlement. Elie Kedourie acted as rapporteur and the participants included, among others, Cypriot leaders G. Clerides and R. Denktash; former officials from Greece, Turkey, the UK and the US, and a number of distinguished scholars. The problem is identified as primarily a political and constitutional one, and its solution must be of the same character. Constitutional areas that can be amenable to amendments are identified and suggestions made, their thrust being to minimize the occasions on which Greek and Turkish Cypriots 'are placed in position to exercise power over each other'.

Foreign Relations. United Nations and Cyprus

United Nations and Cyprus

317 **Report of the United Nations mediator on Cyprus to the secretary general.**
Galo Plaza. *United Nations Security Council Official Records, Supplement,* Jan.-June 1965. (Doc. S/6253, 26 March 1965).

The Plaza Report remains one of the central documents of recent Cypriot political history. It provides a concise and comprehensive background to the problem and a detailed and candid analysis of the positions of the parties concerned regarding a peaceful and agreed solution. Without offering precise recommendations or even suggestions, the UN mediator makes apparent certain directions that the parties concerned, primarily the Cypriots, may wish to explore in their search for a solution. Some of the directions suggested remain relevant to this date despite the 1974 upheaval. A comprehensive list of all documents pertaining to Cyprus is compiled in the *United Nations Security Council Index,* published annually. These are published in quarterly *Supplements of the Official Records of the Security Council.* Resolutions of the Security Council are to be found in *Resolutions and Decisions of the Security Council,* published in yearly volumes, and those of the General Assembly in *Resolutions and Decisions Adopted by the General Assembly,* also published annually. The texts of the debates in the Security Council and the General Assembly on Cyprus are to be found in *Provisional Verbatim Records, Verbatim Records* and *Official Records* of the appropriate body.

318 **The United Nations Force in Cyprus.**
James A. Stegenga, foreword by Inis L. Claude, Jr. Columbus, Ohio: Ohio State University Press for the Mershon Center for Education in National Security, 1968. viii + 227p. maps. bibliog. tables.

This is the most comprehensive account of the creation and deployment of the United Nations Force in Cyprus (UNFICYP). In his interim assessment on the effectiveness of the force Mr. Stegenga concludes that UNFICYP has been a model of efficiency, has made a positive contribution to peace on the island, and could serve as a model for future UN forces deployed in analogous circumstances. He points out nevertheless that UN forces have a limited capacity to affect the peacemaking process and are not a substitute for traditional diplomacy.

319 **UN peacekeeping: the Cyprus venture.**
James A. Stegenga. *Journal of Peace Research,* vol. 7 (1970), p. 1-15.

A subsequent look at UN peacekeeping in Cyprus with a rejoinder to the critics of the author's earlier book (see the preceding item).

Foreign Relations. United Nations and Cyprus

320 **Cyprus: episode in peacekeeping.**
James M. Boyd. *International Organization*, vol. 20, no. 1 (1966), p. 1-17.

Based primarily on UN documentation, this article discusses the creation and deployment of the United Nations Force in Cyprus (UNFICYP), addresses its 'pluses and minuses' after two years of operations, and through UNFICYP's experience makes general remarks on the future of peacekeeping.

321 **A view from within: the role of small states and the Cyprus experiences.**
Andreas J. Jacovides. Nicosia: Public Information Office, 1969. 47p.

In the context of assessing the prospects for a more effective United Nations peacekeeping effort, details and other relevant information on the establishment of the United Nations peacekeeping force in Cyprus (UNFICYP) are provided. The author, a Cypriot diplomat and lawyer, was actively involved (representing his government) in the establishment of UNFICYP.

322 **The international regulation of civil wars.**
Edited by Evan Luard. New York: New York University Press, 1972. 240p.

A contribution by Anne Duncan-Jones entitled 'The civil war in Cyprus' is part of this volume (p. 148-68). Essentially it is an evaluation of the UN efforts regarding the Cyprus conflict. It concludes that the role of the UN peacekeeping force was successful, especially in its mission as an 'impartial observer'. Suggests that it is hard to evaluate UNFICYP's two other functions of maintaining law and order and contributing to the return of normal conditions. Salutes the appointment of Osorio-Tafall as special representative with the mandate to promote an agreed settlement, not to impose a UN settlement.

323 **United Nations peacekeeping and peacemaking and the Cyprus Question.**
Van Coufoudakis. *Western Political Quarterly* (USA), vol. 29, no. 3 (Sept. 1976), p. 457-73.

The article examines how the Cyprus Question affected the UN and the organization's response to the various phases of the problem; why the parties to the dispute sought, endorsed, tolerated or opposed the UN's involvement; and how the UN's response was affected by the politics of the superpowers, the goals of the parties and their relations with the superpowers.

Foreign Relations. United Nations and Cyprus

324 **American foreign policy and the UN peacekeeping force in Cyprus.**
T. W. Adams, Alvin J. Cottrell. *Orbis,* vol. 12, no. 2 (summer 1968), p. 490-503.

The deployment and operation of the UN peacekeeping force in Cyprus (UNFICYP) is evaluated in the context of Western and American security interests in the eastern Mediterranean. Much of the material and analysis has appeared in previous publications of the two authors.

325 **The impartial soldier.**
Michael Harbottle, foreword by K. G. Younger. London, New York, Toronto: Oxford University Press, for the Royal Institute of International Affairs, 1970. viii + 210p. maps. bibliog. illus.

An authoritative account of the peacekeeping and peacemaking process in operation in Cyprus, by the chief of staff of the United Nations Force in Cyprus (UNFICYP) during the years 1966-68. After a brief background on the organization and deployment of UNFICYP, the author relates particular incidents, violent or otherwise, and the instrumental role played by the various agencies of UNFICYP in defusing them. Of particular importance is the author's account of the background and causes of the 1967 Ayios Theodoros-Kophinou crisis. A revealing chapter on General Grivas and his influence on events is included.

326 **Peace soldiers: the sociology of a United Nations military force.**
Charles C. Moskos. Chicago: University of Chicago Press, 1976. xi + 171p. charts. apps.

A scholarly, sociological study of the UN peacekeeping force (UNFICYP) in Cyprus between 1963-69. The author, a respected sociologist of the armed forces, applies Janowitz's concept of 'constabulary ethic' to UNFICYP. Documentary materials in the history of operations and field observations in Cyprus by the author are the data sources. A good source for the history, concepts and principles of UN peacekeeping, as well as the organization, composition and operation of UNFICYP. Moskos argues that UNFICYP showed great success in its peacekeeping operations given the limited role and power of its mandate.

Foreign Relations. United Nations and Cyprus

327 **The thin blue line: international peacekeeping and its future.**
Indar Jit Rikhye, Michael Harbottle, Bjørn Egge. New Haven, Connecticut; London: Yale University Press, 1974. 353p. maps. bibliog.

In the context of this study, sponsored by the International Peace Academy, UN peacekeeping in Cyprus is dealt with in chapter 7 (p. 97-119) as one of three case studies, from which general conclusions are drawn (the other two are Middle East-UNEF 1956 and Congo-ONUC). The essay on Cyprus deals with the causes that necessitated the deployment of UNFICYP in 1964, its mandate and its mode of operation in the context of the local confrontation: preventing action through interposition, and political reconciliation through follow-up action. Overall the authors underscore, *inter alia*, the various advantages of peacekeeping operations on the island that resulted from the logistical support provided by the British bases and the successful use of military and civilian components and of mixed nationality task forces in operations. UNFICYP's role is viewed as positive, its limitations flowing out of its restrictive mandate.

328 **The strategy of third party intervention in conflict resolution.**
Michael Harbottle. *International Journal* (Canada), vol. 35, no. 1 (winter 1980), p. 118-31.

An experienced soldier turned scholar, the author served as chief of staff of the United Nations peacekeeping force in Cyprus from 1966-68. Through his experience there and by using Cyprus as a case study, he suggests that for a third-party intervention to be successful a split-level approach to the problem should be adopted by the intervening party, one that would act and interact simultaneously on various levels, official and non-official. The objective should be to create a lasting structure for a peaceful settlement (peacemaking) while keeping the peace (peacekeeping). The latter was achieved in Cyprus by 1968 and the problem would have been solved, according to Harbottle, had the right initiatives in laying the structure for peace been taken. To underscore his point, he cites the little-known Cyprus Resettlement Project, undertaken by a Quaker group in 1973-74, that was remarkably successful but was short-lived, swept away by the 1974 crisis.

329 **Cyprus – conflict and resolution.**
A. Paul Hare. Cape Town: University of Cape Town, 1974. 11p. (New Series, no. 25).

In August 1972 a small group of volunteers from India, the US, the UK and South Africa, all committed to peace and social change without violence, established a 'non-military peace contingent' which worked in conjunction with the United Nations to help restore peaceful conditions in Cyprus. The Cyprus Resettlement Project grew out of this, and in cooperation with the Cyprus government and Turkish Cypriot leadership it began a limited project of resettling Turkish Cypriots in their former villages. This little-known attempt at peacemaking is recounted here in the context of theoretical observations for conflict resolutions through a 'non-military peace contingent'.

Cyprus Question, 1974-

330 The wrong horse: the politics of intervention and the failure of American diplomacy.
Laurence Stern. New York: Times Books, 1977. 170p.

This is a work critical of post-Second World War American foreign policy in the eastern Mediterranean – Greece and Cyprus. Part 2 (p. 77-162) deals almost exclusively with the 1974 Cyprus crisis and its consequences, particularly the congressional revolt against the US administration as manifested in the imposition of the partial arms embargo against Turkey. Based primarily on the author's article 'Bitter lessons: how we failed in Cyprus' (see the following item), the section on Cyprus provides hitherto unknown details of the Greek junta's subversive activities against the Makarios government, of the animosity against Makarios held by numerous officials in successive American administrations, of the pivotal role played by their secretary of state Kissinger during the 1974 crisis, and of the battle of the embargo in the US Congress. Written in a lucid and lively form, Stern's work is of seminal importance.

331 Bitter lessons: how we failed in Cyprus.
Laurence Stern. *Foreign Policy*, no. 19 (summer 1975), p. 34-78.

A comprehensive examination of American involvement in subversive activities and the subsequent Turkish invasion of Cyprus in 1974. It draws on the author's authoritatve knowledge of the Washington political scene in the Nixon years.

332 Detente and destabilization: report from Cyprus.
Christopher Hitchens. *New Left Review*, no. 94 (Nov.-Dec. 1975), p. 61-73.

Describing Cyprus as 'a locus classicus of destabilization in the age of detente', the author suggests that the 1974 events were long in the making through the persistent attempts of the West to eliminate Cypriot independence which was viewed as inimical to Western interests. This was finally achieved through the systematic manipulation of racial and religious hostilities in Cyprus and as a result of the predatory militarism of the Greek and Turkish régimes. The article is also critical of the Cypriot leftist parties, especially AKEL, for failing to renounce enosis, assert itself politically, and prepare for the confrontation with the external and internal force of reaction.

333 Violence at a distance: Greece and the Cyprus crisis.
J. Bowyer Bell. *Orbis*, vol. 18, no. 3 (fall 1974), p. 791-808.

Bell's account concentrates on the role the Papadopoulos and Ioannides military régimes played in promoting the subversion in Cyprus through EOKA-B that climaxed in the July 1974 crisis. The analysis remains narrow in perspective, failing to account for the wider implications and the role of other powers in the regional and global struggle in the eastern Mediterranean.

Foreign Relations. Cyprus Question, 1974-

334 **The problem of Cyprus.**
Marios L. Evriviades. *Current History* (USA), vol. 70, no. 412 (Jan. 1976), p. 18-21, 38-42.

Based on interviews with some of the participants in Greece, Cyprus and the United States, and on information that resulted from US congressional hearings, this article traces and analyses the salient elements in Greek and American policies towards Cyprus on the eve of the 1974 crisis. The externally financed subversion against Cyprus is also documented.

335 **Cyprus: the 'quiet' civil war.**
Daniel B. Drooz. *Times of Israel,* vol. 1, no. 5 (April 1974), p. 42-47.

An interesting article written a few months before the 1974 crisis. It concentrates on the strife within the Greek Cypriot community and expresses strong Israeli sympathy towards General George Grivas and his EOKA-B underground. Special inserts on Cypriot-Israeli relations and on the international spying that flourishes in Nicosia are included.

336 **United Nations Monthly Chronicle.**
Vol. 11, no. 8 (Aug.-Sept. 1974).

Almost the entire issue dwells on the 1974 Cyprus crisis. It provides a convenient summary of Security Council debates on the issue and gives the texts of the numerous resolutions adopted during July and August.

337 **Cyprus against Turkey. (Application nos. 6780/74 and 6950/75): report of the commission.**
Strasbourg, France: European Commission of Human Rights, Council of Europe, 1976. 2 vols.

This two-volume report (the appendixes comprise volume 2) adopted by the commission on 10 July 1976 remained a classified document until 31 August 1979. It documents the two applications submitted by Cyprus to the European Commission of Human Rights contending that by its invasion of Cyprus and subsequent acts on the island Turkey was in violation of various provisions of the European Convention on Human Rights. Turkey argued that the applications were inadmissible and refused to participate in the inquiry. The applications were declared admissible nonetheless. The seventeen-member commission, under their British president James Fawcett, found Turkey guilty of violating several of the provisions of the European Convention on Human Rights pertaining to murder, rape and looting during its 1974 invasion. For the filing of the original complaints see the Council of Europe's *Yearbook of the European Convention on Human Rights* (vol. 18 (1975), p. 82-126).

Foreign Relations. Cyprus Question, 1974-

338 **Cyprus '74: Aphrodite's other face.**
Edited by Emmanuel C. Casdaglis. Athens: National Bank of Greece, 1976. 221p. map. illus.

This is a sad volume, illustrating Cyprus's history and culture and contrasting through black-and-white photography and children's drawings the tragedy that befell the 'sweet land' with the 1974 Turkish invasion.

339 **Cyprus 1974: days of disaster.**
Andros Pavlides, Dimitris Andreou, photographs by Doros Partassides, translated by Lana der Parthogh. Nicosia: Cyprus Broadcasting Corporation [n.d.]. 136p.

A moving glimpse into the horrifying experience of the people of Cyprus in the summer of 1974 as captured by superbly expressive black-and-white photographs. The bilingual (Greek and English) album is introduced by a chronicle of the events of the Turkish invasion from 20 July to 20 August 1974. The collaborators, all employed at the Cyprus Broadcasting Corporation, lived through all stages of the war at close range, and with their book they have provided one of the best visual documentary records of the tragedy.

340 **Conference proceedings: U. S. foreign policy toward Greece and Cyprus: the clash of principle and pragmatism.**
Edited by Theodore A. Couloumbis, Sallie M. Hicks. Washington, DC: Center for Mediterranean Studies and American Hellenic Institute, 1975. 159p.

The second part of this conference deals with the question of Cyprus, especially in the context of US foreign policy. The papers read and discussed are: 'Cyprus: the nature of ethnic conflict' (Paschalis M. Kitromilides); 'Kissinger's tilt on Cyprus: the new style of crisis diplomacy' (Nikolaos A. Stavrou); 'United States foreign policy and the Cyprus Question: a case study in cold war diplomacy' (Van Coufoudakis).

341 **Essays on the Cyprus conflict.**
Edited by Van Coufoudakis. New York: Pella Publishing, 1976. xviii + 51p.

The essays in this monograph, dedicated to the memory of Professor Stephen G. Xydis, were first presented at the Middle East Studies Association conference in Louisville, Kentucky (November 1975). They are: 'The role of Turkey in Greek-Turkish Cypriot communal relations' (M. A. Ramady); 'The United States and the Cyprus Question 1974-1975' (John C. Campbell); and 'The dynamics of political partition and division in multiethnic and multireligious societies – the Cyprus case' (Van Coufoudakis).

Foreign Relations. Cyprus Question, 1974-

342 **Cyprus reviewed.**
Edited with an introduction by Michael A. Attalides. Nicosia:
Zavallis Press, 1977. xi + 279p. maps.

The papers presented at a seminar held in Nicosia in 1976 on the Cyprus problem are conveniently collected in this volume. They are: 'Argaki: the uprooting of a Cypriot village' (Peter Loizos); 'Cyprus: what kind of problem?' (Alexander G. Xydis); 'From coexistence to confrontation: the dynamics of ethnic conflict in Cyprus' (Paschalis M. Kitromilides); 'The Turkish Cypriots: their relations to the Greek Cypriots in perspective' (Michael A. Attalides); 'United States foreign policy and the Cyprus Question: a case study in cold war diplomacy' (Van Coufoudakis); 'The impact of Greek Americans upon United States foreign policy: illusion or reality?' (Theodore A. Couloumbis, Sallie M. Hicks); 'The Cyprus problem and the United Nations' (Andreas J. Jacovides); 'The United States and the Mediterranean triangle (Greece, Turkey, and Cyprus): a new phase' (Harry J. Psomiades); 'The problem of Cyprus and constitutional solutions' (Polyvios G. Polyviou); 'The unity of the economy and the economics of separation' (N. S. Symeonides).

343 **Small states in the modern world: the conditions of survival.**
Edited by Peter Worsley, Paschalis Kitromilides. Nicosia:
Cyprus Sociological Association and New Cyprus Association,
1979. rev. ed. xviii + 261p.

A collection of papers originally presented at a 1976 conference on the survival of small countries. It contains mostly papers considering the general question of small state survival in the perspective of the Cyprus experience, and the volume includes several contributions on the Cyprus Question. Among the issues treated in connection with Cyprus are those of communalism (Peter Worsley), the theory of nationalism (Tom Nairn), the international determinants of domestic conflict (A. Pollis, N. Kadritzke, W. Wagner), the ideological dimensions of ethnic conflict (P. Kitromilides) and the uses of international law, organization and peacekeeping (A. J. Thomas, Ann Van Wynen Thomas, Michael Harbottle).

344 **Greek-American relations: a critical review.**
Edited by T. A. Couloumbis, John D. Iatrides. New York:
Pella Publishing, 1980. 263p. bibliog.

An article by Van Coufoudakis in this volume, 'American foreign policy and the Cyprus problem, 1974-1978: the "theory of continuity" revisited' (p. 131-47), argues that the same strategic considerations that motivated US policy towards Cyprus in the 1960s and early 1970s continue to dominate US policy in the late 1970s. The volume also contains an incomplete bibliography on the Cyprus conflict (p. 234-39).

Foreign Relations. Cyprus Question, 1974-

345 **Cyprus.**
Dis Politika (Ankara), vol. 4. no. 2-3 (Feb. 1975).
This entire issue is devoted to the Cyprus problem and was prepared in the aftermath of the 1974 crisis. It contains articles sympathetic to Turkey's position on the background to the conflict, the 1974 crisis, and Turkish, US and Soviet relations as these have been influenced by the Cyprus conflict. Of particular interest are the contributions of Turkish diplomats and politicians such as Haluk Ulman's '1974 Geneva Conference on Cyprus'; Kamran Inan's 'Cyprus, 1974 crisis'; Haluk Bayulken's 'Cyprus Question and the United Nations'; and Nihat Erim's 'Reminiscences on Cyprus'.

346 **Cyprus: the tragedy and the challenge.**
Polyvios G. Polyviou. London: John Swain & Sons [n.d.].
204p. maps. apps. Reprinted, with postscript, Washington, DC: American Hellenic Institute, 1975. 222p.

347 **Cyprus: in search of a constitution.**
Polyvios G. Polyviou, foreword by H. W. R. Wade. Nicosia: Chr. Nicolaou & Sons, 1976. 450p. map. apps.

348 **Cyprus: conflict and negotiation 1960-1980.**
Polyvios G. Polyviou. London: Gerald Duckworth; New York: Holmes & Meier, 1980. 246p. maps.
The first two of the three works cited above grew out of the 1974 Turkish invasion. The author, a lawyer, served on the Cypriot delegations, headed by the then acting president of Cyprus, G. Clerides, that went to Geneva for the ill-fated July-August 1974 negotiations between Turkey, Greece, Great Britain and the two Cypriot communites. The first work, written hastily (by the author's own admission), provides ideas and suggestions concerning the country's political and constitutional reconstruction, chronicles the Turkish invasion, addresses its legal consequences, and reveals much of the backstage manoeuvring at Geneva in 1974. The second volume provides a detailed account of the four phases of the intercommunal discussions (1968-74) based for the most part on a systematic transcription of the repeated proposals of the two sides: it gives a sense of the evolution of the respective positions in this period up to the eve of the *coup* and the invasion. As may be expected, the works are often repetitive, especially when addressing the constitutional issues. The last one advocates, *inter alia*, the controversial thesis that prior to the cataclysmic events of 1974 an agreement had been reached by the two interlocutors, Clerides and Denktash, but was swept away by the July crisis.

Foreign Relations. Cyprus Question, 1974-

349 **Cyprus: nationalism and international politics.**
Michael A. Attalides. Edinburgh: Q Press; New York: St. Martin's Press, 1979. xi + 226p. bibliog.

This is a lucid book dealing with the growth and eventual collision of two nationalist movements in Cyprus. It pays due attention to the possibility of the development of an alternative to conflict in the form of a common Cypriot identity – a development precluded by the contradictions of Cypriot politics and the involvement of foreign powers in the affairs of the island. The book contains a useful bibliography on the Cyprus Question.

350 **U.S. foreign policy and the Cyprus Question: an interpretation.**
Van Coufoudakis. *Millenium: Journal of International Studies* (UK), vol. 5, no. 3 (winter 1976-77), p. 245-68.

The article covers the period of 1963-74. On the basis of new and unpublished information the article analyses the motivations of US foreign policy, the methods used in the promotion of US interests, and the role played by Greece in American policy schemes toward Cyprus. The aim of US policy has been the limitation of Cypriot independence through solutions amounting to a Greco-Turkish partition of the republic.

351 **Cyprus: the time bomb of the Mediterranean.**
Edited by Julian Critchley, research by William Park. London: Atlantic Information Centre for Teachers, 1975. 24p. (Crisis Paper no. 40).

Selected articles from newspapers and journals from all over the world are incorporated in this brief, covering the 1974 crisis on the island.

352 **The Cyprus conflict: national identity and statehood.**
Zenon Stavrinides. Wakefield, England: the author, 1976. 1 + 134p.

This is a short political history of post-independence Cyprus which is highly critical of the internal and foreign policies of Archbishop Makarios and of his advisers. Although the work contains some valid and long-overdue criticisms of those policies, it also contains egregious errors in quotations and documentation, thus diminishing its value as a serious work.

353 **Interview with history.**
Oriana Fallaci, translated by John Shepley. New York: Liveright, 1976. Reprinted, Boston, Massachusetts: Houghton Mifflin, 1977. 376p.

Archbishop Makarios is among those interviewed by this famous Italian journalist (chapter 13, p. 310-31). This extremely perceptive interview was conducted in the autumn of 1974, before Makarios's return to Cyprus following the July crisis. Aside from its historical importance the interview reveals fascinating aspects of the archbishop's personality and of his views, religious and secular. Originally published as *Intervista con la storia* (Milan, Italy: Rizzoli, 1974).

Foreign Relations. Cyprus Question, 1974-

354 **Policy or law for Cyprus.**
W. M. Dobell. *International Journal,* vol. 31, no. 1 (winter 1975-76), p. 146-58.

The article examines the positions of the parties on the various legal issues and controversies that emerged in the aftermath of independence, and contrasts them with subsequent positions as these were shaped by the various crises, particularly that of 1974.

355 **The Cyprus crisis 1974-75: political and juridical aspects.**
Ann Van Wynen Thomas, A. J. Thomas. *Southwestern Law Journal,* vol. 29 (1975), p. 513-46.

A good survey of the 1974 crisis and its background, examining its historical, political and legal aspects. Special attention is paid to the Cyprus issue as a UN problem.

356 **NATO and the Cyprus crisis.**
David Rudnick. *Round Table,* no. 266 (April 1977), p. 182-90.

This is a general and not particularly suggestive overview of the reactions within NATO, the EEC and the US Congress to the 1974 crisis.

357 **Can the Cyprus problem be solved?**
Stanley Mayes. *Round Table,* no. 273 (Jan. 1979), p. 81-87.

A veteran observer of the Cyprus scene analyses the salient elements of the 1978 Western initiative for a solution put together by the US, the UK and Canada and submitted under the umbrella of the United Nations. The plan proved unacceptable to both sides.

358 **Cyprus and the U.N.: a case for non-military collective measures.**
Christina K. Navarro. *Indiana Law Journal,* vol. 54, no. 1 (1978-79), p. 125-63.

Using the case of Cyprus and the lack of any progress towards a solution based on charter principles in the aftermath of the 1974 crisis, the author calls into question the traditional non-coercive efforts of the UN as vehicles for dispute resolution. Details of the UN involvement in the conflict are given, and the case is made for the use of non-military coercive measures (under chapter 7 article 41 of the UN charter) as a potential dispute resolution mechanism applicable to the Cyprus case.

359 **Greek-Turkish conflict over Cyprus.**
Glen D. Camp. *Political Science Quarterly,* vol. 95, no. 1 (spring 1980), p. 43-70.

This article provides an overview of the conflict as it emerged following the Zurich-London accords, through the turbulent decade of the 1960s and up to and including the 1974 crisis. It is the author's conclusion that Turkey, holding the upper hand, has lost interest in any solution short of partition and under the circumstances it prefers the current stalemate which the author views as inherently unstable.

Foreign Relations. Cyprus Question, 1974-

360   **The Cyprus Question: its dimensions, implications and prospects for a solution.**
Andreas J. Jacovides. Washington, DC: Center for Mediterranean Studies, American University, 1980. 19p. (Occasional Paper no. 1).

Reflecting the official viewpoint, this is an address by the ambassador of Cyprus to the US. It emphasizes the existence of an acceptable framework for a Cyprus solution, based on the high-level agreements between Makarios and Denktash (1977) and Kyprianou and Denktash (1979), and the fact that a Cyprus solution would serve the interests of all concerned.

361   **The Cyprus deadlock: forever or another day?**
Dennison I. Rusinow. Hanover, New Hampshire: American Universities Field Staff, 1981. 23p. map. bibliog. (AUFS Reports, 1981, no. 11, Europe).

A detached and at times impressionistic brief report on developments in Cyprus since the 1974 crisis. It identifies, at times very perceptively, the various obstacles, psychological and otherwise, that need to be resolved so that the inter-communal talks can be moved off dead centre and towards a long-term solution.

362   **Cyprus – past and future: a personal perspective.**
Lord Caradon, introduction by John Brademas. Muncie, Indiana: Ball State University, 1980. iv + 11p. (Sixth Stephen J. Brademas, Jr., Lecture).

The last British governor of Cyprus reminisces about his long involvement with the island and suggests a number of ways to move negotiations off dead centre and towards reconciliation between the two communities. He recalls a proposal he advocated for the appointment of a conciliation mission by the UN Security Council, composed of a Western, an Eastern and a Third World country, all of which should not have been connected with Cyprus in the past, and which should put forward an impartial plan for peace. He also recognizes Britain's special obligations on the island and suggests that she could lead an initiative for a viable solution.

363   **The challenge of peace.**
Kurt Waldheim. New York: Rawson, Wade; London: Weidenfeld & Nicolson, 1980. 158p.

Chapter 7 (p. 61-78) of the secretary-general's book is devoted to Cyprus and deals mostly with the events following the 1974 crisis and the UN's and Waldheim's personal diplomacy to give impetus to the Cypriot intercommunal talks. As with the whole work there are no revelations, and in the UN's tradition much remains unsaid. The French original was published in 1977, and a German edition in 1978.

363a   **The Cyprus problem.**
Nikos Kranidiotis. Athens, 1975. 78p. maps.

A senior Cypriot diplomat considers the character of the Cyprus Question as it appeared after the Turkish invasion.

Foreign Relations. Congressional and parliamentary publications

Congressional and parliamentary publications

364 **Crisis on Cyprus: 1974. A study mission report.**
Subcommittee to Investigate Problems Connected with Refugees and Escapees, Committee on the Judiciary, US Senate; preface by Edward M. Kennedy. Washington, DC: US Government Printing Office, 1974. 116p. map. illus. apps. (93rd Congress, 2nd Session, 11 Oct. 1974).

365 **Crisis on Cyprus: 1975: one year after the invasion. A staff report.**
Subcommittee to Investigate Problems Connected with Refugees and Escapees, Committee on the Judiciary, US Senate; preface by Edward M. Kennedy. Washington, DC: US Government Printing Office, 1975. 142p. map. illus. apps. (94th Congress, 2nd Session, 20 July 1975).

366 **Crisis on Cyprus: 1976: crucial year for peace. A staff report.**
Subcommittee to Investigate Problems Connected with Refugees and Escapees, Committee on the Judiciary, US Senate; preface by Edward M. Kennedy. Washington, DC: US Government Printing Office, 1976. 103p. map. illus. apps. (94th Congress, 2nd Session, 19 Jan. 1976).

During the 1974 crisis and its immediate aftermath, the Senate Subcommittee to Investigate Problems Connected with Refugees and Escapees of the Committee on the Judiciary, chaired by Senator Kennedy, closely followed the humanitarian problems in Cyprus by holding public hearings and by dispatching a study mission to the eastern Mediterranean. The study mission spent a week in Cyprus and it also travelled to Ankara, Athens, Geneva and London. The first of the three reports cited above is the immediate outcome of the mission's field work, and all three concern themselves with the events that led to the anti-Makarios *putsch*, the Turkish invasion, the consequences, and the island's humanitarian needs. The mission's findings and its recommendations, together with notes on the US policy *vis-à-vis* the crisis, are included. All three reports are indispensable for an understanding of the 1974 crisis and of the motivation and actions of US policy-makers. Additionally, the rich appendixes in all the reports contain a gold mine of information. Reprints of journalistic and scholarly articles on the crisis are included, together with official statements as well as written exchanges between the subcommittee and State Department officials including Secretary Kissinger. A chronology of events (1974-75) prepared by the Library of Congress is included in the last two reports.

Foreign Relations. Congressional and parliamentary publications

367 **World hunger, health, and refugee problems: part 5. Human disaster in Cyprus, Bangladesh, Africa. Hearing.**
Subcommittee to Investigate Problems Connected with Refugees and Escapees, Committee on the Judiciary, US Senate; Subcommittee on Health, Committee on Labor and Public Welfare, US Senate. Washington, DC: US Government Printing Office, 1974. 208p. maps. apps. (93rd Congress, 2nd Session, 20 Aug. 1974).

368 **Humanitarian problems on Cyprus. Hearing.**
Subcommittee to Investigate Problems Connected with Refugees and Escapees, Committee on the Judiciary, US Senate.
Washington, DC: US Government Printing Office, 1974.
136p. map. apps. (93rd Congress, 2nd Session, 26 Sept. 1974).

369 **Humanitarian problems on Cyprus: part 2. Hearing.**
Subcommittee to Investigate Problems Connected with Refugees and Escapees, Committee on the Judiciary, US Senate.
Washington, DC: US Government Printing Office, 1975. 68p.
map. apps. (93rd Congress, 2nd Session, 17 Dec. 1974).

In the three items cited above, part of the record in the 20 August hearing and the whole record in the 26 September and 17 December hearings are devoted to the humanitarian and other problems that resulted in Cyprus as a result of the 20 July Turkish invasion. Expert witnesses and high-ranking US administration officials provide testimony on the humanitarian problems in Cyprus, the political situation there and the foreign policy of the US *vis-à-vis* the crisis. The appendixes provide a rich reproduction of articles and editorials about the crisis from the American and international press and official (especially US) documents and correspondence pertaining to it.

370 **Cyprus - 1974. Hearings.**
Subcommittee on Europe, Committee on Foreign Affairs, US House of Representatives. Washington, DC: US Government Printing Office, 1974. 85p. map. apps. (93rd Congress, 2nd Session, 19-20 Aug. 1974).

A record of the House Subcommittee on Europe on the 1974 crisis. It includes testimony by the assistant secretary of state for European affairs, A. Hartman, and former under-secretary of state, G. Ball. The appendixes include parts of the 1960 Zurich-London accords, articles from the American and international press, other statements and a chronology.

Foreign Relations. Congressional and parliamentary publications

371 **Europe, south and east: redefining the American interest. Report.**
Study Mission to Portugal, Greece, Yugoslavia, and Hungary, Committee on Foreign Affairs, US House of Representatives. Washington, DC: US Government Printing Office, 1975. 28p. (94th Congress, 1st Session).

The study mission visited Cyprus in January 1975. In analysing and assessing US-Greek relations, this report emphasizes, *inter alia*, the situation in Cyprus and its effects on Greek politics and Greek-American relations. The report is critical of past US policy towards Greece, especially US support for the Greek junta which in turn, through its misadventure against Cyprus in 1974, precipitated the 1974 crisis.

372 **Greece and Cyprus, 1975. Report.**
Claiborne Pell, prepared for the Committee on Foreign Relations, US Senate. Washington, DC: US Government Printing Office, 1975. 15p. app. (94th Congress, 1st Session, Nov. 1975).

The outcome of Senator Pell's official visit to Greece and Cyprus in late 1975. This report gives the senator's views and recommendations on the problems facing Greece in the aftermath of the collapse of the seven-year dictatorship and those facing Cyprus after the Turkish invasion. A useful chronology on Cyprus is appended.

373 **Greece and Turkey: some military implications related to NATO and the Middle East.**
John M. Collins; Congressional Research Service, Library of Congress; prepared for the Special Subcommittee on Investigations, Committee on Foreign Affairs, US House of Representatives. Washington, DC: US Government Printing Office, 1975. 63p. annex. (94th Congress, 1st Session, 28 Feb. 1975).

This study was requested in the summer of 1974 as the Cyprus crisis became a major foreign policy concern in Washington, and was prepared by John M. Collins, senior specialist in national defence of the Congressional Research Service. It deals with Cyprus in an indirect and tangential way — in the context of examining US base facilities and military relations with Greece and Turkey, and their implications for NATO and the Middle East. The annex is rich in material documenting the historical evolution of US and Greek and Turkish relations since the Truman Doctrine.

Foreign Relations. Congressional and parliamentary publications

374 **Suspension of prohibitions against military assistance to Turkey. Hearing.**
Committee on International Relations (Foreign Affairs),
US House of Representatives. Washington, DC: US Government Printing Office, 1975. 158p. apps. (94th Congress, 1st Session, 10 July 1975).

By using US-supplied weapons during the 1974 invasion of Cyprus, Turkey failed to comply with the provision of article 4 of the bilateral Agreement on Aid to Turkey of July 1947 and with the provisions under title 2 of the 1961 Foreign Assistance Act which stipulated that these weapons should be used only for defensive purposes. As a result, and while bitterly opposed by the Ford-Kissinger administration, the US Congress imposed, in February 1975, a partial arms embargo against Turkey. These hearings treat that subject by considering House Resolution 8454 — a bi-partisan congressional initiative aimed at easing the embargo, strengthening NATO and, according to its sponsors, creating favourable conditions for a Cyprus solution. The record includes the testimony of administration officials, that of congressional opponents and proponents of the measure, and of various other partisans.

375 **To promote improved relations between the United States, Greece and Turkey, to assist in the solution of the refugee problem of Cyprus, and to otherwise strengthen the North Atlantic alliance. Report: together with opposing, supplemental, dissenting, additional and separate views on S. 846.**
Committee on International Relations (Foreign Affairs),
US House of Representatives. Washington, DC: US Government Printing Office, 1975. 17p. (Report no. 94-365).

376 **Authorization of appropriations for the Board for International Broadcasting and partial lifting of the Turkish arms embargo. Hearing (on S. 2230).**
Committee on International Relations (Foreign Affairs), US House of Representatives. Washington, DC: US Government Printing Office, 1975. 17p. (94th Congress, 1st Session, 17 Sept. 1975).

Foreign Relations. Congressional and parliamentary publications

377 To authorize appropriations for the Board for International Broadcasting for fiscal year 1976; and to promote relations between the United States, Greece and Turkey to assist in the solution of the refugee problem on Cyprus, and to otherwise strengthen the North Atlantic alliance. Report: together with opposing, separate, supplemental, and additional views on S. 2230.
Committee on International Relations (Foreign Affairs), US House of Representatives. Washington, DC: US Government Printing Office, 1975. 43p. (Report no. 945500).

The two reports and the hearing bills cited above are designed, *inter alia*, to bring about a partial lifting of the Turkish arms embargo. Both records include the supporting views of the Ford administration, the supporting and dissenting views of committee members and related material and press clippings. They all provide valuable details on the pertinent issues and the debate between the administration and the US Congress over the arms embargo in particular, but more generally over the role of Congress in US foreign policy.

378 U.S. intelligence agencies and activities. Hearings and proceedings: parts 1-6.
Select Committee on Intelligence, US House of Representatives. Washington, DC: US Government Printing Office, 1975-76. 2315p. charts. apps. (94th Congress, 1st and 2nd Sessions, July 1975-Feb. 1976).

The 1974 crisis on Cyprus was one of the cases examined by the House Select Committee on Intelligence, set up in 1975 under chairman Otis Pike, to investigate the intelligence-gathering activities of the US government. As a result an impressive amount of material, official documents and testimony on the events surrounding the Greek-executed *putsch* against Archbishop Makarios and the subsequent Turkish invasion have been made available for the record. The emphasis is to assess the role and performance of US intelligence agencies – the Central Intelligence Agency is scrutinized and criticized in the case of Cyprus. Material supplied for the record by the CIA, however, such as its *Post mortem report and examination of the intelligence community's performance before and during the Cyprus crisis of 1974,* though a most revealing document, is 'sanitized'. Almost all materials pertaining to Cyprus can be found in parts 2 and 4. The Pike documents are by no means the complete record of US actions and policy objectives in the eastern Mediterranean, but they are essential for the serious researcher. However, the committee's final report, a crucial document containing its findings and recommendations, is not part of this record. The House voted against its publication until the Executive had an opportunity to review it and possibly censor all or parts of it. Nonetheless this final report was leaked to the weekly *Village Voice* (USA) and was published in two special supplements on 16 and 23 February 1976. This final report was subsequently published as *CIA: the Pike Report*, with an introduction by Philip Agee (Nottingham, England: Spokesman Books, 1977, 284p.).

Foreign Relations. Congressional and parliamentary publications

379 **Report from the Select Committee on Cyprus: together with the proceedings of the committee, minutes of evidence and appendices.**
House of Commons. London: HM Stationery Office, 1976.
li + 131p. apps. (Session 1975-76, HC no. 331).

380 **The Select Committee on Cyprus: minutes of evidence, 19th February 1976.**
House of Commons. London: HM Stationery Office, 1976, p. 53-68. (Session 1975-76, HC no. 206-i).

381 **Report from the Select Committee on Cyprus: observations by the government.**
House of Commons. London: HM Stationery Office, 1976.
8p. (Session 1975-76, Cmnd. no. 6579).

Somewhat but not quite analogous to the American congressional hearings, the three above reports on Cyprus from a British select parliamentary committee provide a valuable record of the 1974 crisis and especially of the policies, motivations, decisions, and actions, or lack thereof, of the British government. Recommendations are made on what positive actions the British government can take to help the general situation in Cyprus, especially to improve the lot of British subjects residing there. The appendixes are rich in material including various documents and memoranda pertaining to the crisis.

382 **Cyprus as an issue in Greek-Turkish relations.**
Richard M. Preece. Washington, DC: Congressional Research Service, Library of Congress, 1978. 23p. bibliog. (Issue Brief no. 1B74128).

This issue brief originally prepared in 1974 and updated in 1978 provides a capsule summary of the Cyprus problem with special emphasis on the 1974 crisis. It was written for the benefit of congressional members and committees and raises various policy questions with regard to US interests in the eastern Mediterranean. A most useful chronology and a bibliography on congressional hearings are appended.

383 **The military aspects of banning arms aid to Turkey. Hearing.**
Committee on Armed Services, US Senate. Washington, DC: US Government Printing Office, 1978. 104p. app.
(95th Congress, 2nd Session, 28 June 1978).

In the context of the Carter administration's efforts to have the partial Turkish arms embargo lifted, hearings on the matter were held by the Senate Armed Services Committee. The emphasis was, *inter alia*, on the embargo's military consequences from the point of view of NATO effectiveness and US global interests. High administration and Pentagon officials were among those testifying in favour of lifting the embargo. With regard to Cyprus, proponents agreed that the embargo had served its purpose and was becoming counter-productive as a means of extracting concessions from Turkey.

Foreign Relations. Congressional and parliamentary publications

384 **Turkey's problems and prospects: implications for U.S. interests. Report.**
Foreign Affairs and National Defense Division, Congressional Research Service, Library of Congress; prepared for the Subcommittee on Europe and the Middle East, Committee on Foreign Affairs, US House of Representatives. Washington, DC: US Government Printing Office, 1980. 68p. maps. apps. (96th Congress, 2nd Session, 3 March 1980).

While in the main this report deals with US-Turkish relations and Turkey's numerous internal problems, the problem of Cyprus is addressed in the context of Greco-Turkish relations. Policy suggestions for dealing with the various problems including Cyprus are made.

385 **Turkey, Greece and NATO: the strained alliance. A staff report.**
Committee on Foreign Relations, US Senate. Washington, DC: US Government Printing Office, 1980. 64p. maps. charts.
(96th Congress, 2nd Session).

Prepared by the committee's professional staff who visited Turkey, Greece and Cyprus. This is an erudite study of Greco-Turkish relations and of the Cyprus problems in the context of the NATO alliance and Western interests. Cyprus is treated in chapter 6 (p. 47-53) and the possibility is raised of the use of American good offices in the search for a solution.

386 **Perspectives on NATO's southern flank. Report.**
Committee on Foreign Relations, US Senate. Washington, DC: US Government Printing Office, 1980. 46p. apps.
(96th Congress, 2nd Session).

In this Senate delegation report emanating from a visit (3-13 April 1980) to the area, the problem of Cyprus is addressed in the sections dealing with Turkey (p. 7-18) and Greece (p. 19-26). Turkish and Greek perspectives are provided. A background on Cyprus is provided in the appendixes, which also include the Western framework for a solution proposed in November 1978 by the United States, Canada and the United Kingdom.

Ethnic Groups and Ethnic Relations

387 The Cypriot Turks.
C. F. Beckingham. *Journal of the Royal Central Asian Society*, vol. 43, pt. 2 (1956), p. 126-30.

A study of the ethnological origins and ethnographic characteristics of the Turkish Cypriot community.

388 The Turks of Cyprus.
C. F. Beckingham. *Die Welt des Islams*, n.s., vol. 5, no. 1-2 *Institute of Great Britain and Ireland*, vol. 87, pt. 2 (July-Dec. 1957), p. 165-74.

A study of the social demography, history, language and religion of the Turkish community of Cyprus.

389 Islam and Turkish nationalism in Cyprus.
C. F. Beckingham. *Die Welt des Islams*, n.s., vol. 5, no. 1-2 (1957), p. 65-83.

A valuable study of the religious and cultural history of the Turkish Cypriot community in the first half of the 20th century, and of the uses to which the Islamic identity of the community was put in order to belatedly develop a militant nationalist and anti-Greek movement.

390 Turkish newspapers and magazines published in Cyprus 1888-1915.
Beria Remzi Ozoran. Ankara: Ayyildiz Matbaasi, 1969. 11p.

Information on fourteen Turkish-language newspapers published in Cyprus in 1888-1915 of which some supported the Young Turks and others the traditionalists.

391 Turkish art in Cyprus.
Emel Esin. Ankara: Ayyildiz Matbaasi, 1969. 35p. 32 plates.

On Turkish Cypriot artistic tradition from p. 14 onward, examining calligraphy, painting and Turkish monuments of Cyprus. The book is marred by the overemphasis of Turkish influences on different cultural monuments in Cyprus.

Ethnic Groups and Ethnic Relations

392 **An investigation into matters concerning and affecting the Turkish community in Cyprus: interim report.**
Committee on Turkish Affairs, 1949. Nicosia: Government Printing Office, 1949. 68p.

A thorough survey of the institutions of the Turkish community in Cyprus covering family law, *sheri* (Islamic religious law) courts, the Muftiship, *evcaf* (administration of Muslim religious properties) and education, providing short histories of the development and condition of these institutions under British rule and suggesting specific measures for improvements consonant with the aspirations of Turkish Cypriots at the time.

393 **Une communauté insulaire en Mediterrannée orientale: les Turcs de Chypre.** (An insular community in the eastern Mediterranean: the Turks of Cyprus.)
Emile Y. Kolodny. *Revue de Géographie de Lyon*, vol. 45, no. 1 (1971), p. 5-56.

A study of the demographic and historical evolution of the Turkish Cypriot community in the context of the overall evolution of the population of Cyprus, its spatial distribution up to 1960 and the changes in traditional demographic and geographical patterns brought about by ethnic confrontation in the 1960s. Of special importance is the examination of the archaic economic structures of the Turkish Cypriot community and their adaptation by turning their economy into an appendage of the mainland Turkish economy to meet the requirements of changing political circumstances. This is a representative study of the condition of the Turkish Cypriots just prior to the 1974 invasion, which has radically altered it.

394 **The crypto-Christians of Turkey.**
R. M. Dawkins. *Byzantion*, vol. 8 (1933), p. 247-75.

The Cypriot sect of Linobambakoi is discussed in this important article as a local manifestation of the broader phenomenon of crypto-Christianity in the Ottoman Empire. On the basis of the evidence available to the author, it is suggested that the Linobambakoi were Christians who chose to practise the rites of Islam in order to derive the benefits of the ruling element of the empire. The termination of Ottoman rule (1878) removed their reason for existence and by the early 20th century the group had practically disappeared, most of its members declaring openly for either Islam or Christianity.

395 **Les Maronites de Chypre.** (The Maronites of Cyprus.)
J.-M. Cirilli. Lille, France: Imprimerie de l'Orphelinat de Don Bosco, 1898. 30p.

A brief history of the Maronite community in Cyprus from the Turkish occupation to the end of the 19th century by the general vicar of the Maronites in Cyprus. It stresses the persecution of this Christian community by both the Turks and the Greeks, refers to Catholic aid extended to the community in the 18th century, and describes the condition and needs (mostly educational and economic) of Cypriot Maronites on the eve of the 20th century.

Ethnic Groups and Ethnic Relations

396 The Maronites of Cyprus.
Edward Brown. *Eastern Churches Quarterly* (USA), no. 2 (Jan. 1937), p. 10-12.

A historical note on the Maronite community of Cyprus identifying the variations between them and other Maronites of Lebanon and Syria. The chief difference is identified as linguistic. The Cypriot Maronites speak Greek and conduct their liturgy in Greek despite the efforts of Maronite monks to revive and sustain the use of Arabic.

397 A brief history of the Armenians of Cyprus.
Noubar Maxoudian. *Armenian Review*, vol. 27, no. 4 (1975), p. 398-416.

A useful account of the origins and development of the Armenian presence in Cyprus.

398 Les petites minorités à Chypre (Maronites, Arméniens et 'Latins'). (The small minorities in Cyprus: Maronites, Armenians and 'Latins'.)
Paul Sergy. *Revue Française d'Etudes Politiques Mediterranéennes*, no. 18-19 (June-July 1976), p. 75-82.

This is part of a survey of the Cyprus problem published in this issue. It gives a general overview of the three Christian minorities of Cyprus, of which two, the Maronites and the Latins, have traditionally formed one of the concerns of French policy in Cyprus.

399 Nineteenth century Jewish colonies in Cyprus.
John M. Shaftesley. *Jewish Historical Society of England Transactions*, vol. 22 (1968-69), p. 88-107.

A historical account of Jewish settlements in Cyprus after the British occupation, with special reference to the colonies of Margo and Kouklia.

400 Peaceful co-existence in Cyprus under British rule (1878-1959) and after independence: an outline.
Costas P. Kyrris. Nicosia, 1977. 191p.

A rich collection of instances of inter-ethnic cooperation in different areas of the social life of Cyprus, illuminating the character of interaction in a bi-communal society. The exposition is unsystematic and the author's interpretation of the evidence may not be always unexceptionable, but as a source of information and empirical details this is a very useful book.

Ethnic Groups and Ethnic Relations

401 Intergroup conflict and British colonial policy: the case of Cyprus.
Adamandia Pollis. *Comparative Politics,* vol. 5, no. 4 (July 1973), p. 575-99.

The author argues that initial apolitical differences between the Christian and Moslem population of Cyprus were intentionally institutionalized by the British colonial government. These policies tended to exacerbate the antagonism between the two groups and eventually contributed to the political hostility between them. Numerous examples from British colonial practices, in Cyprus and elsewhere, are cited in support of the author's thesis.

402 Ethnic conflict in a strategic area: the case of Cyprus.
Paschalis M. Kitromilides, Theodore Couloumbis. In: *Ethnicity in an international context: the politics of disassociation.* Edited by A. Said, L. Simmons. New Brunswick, New Jersey: Transaction Books, 1976, p. 167-202.

After a survey of the historical background and sociological, cultural and political dimensions of ethnic conflict in Cyprus, the authors describe the increasing internationalization of the Cyprus Question and argue the case that the confrontation between the Greek and Turkish Cypriots has been exacerbated by the intervention of outside powers in the domestic affairs of the strategically situated island. The chapter is followed by extensive references to pertinent bibliographical and other source material. A longer version with more details on the 1974 crisis and its aftermath appeared in *Greek Review of Social Research* (no. 24 (1975), p. 270-91).

403 The progress of Greek nationalism in Cyprus, 1878-1970.
Peter Loizos. In: *Choice and change: essays in honour of Lucy Mair.* Edited by J. Davis. London: London School of Economics, 1974, p. 114-33. (LSE Monographs on Social Anthropology, no. 50).

An attempt to periodize the evolution of the Greek Cypriot movement for union with Greece and to explain its persistence even after the achievement of independence. The tenacity of the claim is explained as a statement of Greek cultural identity in a plural society.

Ethnic Groups and Ethnic Relations

404 Muslim-Christian conflicts: economic, political and social origins.
Edited by Suad Joseph, Barbara L. K. Pillsbury. Boulder, Colorado: Westview Press; Folkestone, England: Wm. Dawson & Sons, 1978. 245p. gloss.

Peter Allen's essay 'Bicommunal separatism in Cyprus' (p. 209-34) is essentially a historical overview of Greek-Turkish relations on Cyprus to support the thesis that the present situation on the island, i.e. the complete separation of the two communities, is the culmination of separatist tendencies dating back to the first settlement of Turks on Cyprus in 1572. It considers religion to be a key factor in the promotion of separatism, and downplays the importance of outside influences. The article displays some carelessness with regard to facts, e.g. Rauf Denktash was not elected vice-president of Cyprus in 1960 — Dr. Fazil Kutchuk was.

405 Status of intercommunal relationships on Cyprus.
Bayard King. Washington, DC: Department of State, Senior Seminar in Foreign Policy, 1972-73. 14p.

This study is based on field research in Turkey, Cyprus, Greece and the United Kingdom. The author analyses the position of the main protagonists, discusses internal political developments and suggests that, with neither side willing to accept the other's suggested solution, 'a final solution may depend on an agreement between Greece and Turkey on the future course of Cyprus'.

406 Cyprus.
Minority Rights Group, with an alternative analysis by Peter Loizos. London: Minority Rights Group, 1976. 28p. maps. apps. (Report no. 30).

This two-part report was prepared by a journalist who lived in Cyprus for a number of years but who wished to remain anonymous (part 1), and by Dr. Loizos, a Briton of Cypriot descent (part 2). The two parts provide a contrasting interpretation of recent Cypriot history and of the causes that brought about the 1974 crisis. In their suggestions for the future, the first author argues that only a federal system, a proposal by Turkey, can be viable; the second author identifies a number of key issues (refugees, territory, constitutional guarantees) that must be addressed substantively for a viable system to emerge.

407 Minorities in history.
Edited by A. C. Hepburn. New York: St. Martin's Press, 1979. 251p.

Cyprus is discussed by A. E. Alcock in his essay 'Three case studies in minority protection: South Tyrol, Cyprus, Quebec' (p. 189-225). The essay is a shortened version of a paper commissioned for the Northern Ireland Constitutional Convention, 1975. After discussing the three cases separately, the author offers certain guidelines by way of conclusions as to the best formula for majority-minority relations. The analysis is rather superficial as presented in this version of the essay and at times the general conclusions don't seem to be consistent with the conclusions of the specific cases. The essay on Cyprus is rather sketchy, with some factual errors, e.g. George Papandreou was the Greek prime minister in 1963-67 and not his son Andreas.

Ethnic Groups and Ethnic Relations

408 **Dr. Ihsan Ali: Turkish Cypriot leader and champion of peaceful coexistence.**
Nicosia: Public Information Office, 1979. 50p. illus.

An illustrated record of the life and activities of Dr. Ihsan Ali on behalf of the cause of Greek-Turkish cooperation in Cyprus. It contains a series of letters and statements by Ihsan Ali presenting his views on the problem of Cyprus.

409 **The symbiosis of the two communities.**
Takis Evdokas. Nicosia: Socio-Psychological Research Group, 1978. 42p. bibliog.

This is a psycho-political approach to the Cyprus problem by a Greek Cypriot psychologist who himself played a prominent role in internal Cypriot politics. Examples on the symbiotic existence of Greek and Turkish communities in Cyprus during the Ottoman (1571-1878) British (1878-1960) and post-independence periods (1960-74) are used to counter the argument that coexistence in Cyprus is impossible. Hatred, it is posited, was promoted through conscious policies, and served as the 'supportive element' in the creation of the 'relative psychological presuppositions' among the two communities in the pursuit of well-defined political objectives: the continuation of British colonialism in the late 1950s and the enforcement of a partitionist solution in the 1960s and 1970s.

410 **Cyprus – war and adaptation: a psychoanalytic history of two ethnic groups in conflict.**
Vamik D. Volkan, foreword by John E. Mack. Charlottesville, Virginia: University of Virginia Press, 1979. xxi + 192p. maps. bibliog.

A psycho-history of the Cyprus conflict by a Turkish Cypriot psychiatrist, drawing on the author's personal experiences and those of other Turkish Cypriots before and after the 1974 crisis. This is the only book of its kind on the Cyprus problem.

411 **Cyprus: an analysis of the Cypriot political discord.**
Halil Ibrahim Salih. Brooklyn, New York: Theo Gaus' Sons, 1968. vii + 184p. bibliog. apps.

412 **Cyprus: the impact of diverse nationalism on a state.**
Halil Ibrahim Salih. University, Alabama: University of Alabama Press, 1978. x + 203p. map. bibliog. illus. apps.

In his 1968 work (see the preceding item) the author concludes that for peace to prevail on Cyprus the island must be partitioned into Greek and Turkish sections. This, he argues, will allow the Greeks to unite their 'Cyprus' with Greece and allow 'Turkish Cyprus' to feel secure by joining Turkey. In his 1978 work he stresses the separateness of the two communities and the Turkish Cypriot concern for security, and advocates a federal/confederal system of government as the most desirable solution. About half the book consists of documents pertaining to the Cyprus problem.

Languages and Dialects

413 **On the sounds and inflections of Cyprian dialect.**
C. E. Bennett. *University Studies* (University of Nebraska), vol. 1, no. 11 (Oct. 1888), p. 131-94.
This is a study of the phonetics and inflections of ancient Cypriot Greek as recorded in literary and epigraphical evidence surviving at the time of writing. It is primarily of interest to the history of Cypriot linguistics.

414 **Homeric words in Cyprus.**
C. M. Bowra. *Journal of Hellenic Studies*, vol. 54 (1934), p. 54-74.
A study of Homeric words in the ancient Cypriot syllabary by a leading classicist.

415 **Ta en diaspora.** (Dispersed writings.)
Kyriakos P. Hadjioannou. Nicosia, 1969. 583p.
A collection of the author's papers which include a series of studies on the evolution of the Cypriot dialect in its ancient, mediaeval and earliest modern phases.

416 **Etude du dialecte chypriote moderne et médiévale.** (A study of the mediaeval and modern Cypriot dialect.)
Mondry Beaudouin. Paris: E. Thorin, 1884. 148p. (Bibliothèque des Ecoles Françaises d'Athènes et de Rome, no. 36).
A historical perspective on the peculiarities of the Cypriot dialect, stressing the importance of its study for the understanding of the evolution of modern from ancient Greek. Some attention is paid to foreign elements in the Cypriot dialect (French, Italian and Turkish). The main focus is on the phonetics, morphology and syntax of Cypriot Greek. Published sources in mediaeval Cypriot Greek and other contemporary studies of the dialect are effectively utilized.

Languages and Dialects

417 **Cypriot Greek: its phonology and inflections.**
Brian Newton. The Hague, Paris: Mouton, 1972. 205p.
19 maps. bibliog.

A modern linguistic study of the Greek dialect spoken by the vast majority of the inhabitants of Cyprus. The book examines the phonology and nominal and verbal inflections of the dialect spoken in the central plain of the island and then goes on to examine other regional sub-dialects. A selection of texts illustrates these local variations, and nineteen maps display the pattern of sub-dialect distribution.

418 **A descriptive analysis of Cypriot Maronite Arabic.**
Maria Tsiapera. The Hague, Paris: Mouton, 1969. 59p.

A concise grammar of the Arabic dialect spoken by the Cypriot Maronite community in the Kormakitis region. The book deals with the technical aspects of grammar following the methodology of modern linguistics, and offers a brief introduction on the Maronite community of Cyprus.

Religion

419 **A history of the Orthodox Church of Cyprus.**
John Hackett. London: Methuen, 1901. Reprinted, New York: Burt Franklin, 1972. xviii + 720p. + 10 plates. 2 maps. apps.

An unsurpassed masterful history of Christianity, not simply of ecclesiastical institutions, in one of the most ancient abodes of the Christian faith. Drawing on meticulous research in a wide range of primary sources, the author reconstructs the history of the introduction of Christianity in Cyprus by the Apostles Paul and Barnabas in AD 45 and brings the story down to the British occupation of 1878. It examines the history of the church and religious life in the centuries of Byzantine rule and under the foreign occupations of the Latins and the Turks. In addition to the events of external history, it pays careful attention to the inner life and organization of the church and to Cypriot monasticism and hagiology, and in conclusion it examines in detail the history of the Latin Church in the periods of Lusignan and Venetian rule. The volume includes useful appendixes, addenda and index. A Greek translation by Ch. Papaiannou was published in Athens (1923-32, 3 vols).

420 **St. Paul in Ephesus and the cities of Galatia and Cyprus.**
Otto Friedrich August Meinardus. New Rochelle, New York: Caratzas Brothers, 1979. 141p. illus.

An illustrated account of the itineraries of Saint Paul in Asia Minor, including his visit and preaching in Cyprus in AD 45.

421 **The claim of Antioch to ecclesiastical jurisdiction over Cyprus.**
Glanville Downey. *Proceedings of the American Philosophical Society,* vol. 102, no. 3 (June 1958), p. 224-28.

A consideration of the abortive attempts of the patriarchs of Antioch in the 5th century AD to extend their control over the Church of Cyprus.

Religion

422 The Church of Cyprus during the period of the Arab wars, A.D. 649-965.
A. I. Dikigoropoulos. *Greek Orthodox Theological Review,* vol. 11, no. 2 (winter 1965-66), p. 237-79.

A study of the ecclesiastical condition of Cyprus during one of the darkest and most controversial periods in the history of the island. It discusses the ecclesiastical organization, episcopal lists and status of the Church of Cyprus *vis-à-vis* the other patriarchates, its relations with temporal authorities, its religious policies and the role of monasticism.

423 A study in Roman Catholic and Greek Orthodox Church relations on the island of Cyprus between the years A.D. 1196 and 1360.
H. J. Magoulias. *Greek Orthodox Theological Review,* vol. 10, no. 1 (summer 1964), p. 75-106.

An account of religious conflict in Cyprus arising from the attempts of the Roman Catholic hierarchy established in Cyprus along with the Lusignan dynasty to force conversion on the Greek Orthodox laity and clergy of the island. The article focuses on the period from the establishment of the Latin Church in 1196 to the attempt at forced conversion of the Cypriots by the apostolic legate Pierre de Thomas in 1360.

424 The tribulations of the Greek Church in Cyprus 1196-1280.
J. Gill. *Byzantinische Forschungen,* vol. 5 (1977), p. 73-93.

A survey of the persecution of the Orthodox Church of Cyprus by the Catholic hierarchy during the first century of Latin rule in the island. The study focuses on the attempts of Pope Innocent IV to achieve a more palatable state of religious affairs (it ignores the historical context of Innocent IV's toleration of the Greeks and presents him as 'ecumenical and open minded far in advance of his contemporaries') through some initiatives of toleration. The article was reprinted as the fourth study in the author's *Church union: Rome and Byzantium* (London: Variorum Reprints, 1979).

425 Archbishop Sophronios III (1865-1900) and the British.
Andreas Tillyrides. *Kypriakai Spoudai,* vol. 42 (1978), p. 129-52.

An account of Archbishop Sophronios's relations with some of his contemporary British officials, including interesting details on his visit to Britain in 1889. It is followed by the texts of letters exchanged between the archbishop and British officials on various occasions.

Religion

426 A report on the archiepiscopal question.
Spyros Araouzos. Nicosia: Kypriakos Syllogos, 1908. 13p.

A brief account of the major ecclesiastical conflict that split the Church of Cyprus during the first decade of the 20th century over the issue of succession to the archiepiscopal throne. The author, one of the most serious-minded political figures in Cyprus, was sympathetic with the party of the bishop of Kyrenia.

427 Church and state in Cyprus.
Frank R. Walsh, Maria Tsiapera Walsh. *Texas Quarterly*, vol. 3, no. 3 (autumn 1960), p. 268-73.

This brief article, written in the year Cyprus became independent with an archbishop as its first president, familiarizes the American reader with the long involvement of the Orthodox Church in the history of the island. That the country's leadership should have come from the church is explained in terms of this historical tradition.

428 Orthodox Church and civil authority.
Theodore Papadopoullos. *Journal of Contemporary History*, vol. 2, no. 4 (Oct. 1967), p. 201-09.

An investigation of the historical preconditions of the political involvement of the Orthodox Church of Cyprus. The temporal activities of the Cypriot church are explained in connection with the historic civil functions taken over by the Eastern Orthodox Church in the period of Ottoman captivity.

429 The churches and saints of Cyprus.
Claude Delaval Cobham. London, 1910. viii + 43p.

In this brief compilation, a leading scholar of the history and traditions of Cyprus has recorded in a series of catalogues some principal aspects of the religious life of the island. The book comprises the following lists: 1. churches found in the villages and cities of Cyprus; 2. feasts and titles of the Virgin Mary — along. with the places where each epithet had been in use; 3. villages with a church of St. George; 4. monasteries in each district; 5. fairs and their dates; 6. saints and places associated with them.

430 Saints de Chypre. (Saints of Cyprus.)
Hippolyte Delahayé. *Analecta Bollandiana*, vol. 26 (1907), p. 161-301.

A survey of the sources of Cypriot hagiography is preceded by nine previously unpublished texts of Cypriot hagiology. This long and important study of the religious tradition of Christian Cyprus closes with a discussion of the *Panigyricon* of one of the most famous saints of Cyprus, Neophytos the Recluse.

Religion

431 **Cypriote shrines.**
Harry C. Luke. London: Faith Press, 1920. 47p.

A well-written bird's-eye view of the leading places of Christian and Muslim worship in Cyprus, designed to familiarize the general reader with the religious life of the island. The author discusses three ancient holy places (Saint Katherine's Prison, Hagia Phaneromene and the Khalat-i-Sultan Tekyé) and the monastery of Stavrovouni, the three Stavropegiac monasteries (Kykko, Makhairas, Saint Neophytos) and the Kirklar Tekyé in Nicosia.

432 **The holy, royal monastery of Kykko founded with a cross.**
Chrysostomos, Abbot of Kykko, preface by Archbishop Makarios III, translated by D. W. Phillips, S. A. Sophroniou.
Kykko, Cyprus: the Holy Monastery of Kykko, 1969. 122p. illus.

A survey of the history, spiritual traditions and treasures of the oldest and most important monastery in Cyprus. The book is richly illustrated and conveys a good sense of Kykko's centrality in the religious life of Cyprus.

433 **The Encleistra and Saint Neophytos.**
Ioannis P. Tsiknopoullos. Nicosia: Monastery of Saint Neophytos, 1965. 128p. illus.

An illustrated history and description of one of the leading monasteries in Cyprus and its art treasures. It includes a spiritual biography of the founder and patron saint of the monastery, the 12th century Cypriot hermit and scholar Neophytos.

434 **The monastery of St. Neophytos at Paphos.**
A. Stylianou, J. Stylianou. Nicosia: Monastery of St. Neophytos, 1970. 15p. bibliog. illus.

An illustrated description of the wall-paintings of the hermitage (12th century) and of the main church (early 16th century) at Saint Neophytos monastery.

435 **Relics in the churches and monasteries of Cyprus.**
Otto Meinardus. *Ostkirchliche Studien*, vol. 19 (1970), p. 19-43.

A survey listing 136 saints and 260 sacred relics kept in 31 collections in Cyprus.

Social Conditions

Labour

436 Labour conditions in Cyprus during the war years, 1939-1945.
C. A. Ashiotis. Nicosia: Government Printing Office, 1945. 12p.

A report on pre-war wages and conditions of employment, improvements and labour legislation introduced during the war, and conditions prevailing in government employment at the end of the war.

437 The development of labour relations in Cyprus.
John L. Slocum. Nicosia: Proodos Press, 1972. 95p. bibliog.

Outside colonial and post-independence government reports, this work is the only one available on such an important topic. The first two chapters recount briefly the history of labour relations from 1936-71, with the period to 1956 dealt with by Aristodemos Avraamides. The rest of the work analyses the basic bargaining agreement in force and addresses such subjects as industry-wide bargaining, the termination of employment law, and collective bargaining for government employees.

438 Labour Review.
Nicosia: Public Information Office with the Ministry of Labour and Social Insurance, 1977- . bimonthly.

A bilingual (Greek and English) publication featuring labour and industrial news, statistical data, and occasionally articles by foreign experts. Supersedes the *Quarterly Review* (1962-74).

Welfare

439 Report to the government of Cyprus on social security and related schemes.
International Labour Organization. Geneva: ILO, 1967. 55p.

This technical report offers advice to the government on various social security

Social Conditions. Social problems

schemes, including holidays with pay, redundancy funds, provident funds, pension funds, and their effect on the economy. Where necessary, it also offers advice on the administrative aspects for the legislation pertaining to these schemes.

440 **Report to the government of the Republic of Cyprus on the development of medical care within the framework of a social security scheme.**
International Labour Organization. Geneva: ILO, 1966. 36p.

An expert in the field examines the possibility of introducing medical care for the insured working population and offers an outline of a medical care scheme based on the insurance approach.

441 **Social welfare in Cyprus.**
John Triseliotis. London: Zeno, 1977. v + 179p. bibliog. tables. apps.

This is a study of the policies and programmes of the main Cypriot social services — education, health, housing, income maintenance and personal services. While some background on the historical precedent of philanthropy and 'charitable activity' are given, the emphasis is on the development of the social service sector after the Second World War and especially in post-independence Cyprus.

442 **Research for social welfare: six case studies in Cyprus.**
Edited by L. G. Moseley. London: Bedford Square Press, 1979. 143p.

The book brings together studies on social welfare administration, child care, voluntary services, community and youth work and time allocation and a report on community studies by J. H. A. Botting, B. Glastonbury, L. G. Moseley and B. K. Taylor.

443 **A critical analysis of policies relating to regional development and income distribution in Cyprus (1960-1971).**
C. Apostolides. *Geographical Chronicles,* vol. 8-9, no. 14-15 (July 1978-June 1979), p. 53-84.

An appraisal of the policies designed to reduce income disparities and regional inequalities in Cyprus.

Social problems

444 **Criminality in Cyprus.**
P. Machlouzarides. Nicosia, 1973. 193p. tables. graphs. apps. (mimeo.)

A very important and informative historical study of the incidence and character of crime, as well as of methods of crime control in Cyprus, by an experienced

Social Conditions. Social problems

chief superintendent of the Cyprus police force. The work, in two mimeographed fascicles, draws on the records of the Cyprus police and covers the period up to 1960. The first part surveys crime to 1900 and the second examines the period 1901-60. Many tables, graphs and accounts of outstanding individual cases are included in the appendixes.

445 Cypriot woman: rise and downfall.
Helen Nikita. Nicosia: Social Research Centre, 1975. 20p.

An account of the reversals suffered by Cypriot women as a consequence of the Turkish invasion, issued on the occasion of the International Women's Year.

446 Cyprus witness.
Edited by I. K. Mazarakis. Athens: Panhellenic Committee for Solidarity with Cyprus, 1976. 78p.

A record of the tribulations inflicted on the population of Cyprus by the Turkish invasion, based on excerpts from officially verified statements of war prisoners and of refugees from Turkish-occupied Cyprus. It includes complete lists of missing and unaccounted-for persons.

447 The refugees of Cyprus: a representative socio-psychological study.
T. Erdokas (and others). Nicosia: Theopress, 1976. viii + 174p. tables.

A group of Greek Cypriot social scientists from the Social-Psychological Research Group set out to study and analyse the effects, psychological and otherwise, of the 1974 Turkish invasion on representative groups of Greek Cypriot refugees. The methodology used, the pertinent questionnaires and the results are collected in this volume.

448 Living conditions of the enclaved Greek Cypriots.
Nicosia: Public Information Office, 1979. 12p.

A report on property seizures, forced labour, restriction on movement, communication, medical care, education and religious practice and the infliction of oppression and atrocities by the invading Turkish troops and mainland Turkish settlers on the Greek Cypriots who remained in their villages in the Karpass. As a consequence, from about 20,000 cut off by the invasion in 1974 only about 2,000 remained in 1979.

449 The case of the missing Cypriots.
Nicosia: Pancyprian Committee of Parents and Relatives of Undeclared P.O.W.s and Missing Persons, 1977. 52p. illus.

An illustrated documentary record of the major social problem left behind by the Turkish invasion of Cyprus. In the wake of the war in the summer of 1974 about 2,000 persons remained unaccounted for, and their fate is still unknown despite all efforts to trace them.

Society and Social Change

450 **Census of population and agriculture 1946: report.**
D. A. Percival. London: Crown Agents for the Colonies, 1949. 92p.

On the basis of the findings of the 1946 census, the compiler of this report analysed social and economic trends since the previous census of 1930 and provided a detailed statistical portrait of Cypriot society at the end of the Second World War.

451 **Honour and shame in a Cypriot highland village.**
Jean G. Peristiany. In: *Honour and shame: the values of Mediterranean society*. Edited by Jean G. Peristiany. London: Weidenfeld & Nicolson; Chicago: University of Chicago Press, 1966, p. 171-90.

An influential description of the moral culture of traditional Cypriot society. This essay records the author's appraisal, during field research in the summer of 1954, of the operation of social values as mechanisms of behavioural control in the highland village of Alona in the Pitsillia region.

452 **Introduction to a Cyprus highland village.**
Jean G. Peristiany. In: *Contributions to Mediterranean sociology: Mediterranean rural communities and social change*. Edited by Jean G. Peristiany. Paris, The Hague: Mouton, 1968, p. 75-91.

An anthropological study of ecology and economic life, social structure, authority and status, relations with neighbouring villages, kinship, parenthood and old age in Alona. The report is based on field research conducted in the summer of 1954 and it therefore offers a first-hand perspective on traditional institutions and values.

Society and Social Change

453 Regional variation in modern Greece and Cyprus: toward a perspective on the ethnography of Greece.
Edited by Muriel Dimen, Ernestine Friedl. *Annals of the New York Academy of Sciences*, vol. 268 (10 Feb. 1976), 465p.

Part 6 (p. 344-81) focuses on Cyprus, with contributions by Jean G. Peristiany surveying anthropological, sociological and geographical fieldwork in Cyprus; Peter Loizos on anthopological research possibilities; and, most notably, an analysis of forms of peasant incorporation by M. Attalides which examines the ways in which the peasantry of the Karpass region was integrated into Greek Cypriot nationalism. The latter's article entitled 'Forms of peasant incorporation in Cyprus during the last century' is reprinted in *Patrons and clients in Mediterranean societies*, edited by E. Gellner and J. Waterbury (London: Duckworth, 1977, p. 137-55).

454 The Greek gift: politics in a Cypriot village.
Peter Loizos. Oxford, England: Blackwell, 1975. xvii + 326p. bibliog. tables. apps.

An anthropological monograph focusing on the village of Argaki in the Morphou plain in Cyprus. In addition to the usual anthropological themes of the structure of village life and kinship, the study pays special attention to the pressures of the broader society on the rural community. As such it provides an angle on Cypriot politics in the 1960s from the vantage point of rural grassroot concerns. This allows the reader to grasp the ways in which broader conflicts were localized and conversely the methods through which local initiatives attempt to cope with the society beyond the confines of the village.

455 Changes in property transfer among Greek Cypriot villagers.
Peter Loizos. *Man*, vol. 19, no. 4 (1975), p. 503-23.

A study of dowry and inheritance as means of property transfer in Cypriot peasant society. It shows how economic change has replaced traditional agricultural property with the construction of a house as the primary form of dowry.

456 Changing configurations of Greek Cypriot kinship.
Michael Attalides. In: *Kinship and modernization in Mediterranean society*. Edited by Jean G. Peristiany. Rome: Center for Mediterranean Studies, American Universities Field Staff, 1976, p. 73-90.

A study of the impact of socio-economic modernization on traditional family and kinship ties and behaviour in Cyprus.

Society and Social Change

457 **Lysi: social change in a Cypriot village.**
Kyriakos C. Markides, Eleni S. Nikita, Elengo Rangou. Nicosia: Social Research Centre, 1978. xiv + 219p. maps. tables. diags.

A study of the village of Lysi in the Mesaoria region of central Cyprus, examining the community's ecological, demographic and regional conditions and focusing on the impact of socio-economic modernization on its population. Changing kinship patterns, the social role of education and individual attitudes toward modernity receive special attention. The book includes many tables, maps, graphs and plans.

458 **Social change and urbanization in Cyprus: a study of Nicosia.**
Michael Attalides. Nicosia: Social Research Centre, 1981. 211p. bibliog.

An empirical examination of the urbanization process in the capital of Cyprus. After a consideration of the historical background, the study explores migration and stratification patterns, ecological and kinship structures, social networks and group affiliation. The research is based on a 1971 migrant survey and does not consider the new circumstances brought into the life of Nicosia by the Turkish occupation of northern Cyprus.

459 **Population trends in Nicosia and the changing rural-urban fringe.**
Othon Yiangoullis. *Geographical Chronicles,* vol. 4, no. 7-8 (Jan.-Dec. 1975), p. 67-79.

460 **The people of the Nicosia rural-urban fringe: a case study.**
Othon Yiangoullis. *Geographical Chronicles,* vol. 6, no. 11 (Jan.-June 1977), p. 3-26.

461 **Conceptualization of rural-urban fringe areas and the delineation of Nicosia's fringe.**
Othon Yiangoullis. *Geographical Chronicles,* vol. 8, no. 13 (Jan.-June 1978), p. 28-38.

In the three above articles the author attempts to apply the concept of the rural-urban fringe to the case of Cyprus's developing capital. The first article warns against the dangers of uneven demographic development and argues for the regulation of commuting to Nicosia as a pre-emptive measure. The second article is a study in the sociology of the inhabitants of the Nicosia rural-urban fringe, while the third attempts to develop a conceptual framework for the definition of rural-urban fringe which is applied to the delineation of the fringe of Nicosia.

Society and Social Change

462 **The historical growth of Famagusta and an analysis of its present functions.**
Kyriacos A. Demetriades. *Geographical Chronicles*, vol. 2, no. 3 (July 1972), p. 38-58.

A professional town planner examines the historical evolution of the city of Famagusta in mediaeval and modern times and considers the urban development, economic activities, and the functions of its port which made it into one of contemporary Cyprus's leading urban centres. Famagusta's pre-eminence as an urban centre is attributed to its geographical location in relation to the rest of the island.

463 **Social change and the rise and decline of social movements: the case of Cyprus.**
Kyriacos C. Markides. *American Ethnologist*, vol. 1, no. 2 (May 1974), p. 309-30.

An analysis of the Greek Cypriot anti-colonialist enosis movement. It is concluded that a traditionally rooted movement like enosis cannot maintain its mass appeal if its ideological content remains inflexible at a time of profound secularizing and modernizing changes.

464 **Process and tradition in Cypriot culture history: time theory in anthropology.**
Michael A. Hoffmann. *Anthropological Quarterly*, vol. 45, no. 1 (Jan. 1972), p. 15-34.

An attempt to conceptualize the history of the Greek tradition in Cyprus from the Bronze Age to modern times in terms of models of synchronic, diachronic and long historical time. The nature and persistence of the Greek tradition over 3,300 years is considered in relation to external pressures, Greek cultural identity and recurring confrontations between two major cultural traditions on the island.

Law and Constitution

465 **Cyprus: its medieval jurisprudence and modern legislation.**
Travers Twiss. *Law Magazine and Review*, no. 236 (May 1880), p. 225-65.

An introductory survey of the legal history of Cyprus. It refers to Greek Byzantine law in force in Cyprus before the Latin occupation, to the law of the 'assizes' introduced by the crusaders whereby trial by one's peers (nobles or commons) was instituted, and to the Ottoman legal and administrative system in force in Cyprus at the time of the British occupation.

466 **The Hellenic laws of Cyprus and the 'Hexabiblos' of Armenopoulos.**
Achilleus Emilianides. In: *Tomos K. Armenopoulou*. Thessaloniki, Greece: Faculty of Law and Economics of the University of Thessaloniki, 1952, p. 33-38.

Documentary evidence suggests that Byzantine family law survived in Cyprus under the institutions of Lusignan rule. The adjudication of cases of family law by the Greek Orthodox Church assured the survival of the Byzantine legal tradition under the Franks and subsequent foreign conquerors.

467 **Cyprus: presented to Parliament by the secretary of state for the colonies, the secretary of state for foreign affairs and the minister of defence by command of Her Majesty July 1960.**
London: HM Stationery Office, 1960. 222p. 4 folding maps. (Cmnd. no. 1093).

This is the official British White Paper on Cyprus. It contains the official texts of the Treaties of Establishment, Guarantee and Alliance setting up the Republic of Cyprus, the text of the constitution of the Republic of Cyprus, and a series of statements and official exchange of notes concerning the arrangements and transition to independence.

468 **Constitutions of nations.**
Edited by A. J. Peasle. The Hague: Martinus Nijhoff, 1968. 3rd ed.

The complete text of the constitution of the Republic of Cyprus appears in volume 3, *Europe*, p. 138-216.

Law and Constitution

469 Cyprus: sui generis.
S. A. de Smith. In: *The new Commonwealth and its constitutions*. S. A. de Smith. London: Stevens & Sons, 1964, p. 282-96.

A perceptive analysis of the Cyprus constitution, stressing its idiosyncracies which were dictated by the pressures of bi-communalism.

470 The first Republic of Cyprus: a review of an unworkable constitution.
T. W. Adams. *Western Political Quarterly*, vol. 19, no. 3 (Sept. 1966), p. 475-90.

The 1960 Cypriot constitution, an integral part of the 1959-60 Zurich and London accords, is surveyed in detail, highlighting its unworkable elements that led to the partial breakdown of constitutional order in late 1963.

471 Cyprus, the 'warlike isle': origins and elements of the current crisis.
Thomas Ehrlich. *Stanford Law Review*, vol. 18, no. 5 (1966), p. 1,021-98.

An exhaustive and lucid analysis that concentrates primarily on the legal aspects of the conflict. The author makes extensive use of United Nations documents and of the Security Council debates among the main protagonists to draw his conclusions on the legal rights and obligations of the concerned parties.

472 Constitutional and legal problems in the Republic of Cyprus.
Criton G. Tornaritis. Nicosia: Public Information Office, 1972. 2nd ed. 100p.

In this work the attorney-general of Cyprus examines the legal aspects of the Cyprus problem in its post-independence phase. Included are also opinions and advice on various other legal questions not related to the Cyprus problem such as: 'The legal position of the auditor-general'; 'Convention no. 105 concerning the abolition of forced labour'; 'The Land Consolidation Bill'; 'The legal position of the Armenian religious group'; and 'Some aspects of the canon law of the Greek Orthodox Church and the human rights'.

473 The Turkish invasion of Cyprus and legal problems arising therefrom.
Criton G. Tornaritis. Nicosia, 1975. 101p.

In considering the legal problems posed by the Turkish invasion of Cyprus, the attorney-general of the republic examines the question of federalism and regionalism, and appraises the legal effects and character of the Turkish military action against Cyprus and of the establishment of a Turkish Cypriot federated state.

Law and Constitution

474 Cyprus and its constitutional and other legal problems.
Criton G. Tornaritis. Nicosia, 1980. 2nd ed. 246p. apps.

This volume by the attorney-general of the republic is valuable for its voluminous documentation and legal references with regard to the status of Cyprus before and after independence. On post-independence developments — the 1963 constitutional crisis and the 1974 Turkish invasion — it expresses the government's viewpoint and that of the Greek Cypriot community. Its rich appendixes conveniently group together the official texts of the proposals and counter-proposals of the two Cypriot communities submitted between 1975 and 1979 for a solution in the aftermath of the 1974 crisis.

475 Treaties conflicting with peremptory norms of international law and the Zurich-London agreement.
Andreas J. Jacovides. Nicosia, 1969. 28p.

This paper is divided in two parts. The first is a theoretical treatise discussing whether international law recognizes within its legal order peremptory norms that have the character of *jus cogens*, i.e. rules from which the law does not permit any derogation by agreement between parties *inter se*. The author concludes that sufficient evidence exists that the principles of non-use of force in international relations, peaceful settlement of disputes, non-intervention and sovereign equality fall within the character of *jus cogens*. In the second part, the case of Cyprus is examined and it is concluded that the Zurich-London agreements 'do conflict in a number of respects with peremptory norms . . . [and that this conclusion] can be supported before any international tribunal'.

476 The legal dimension of the Cyprus conflict.
Marios L. Evriviades. *Texas International Law Journal*, vol. 10, no. 2 (spring 1975), p. 227-64.

After tracing the political and legal background to the founding of the Republic of Cyprus, the article examines the legal issues and the legal arguments of the parties concerned during the 1964, 1967 and 1974 crises. With regard to the controversial article 4 of the Treaty of Guarantee, it is the author's contention that it was not the 'agreed intention of all parties', i.e. Great Britain, Greece and Turkey, to jointly or separately use force against Cyprus to re-establish the *status quo ante*. During the 1974 crisis, it is argued that all three guarantor powers failed to fulfill their obligations towards Cyprus, Greece and Turkey by violating what they purported to guarantee and acting contrary to their legal requirements, and Britain by failing to act according to her legal obligation.

Law and Constitution

477 **The statute laws of Cyprus in force on the 1st day of April, 1959.**
Criton George Tornaritis. London: C. F. Roworth, 1959.
rev. ed. 6 vols.

These six volumes prepared on the eve of Cypriot independence codify the legislation passed in Cyprus during the period of the British administration. The 1960 constitution contained an express provision to save the existing laws as long as they were not inconsistent with the constitution. With minor exceptions the laws and statutes included in these volumes are still in force. It includes alphabetical and chronological lists of laws. Prepared under the authority of the Cyprus Laws (Revised Edition) Law, 1959.

478 **Index to the laws of the Republic of Cyprus.**
Nicosia: Government Printing Office, 1971. 588p.

This is a bilingual edition (Greek and English) indexing the laws included in *The statute laws of Cyprus* of 1959 (see the preceding entry) and the laws enacted between 1 April 1959 and 31 December 1971.

479 **Reports of the Supreme Constitutional Court.**
Nicosia: Government Printing Office, 1960-64. annual.

Contains rulings of the Supreme Constitutional Court of the Republic of Cyprus (1960-64).

480 **Cyprus Law Reports.**
Nicosia: Government Printing Office, 1960-64. annual.

Contains rulings of the High Court of the Republic of Cyprus in the period 1960-64 before its merger with the Supreme Constitutional Court to form the Supreme Court of the Republic.

481 **Cyprus Law Reports.**
Nicosia: Government Printing Office, 1965- . annual.

Since 1965 the judgements of the Supreme Court of the Republic of Cyprus have been published in these three annual volumes of which the first contains civil law cases, the second criminal law cases and the third administrative law cases.

482 **Cyprus law reports and monthly publication of judgements of the Supreme Court of Cyprus, 1956-1976.**
Edited by P. Kallis. Nicosia: Government Printing Office, 1977. lxii + 663p.

Index of subject matter and statutes, rules and regulations judicially considered, comprising legislation from the eve of independence through the first sixteen years of the republic.

483 **Cyprus administrative law.**
Zaim M. Nedjati. Nicosia, 1970. xviii + 294p.

This is a manual of administrative law as it developed under the constitutional practice of the Republic of Cyprus. The author draws extensively on case materials in outlining the practice of administrative law in the republic.

Law and Constitution

484 Human rights and fundamental freedoms.
Zaim M. Nedjati. Nicosia, 1972. 228p.

A consideration of the safeguard of basic liberties in Cyprus in the light of legal and constitutional norms.

485 The social and economic rights under the law of the Republic of Cyprus.
Criton G. Tornaritis. Nicosia: Public Information Office [n.d.]. 24p.

Considers the basic freedoms and social rights guaranteed by the constitution of the Republic of Cyprus, citing the evidence of pertinent legal cases. Originally published in *Mélanges Marcel Bridel* (Lausanne, Switzerland: Imprimeries Réunies, 1968, p. 533-56).

486 Expropriation and nationalization of property under the law of the Republic of Cyprus.
Criton G. Tornaritis. Nicosia: Public Information Office, 1970. 23p.

Through an examination of the constitution and laws of Cyprus, it is pointed out that both the individualistic concept of property and the privileges and properties of religious bodies are secured and protected. The silence of the Cyprus constitution regarding nationalization is also discussed.

487 Criminal procedure in Cyprus.
A. N. Loizou, G. M. Pikis. Nicosia: Proodos Press, 1975. 265p.

A treatment of criminal procedure law as practised in the courts of Cyprus. The authors are both senior members of the republic's judiciary. They present the relevant statute and case law and proceed to a comparative examination of English case law, which makes their treatise a valuable contribution to the study of criminal procedure in the British Commonwealth.

488 Sentencing in Cyprus.
George M. Pikis. Nicosia: Proodos Press, 1978. 182p.

An examination of the process of sentencing in the Cypriot courts by a practising judge. It surveys the general principles and purpose of sentencing, modes of punishment, facts relevant to the sentence, imprisonment, and the role of trial and appeal courts. Sentencing procedures for specific offences are examined in detail in the second part of the book.

Economics

489 **The economics of Cyprus: a survey to 1914.**
Diamond Jenness. Montreal: McGill University Press, 1962.
219p. bibliog. apps.

An economic history of Cyprus, surveying the Byzantine, Lusignan and Venetian periods and examining in somewhat greater detail the economics of Ottoman rule in the island. Its main focus is on the first phase of British rule from 1878-1914. It contains useful quantitative appendixes on the growth of agriculture (1879-97), imports and exports (1879-1913) and revenues and expenditures (1879-1913).

490 **The economy of Cyprus.**
A. J. Meyer, Simos Vassiliou. Cambridge, Massachusetts: Harvard University Press, 1962. xii + 94p. map. bibliog.

This is essentially an economic history of Cyprus in the last phase of British rule, free from the technicalities and jargon of economic literature and thus easily accessible to the general reader. It examines the expansion and problems of the Cypriot economy from 1943-60 and the character of the island's agriculture, industry, trade and banking. It stresses the dependent nature of the local economy, but concludes with the optimistic view that this very dependence can be turned to advantage through appropriate planning.

491 **Cyprus: the 'copra-boat' economy.**
A. J. Meyer. *Middle East Journal*, vol. 13, no. 3 (summer 1959), p. 249-61.

An appraisal of the economic prospects of Cyprus on the eve of statehood. It stresses the poverty of the island's natural resources, and, instead of planning for development of the productive sectors of the economy, it advises the economic exploitation of the island's strategic real estate and reliance on such parasitic activities as tourism and emigration. The model of growth suggested here is the exact opposite of that actually adopted in the economic planning of the republic. Reprinted in the author's *Middle Eastern capitalism* (Cambridge, Massachusetts: Harvard University Press, 1959, p. 47-64).

Economics

492 Cyprus: suggestions for a development programme.
William L. Thorp, prepared for the government of the Republic of Cyprus under the United Nations Programme of Technical Assistance. New York: United Nations, 1961. v + 113p. (Document ST/TAO/CYP/1).

This UN-sponsored report contains a comprehensive survey of the Cypriot economy as this stood on the eve of independence in 1960. All sectors of the economy are examined and suggestions for their improvement are made. The water problem is emphasized in particular, and annexes are included with suggested areas for surveys and drilling.

493 A study of the Cyprus economy.
Marjorie W. Hald. Nicosia: Printing Office of the Republic of Cyprus, 1968. 84p. bibliog.

The study considers the geography and resource structure of Cyprus, surveys economic history to 1960, examines the foundations of planning and development laid by the First Five-Year Plan, and appraises the economic outlook and structural problems in the late 1960s.

494 The story of Cyprus Mines Corporation.
David Sievert Lavender. San Marino, California: Huntington Library, 1962. x + 387p. bibliog.

This is the quasi-official history of the Cyprus Mines Corporation, since the first survey of the field in 1912 to the consolidation and expansion of the 1950s. The book is well written and well researched, and offers an important perspective on the social and economic history of Cyprus.

495 Communal conflict and economic considerations: the case of Cyprus.
Stahis S. Panagides. *Journal of Peace Research,* vol. 5 (1968), p. 133-45.

A survey of the economic conditions of the Greek and Turkish Cypriot communities as these have been affected by the communal conflict. It is the author's contention that the benefits of economic integration in Cyprus can help alleviate, though not solve, the political problem and that if Cypriot society fails to integrate economically, social and political instability will increase.

496 Five-year programme of economic development.
President Makarios. Nicosia: Republic of Cyprus, 1961. 38p.

An address to the House of Representatives by the first president of the republic, laying the foundations of economic policy and development guidelines for the new state.

Economics

497 The Second Five-Year Plan (1967-1971).
Nicosia: Planning Bureau of the Republic of Cyprus [n.d.]. 273p.

The basic source concerning development policy and economic planning in the Republic of Cyprus. It includes statistical indicators and other information pertinent to the economic history of the island since independence.

498 The Third Five-Year Plan (1972-1976).
Nicosia: Planning Bureau of the Republic of Cyprus [n.d.]. 396p.

Includes an assessment of economic development in the republic's first decade. Besides planning for growth in different sectors of economic activity, the plan places special emphasis on social policies and human resource development.

499 Third emergency economic action plan 1979-1981 (summary).
Planning Bureau of the Republic of Cyprus, Planning Commission. Nicosia: Republic of Cyprus [n.d.]. 79p.

As with the previous two-year emergency economic action plans which covered the 1975-1978 period, this plan has been prepared within the government's efforts to mobilize and utilize the country's material and human resources with the view of reactivating the country's economy. Following the relative success of the earlier plans, the third one aims, *inter alia*, to combat inflationary pressures and the instability in the balance of payments, to alleviate the labour shortages, and to increase productivity and expand exports.

Trade and Industry

General

500 **The Cyprus economy: a case in the industrialization progress.**
John S. Kaminarides. Nicosia: Socrates Publishing, 1973. 293p. bibliog. tables. apps.

During the 1960s, not withstanding the inter-communal troubles, Cyprus made impressive strides in economic development, especially when compared to other newly independent states. This study treats the subject analysing, albeit in a highly technical fashion, some of the indicators responsible. Non-economic factors, including social and institutional change, and their effects are also addressed.

501 **Manufacturing development in a small country economy: the case of Cyprus.**
Stahis Panagides. *Social and Economic Studies* (Jamaica), vol. 16 (1967), p. 390-405.

An investigation of the manufacturing sector of the economy of Cyprus on the basis of which some policy implications are drawn for manufacturing development in small countries, especially in relation to trade policy.

502 **The mineral resources and mining industry of Cyprus.**
L. M. Bear. Nicosia: Geological Survey Department, 1963. 208p. 3 folding maps. bibliog. illus.

An illustrated and carefully indexed inventory of all known metallic and non-metallic deposits in the subsoil of Cyprus. After a historical introduction and a summary of the geology of Cyprus, it offers valuable information on the mining industry (legislation, taxation, royalties, production and companies) and a detailed professional survey of the metallic and non-metallic mineral deposits of the island.

503 **'Normal' patterns of industrial growth in Cyprus.**
E. I. Demetriades. *Geographical Chronicles*, vol. 6, no. 11 (Jan.-June 1977), p. 41-49.

Trade and Industry. General

504 Capacity utilization in the Cyprus manufacturing sector.
E. I. Demetriades. *Geographical Chronicles*, vol. 7, no. 12 (July-Dec. 1977), p. 18-26.

505 The system and structure of protection of manufacturing in Cyprus.
E. I. Demetriades. *Geographical Chronicles*, vol. 9-10, no. 16-17 (July 1979-June 1980), p. 59-98.

In the three previous articles the author appraises the industrialization policies followed in Cyprus since independence. In the first article through the application to Cyprus of the 'normal' pattern model of industrial growth and in the second through the development of a capacity utilization index for manufacturing, it is shown that despite increases the role of industry in the overall economy has not been what it might have been. The last article calls for a reappraisal of industrial policy, suggesting the replacement of the import substitution followed up to now with export-oriented policies.

506 The process of industrialisation in Cyprus.
E. I. Demetriades. Nicosia: Social Research Centre, 1982. 235p. bibliog.

An analysis of the industrialization process in Cyprus during the period of the First and Second Five-Year Plans, 1962-71. It appraises the basic industrialization strategy – import substitution through protection – and suggests that an export-oriented policy might be crucial for future industrial development.

507 Focus on Cyprus.
New Commonwealth, vol. 49, no. 1 (Jan. 1970), p. 5-12.

A decade after independence this section focuses on Cyprus's development progress. It emphasizes its potential for foreign investment, and gives details on the island's citrus industry – the export leader at the time.

508 Focus on Cyprus.
World Development, vol. 1, no. 9 (Sept. 1973), p. 69-79.

A special report on the economy of Cyprus, considering the prospects of the Third Five-Year Plan, the development of agriculture, the progress of Cyprus Airways since its establishment in 1947, tourism, investment opportunities, industrial development and agricultural exports.

509 Investing in the eastern Mediterranean: Greece, Egypt, Cyprus.
John F. Chown. Bedford, England: Sidney Press, 1977. 168p.

An investor's guide to outlets in the broad geographical area of which Cyprus forms a focal point.

Trade and Industry. Cyprus and the EEC

510 **The way: Cyprus, a base for international operations.**
Nicosia, 1979. 47p.

For foreign businessmen and multinational corporations interested in setting up a base in Cyprus. This booklet provides details on company law, taxation and foreign exchange controls.

511 **The legal aspects of foreign investment in Cyprus.**
Kypros Chrisostomides. Nicosia: Chr. Nicolaou & Sons, 1978. 34p.

An examination of the various legal forms available to foreign investors in Cyprus. Expositions on partnerships, companies, taxation and tax incentives, off-shore companies, restrictions and exchange control, and legal security are included.

512 **Cyprus in international tax planning.**
Chrysses Demetriades, introduction by John Poole. London: Kluwer Publishing, 1980. xvi + 447p. charts. apps.

This is a practical and comprehensive guide for foreign firms and individuals who want to use Cyprus as a base for their international operations and tax planning purposes. It is the only major publication of its kind and fills an information gap with regard to tax laws and other financial amenities and incentives available.

513 **Cyprus Trade and Industry.**
Nicosia: Public Information Office, 1975- . quarterly.

This periodical of the Ministry of Commerce and Industry provides Cypriot entrepreneurs and potential foreign investors with brief articles and news items on Cypriot imports and exports. It also contains reports on tourism, feature articles on specific economic sectors and occasional policy addresses by Cypriot officials.

Cyprus and the EEC

514 **Cyprus and the EEC.**
Titos Phanos. *Revue de la Société d'Etudes et d'Expansion*, vol. 73, no. 262 (Oct.-Dec. 1974), p. 505-13.

A presentation of the terms and significance of the EEC-Cyprus association agreement. The author is a Cypriot official.

Trade and Industry. Cyprus and the EEC

515 **Trade agreements between the EEC and the Arab countries of the eastern Mediterranean and Cyprus.**
George Vassiliou. In: *The EEC and the Mediterranean countries.* Edited by A. Shlaim, G. Yannopoulos. Cambridge, England: Cambridge University Press, 1976, p. 179-99.

A consideration of trade arrangements between the EEC and the states of the eastern Mediterranean including Cyprus.

516 **Associate status with the E.E.C. and its implications for the economy of Cyprus.**
G. S. Chrysomilides. Beirut: Faculty of Agricultural Sciences, American University of Beirut, 1975. 17p. bibliog. tables. app.

This monograph examines the structure and implications for the Cyprus economy of the January 1972 associate status agreement between Cyprus and the EEC. Although the emphasis is on the agricultural sector, the work also addresses the effects on the other sectors, especially that of capital inflows from EEC and non-EEC countries.

517 **The impact of the European Economic Community south enlargement on Cyprus' industry: five discussion papers.**
Viktoria Grevemeyer-Korb, Dieter Kampe, Christin Schmidt, Jutta Wagenseil, Dieter Weiss. Berlin, GFR: German Development Institute, 1979. 130p. bibliog.

The five discussion papers consider respectively marketing and technology, the difficulties of the EEC policy toward south enlargement and its consequences for other Mediterranean countries, a conceptual framework for industrial strategy, trade flows, and the industrial structure and industrial strategy of Cyprus's main competitors within an enlarged EEC.

518 **Cypriot agricultural trade with the EEC: scope for assuring market access.**
Hans Gsanger. Berlin, GFR: German Development Institute, 1979. 54p.

A study of the implications of the EEC's south enlargement for Cypriot agricultural exports.

519 **Cyprus-EEC association agreement.**
Gaston K. Neokleous. Nicosia, 1980. 68p. bibliog.

A study of the association agreement concluded between the European Economic Community and Cyprus, examining Cyprus's foreign trade, the welfare effects of the agreement, an analysis of the mutual concessions involved, and concluding with policy suggestions.

Agriculture

520 **A survey of rural life in Cyprus.**
B. J. Surridge. Nicosia: Government Printing Office, 1930. 91p.

A remarkable analysis of the causes of rural poverty by a government official just prior to the anti-colonial rising of 1931.

521 **Rural indebtedness and agricultural cooperation in Cyprus.**
N. C. Lanitis. Limassol, Cyprus, 1944. 278p. tables. diags.

This is a seminal study of the problem of peasant debts and the role of usury and its consequences in rural Cyprus prior to the Second World War. The relevant data are presented in many useful tables and diagrams. The problems of usury and exploitation provided the stimulus for the creation of the vital cooperative movement which developed into the major factor in the rural economy of Cyprus. Available also in a Greek version, translated by Chr. Christodoulou (Nicosia, 1946. 342p.).

522 **The evolution of the rural land use pattern in Cyprus.**
Demetrios Christodoulou. Bude, England: Geographical Publications, 1959. 230p. bibliog. (World Land Use Survey, Monograph 2).

A seminal study of Cyprus agriculture. It examines the geology and land forms, climate, water resources, soils, vegetation, people and habitations, settlements, land tenure and water rights, finance, rural services, land use, woodland, arable land, types of farming, industrial crops, market gardening and intensive cultivation, viticulture, fruit trees, animal husbandry and land use regions at the close of the colonial era. On the basis of the picture provided here the student of Cyprus agriculture can appraise the progress achieved since independence.

523 **Land ownership in Cyprus.**
George Karouzis. Nicosia: Strabo, 1977. 133p. maps. diags.

A study of the pattern of land ownership in Cyprus with special reference to the distribution of land holdings between the Greek and Turkish communities. The text is documented with diagrams and maps.

Agriculture

524 **Report on aspects of land tenure in Cyprus.**
George Karouzis. Nicosia: Land Consolidation Authority, 1980.
248p. graphs. plans.

The findings of a survey of land tenure patterns in the Paphos, Limassol, Larnaca, Morphou and Polis-Tylliria regions. Richly documented with statistical data, graphs and plans, it considers water rights, time wasted because of fragmentation and dispersion of plots, shape of plots, correlation between existing ownership and operation, land tenure trends, land consolidation and other required measures.

525 **Time wasted and distance travelled by the average Cypriot farmer in order to visit his scattered and fragmented agricultural holding.**
George Karouzis. *Geographical Chronicles*, vol. 1, no. 1 (Jan. 1971), p. 39-58.

A richly documented study of the consequences of plot fragmentation in agricultural ownership in Cyprus.

526 **Rural planning in Cyprus.**
Nicosia: Cyprus Land Consolidation Authority, 1973.
73p. maps. 10 plates. illus.

Featuring many illustrations, maps and plates, this is a report on policies designed to improve working and living conditions for the Cypriot farmer through the initiation of land consolidation and other measures of rural development.

527 **Aspects of the agricultural economy of Cyprus: 1950-1967.**
P. Yiassemides, H. Kunert. Nicosia: Agricultural Research Institute, 1967. 41p. maps.

After an overall consideration of the position of agriculture in the economy of Cyprus, the study examines land use structures and agricultural inputs and outputs, and proposes an econometric model of Cyprus agriculture for the years 1950-65.

528 **Recent trends of agricultural production and productivity in Cyprus.**
Rogiros Chr. Michaelides. Nicosia: Ministry of Agriculture and Natural Resources, 1970. 52p. graphs.

A bilingual report on the progress of agriculture and animal husbandry and on agricultural policies during the republic's first decade by the director general of the Ministry of Agriculture and Natural Resources. It includes many helpful graphs.

Agriculture

529 **Norm input-output data of the main crops of Cyprus.**
Stelios Papachristodoulou. Nicosia: Agricultural Research Institute, 1976. 259p.

A detailed quantitative record of physical and financial input-output data of the citrus, deciduous fruit, vine, banana, vegetable, cereal, groundnut and dry legume crops of Cyprus. The compendium is useful for farm planning and budgeting and for agricultural development project implementation.

530 **Agricultural development and co-operative marketing in Cyprus.**
Paris Andreou. Nairobi: East African Literature Bureau, 1977. 198p.

A study of the progress of Cypriot agriculture and of the major mechanism of marketing agricultural products through the effective development of producers' cooperatives.

531 **Dams of Cyprus.**
C. A. C. Konteatis. Nicosia: Water Development Department, 1974. xxii + 264p. illus. plans.

A technical study of the construction requirements of the numerous dams through which the Water Development Department of the republic attempted to cope with the chronic water supply problems of the island. Four categories of dams are examined: masonry dams, concrete dams, rockfill dams and earthfill dams. The book is illustrated with photographs and plans.

532 **Dry farming and irrigation farming in Cyprus: rural geographical processes until the summer of 1974.**
Gunter Heinritz. *Geographical Chronicles,* vol. 7, no. 12 (July-Dec. 1977), p. 35-41.

An appraisal of the progress of irrigated agricultural production between 1961-74 and of the problems which have remained unresolved.

533 **Traditional forms of animal husbandry and industrial animal production: problems and future prospects.**
Gunter Nagel. *Geographical Chronicles,* vol. 7, no. 12 (July-Dec. 1977), p. 60-65.

A 1973 report on the situation of animal husbandry in Cyprus.

Statistics

534 **Statistical Abstract.**
Nicosia: Department of Statistics and Research, Ministry of Finance, 1955- . annual.

A compendium of comprehensive information on all aspects of the economic and social life of Cyprus. It contains data on physiographic description, area and climate, population and vital statistics, migration and tourism, education, health, justice and crime, labour and employment, social insurance and welfare, national accounts, prices, public finance, banking, saving and currency, transport and communication, agriculture, forestry and fishing, industry, housing and construction, distribution and services, external trade, balance of payments and comparative international statistics. It also includes a map of Cyprus and an index of sources. More specialized monthly and annual reports are also available in each of the above sectors and can be traced by consulting the *List of publications of the Department of Statistics and Research.*

535 **Statistical data by ethnic group.**
Nicosia: Department of Statistics and Research, Ministry of Finance, 1964. maps. figs.

A compilation of six maps and forty-two figures, all of them in colour, presenting geographic, demographic, productivity, ownership, educational and communications data by ethnic group. An indispensable atlas of basic statistical information on ethnic relations in the bi-communal society of Cyprus.

536 **Central Bank of Cyprus Annual Report.**
Nicosia: Central Bank of Cyprus, 1964- . annual.

Offers a balance sheet and a profit and loss account, including a comprehensive view of all sectors of the Cypriot economy and of the country's financial state of affairs.

537 **Bulletin.**
Nicosia: Economic Research Department, Central Bank of Cyprus, 1964- . quarterly.

Provides financial details on the assets and liabilities of the Central Bank and other financial institutions in the country. Useful charts on liquidity, currency notes, coins in circulation, interest rates, balance of payments, foreign trade and imports, the price index, etc. are provided.

Education

538 **Education in Cyprus: some theories and practices in education in the island of Cyprus since 1878.**
W. W. Weir. Nicosia: Cosmos Press, 1952. xix + 312p.

This is one of the most serious studies of the history and problems of education in Cyprus under British rule by an American educator who served for many years in the island. The author discusses the changes brought to Cypriot educational practice by the British occupation, and goes on to examine subsequent developments in terms of four major patterns of external influence on local education: Turkish, Greek, English and American. Some attention is paid to lesser sources of influence and the book concludes with some suggestions on the future educational development of Cyprus.

539 **The educational policy of the English government in Cyprus (1878-1954).**
Costas Spyridakis. Nicosia: Cyprus Ethnarchy Office, 1954. 41p.

A report on the educational policies followed by the British administration in Cyprus from the establishment of British rule to the eve of the anti-colonial revolt. Written from the point of view of Greek Cypriot nationalism, it stresses the attempts of the colonial administration to bring educational institutions under government control and thus de-Hellenize the curriculum.

540 **Church and state in Cyprus education.**
Panayiotis K. Persianis. Nicosia: Holy Archdiocese of Cyprus, 1978. xii + 235p. bibliog.

This is a historical study of the evolution of Greek education in Cyprus in the period of British rule (1878-1960). It focuses on the role of the Greek Orthodox Church of Cyprus in the promotion of educational policies which transformed the educational system of the island into a medium of Greek nationalism, and on the struggles that these attempts precipitated between the church and the British administration. The essence of the author's argument originally appeared in an article entitled 'Church and state in the development of education in Cyprus 1878-1960' in *Educational policy and the mission schools,* edited by Brian Holmes (London: Routledge & Kegan Paul, 1967, p. 241-78).

Education

541 **The political and economic factors as the main determinants of educational policy in independent Cyprus (1960-1970).**
Panayiotis K. Persianis. Nicosia: Paedagogical Institute of Cyprus, 1981. 244p. bibliog.

An examination of economic considerations and political conflicts in the elaboration of educational policies and choices during the republic's first decade.

542 **The Greek secondary education of Cyprus.**
C. Spyridakis. Nicosia: Cyprus Ethnarchy Office, 1959. 36p.

An account of the state of Greek secondary education in Cyprus on the eve of independence by the leading figure in the educational life of the island.

543 **Secondary general education in Cyprus.**
Ministry of Education, Department of Higher and Secondary Education. Nicosia: Kailas Press, 1976. 66p.

This is a brief but extremely useful publication containing a concise and comprehensive itemized summary on all subjects taught at the secondary level of Greek Cypriot public education (age group 12-18). The material taught is divided in two major cycles: that of the gymnasium, i.e. the lower level covering classes 1, 2 and 3; and that of the lyceum, i.e. the upper level covering classes 4, 5 and 6. Education in the lyceum is further separated into three sections: the classical, the scientific and the economic. Timetables on all subjects are provided.

544 **Cyprus school history textbooks.**
Education Advisory Committee, Parliamentary Group for World Government, translated by Barbara Hodge, G. L. Lewis, introduction by J. A. Lauwerys. London: Parliamentary Group for World Government, 1966. 47p.

By comparing extracts from Greek and Turkish Cypriot history textbooks the authors point out that while no falsehoods *per se* are included in the texts the selectivity of events and quasi-events, as well as the emphasis given, contribute to the misunderstanding and antagonism between the communities on the island. It is emphasized nonetheless that this phenomenon is by no means confined to Cypriots. 'For let us be clear', it is emphasized, 'the Cypriots are certainly no worse than others: there would be no difficulty in getting examples like those gathered here from textbooks used in England, the U.S.A., the U.S.S.R., France, Germany or China'.

Education

545 **Establishment of guidance services in developing countries with special emphasis on a guidance program for the secondary schools in Cyprus.**
Zenon E. Georgiades. Nicosia: Violaris Press, 1979. 142p.

The book studies the need for educational planning and the introduction of guidance programmes in Cypriot secondary schools in order to meet the requirements of social change and economic development in the newly founded republic. This is the text of the author's EdD thesis submitted in 1966, and thus reflects educational needs and realities in Cyprus immediately following the establishment of the republic.

546 **The development of the administration of elementary education in Cyprus.**
Andreas G. Anastassiades. Nicosia, 1979. vii + 117p.

A historical account of the organization and administration of elementary education in Cyprus. The main focus is on the educational policies of the British administration, followed by a general survey of the organization of Greek elementary education under the Cyprus republic.

547 **The headmaster in Cyprus.**
K. N. Neokleous. Nicosia [c.1970]. 183p.

A consideration by an experienced headmaster of the role of the headmaster in the operation of the secondary school system in Cyprus.

548 **Basic issues of educational policy.**
Chrysostomos Sophianos. Nicosia [n.d.]. 47p.

An address before the House of Representatives by the minister of education in the last government of President Makarios, outlining the goals of educational and cultural policies and stressing the need of democratization and change in educational practice.

549 **Effective management techniques and procedure in public examinations.**
Mikis I. Zevlaris. Nicosia, 1970. viii + 48 + xiiip.

A historical account of civil service examinations in Cyprus under British rule and under the republic. The book also contains suggestions for improved examination methods.

Literature

550 **Le Pétrarquisme en Chypre: poèmes d'amour en dialecte chypriote, d'après un manuscrit du XVI siècle.** (Petrarchan poetry in Cyprus: love poems in the Cypriot dialect according to a 16th century manuscript.)
Themis Siapkaras-Pitsillides. Athens: Collection de l'Institut Français d'Athènes, 1952. 446p. New ed. 1975; Greek translation, 1976.

A definitive critical edition of the exquisite lyric poetry composed by an unknown author in the Cypriot dialect in the 16th century. Besides the Greek text, a French translation and a commentary, the book includes important historical and philological studies of this poetic achievement.

551 **Poems of Cyprus: a selection from the work of Vassilis Michaelides and Dimitris Lipertis.**
Introduction by Costas M. Prousis, translated by Athan Anagnostopoulos. Nicosia: Printing Office of the Republic of Cyprus, 1970. xv + 120p.

A selection of representative works by the two 'classic' poets of modern Cyprus, both of whom distinguished themselves by expressing Cypriot sensibility in the local dialect. The anthology includes Michaelides' epics 'The ninth of July in Nicosia' (the national epic of Cyprus) and 'The woman of Chios', and the best of Lipertis' lyrics and didactic poems. This is the twenty-ninth book in a series of translations sponsored by the Council of Europe in order to make available to a wider public the literatures of the lesser-known European languages.

552 **The voice of Cyprus: an anthology of Cypriot literature.**
Edited by A. Decavalles (and others). New York: October House, 1966. 192p. plates.

Originally published as nos. 7-8 of *The Charioteer* (1965), this is an anthology of Cypriot verse and prose. It includes texts by the leading representatives of the literary tradition of modern Cyprus, and is illustrated by plates of Cypriot art, mostly of 20th century painting.

Literature

553 **Anthology of Cypriot poetry.**
Edited by Costas Montis, Andreas Christophides, translated by Amy Mims. Nicosia: Proodos Press, 1974. v + 251p.

This anthology offers a substantial introduction to the literary tradition of Cyprus through the centuries, with selections from ancient, mediaeval, folk and modern poetry. The greatest part of the book is devoted to modern poetry of the 19th and mostly of the 20th century, indicating the viability and renewal of an ancient tradition.

554 **The wanderer ballad.**
Kypros Chrysanthis, translated from the Greek by Claude Legagneux. Nicosia [n.d.]. 23p.

A selection from the lyric poetry of one of Cyprus's senior contemporary poets, with a prefatory biographical note by the translator.

555 **The betrayal.**
Kypros Chrysanthis, translated from the Greek by Christos Cameris. Nicosia, 1964. 8p.

A one-act play inspired by the liberation struggle of the 1950s.

556 **Seven poems from Cyprus.**
Translated by Peter Thompson. Nicosia: Pnevmatiki Kypros, 1969. 15p.

A bilingual collection of poems by A. Christophides, K. Chrysanthis, Costas Montis and T. Phylactou.

557 **Poems from the modern Greek.**
Translated by Jack Gaist. Nicosia: Pnevmatiki Kypros, 1976. 42p.

Besides selections from well-known modern Greek poets, the collection includes poems by Kypros Chrysanthis and Costas Montis.

558 **Ores tis Lefkosias stin poiesi ton Kyprion.** (Moments of Nicosia in Cypriot poetry.)
Edited by Nikos S. Spanos. Nicosia: Municipality of Nicosia, 1980. xxiv + 397p. illus.

This is an excellent collection, dealing with the image of Nicosia as it was perceived and poetically recreated in the poetry of successive generations of 19th and 20th century Cypriot poets. The work is further enriched by some pertinent prose selections, and is beautifully illustrated with old engravings, maps and drawings as well as with modern works by leading Cypriot artists.

Literature

559 Collective consciousness and poetry: three moments in the literary tradition of modern Cyprus.
Paschalis M. Kitromilides. *Neo-Hellenika,* vol. 4 (1981).
An essay on the function of poetry as a medium for the expression of collective aspirations through a consideration of three stages in the development of modern Cypriot poetry: 19th century romanticism, the classic work of Vassilis Michaelides and Dimitris Lipertis in the Cypriot dialect, and the poetry of dissent and social criticism by Tefkros Anthias and Thodossis Pierides.

560 George Philippou Pierides: a selection.
Translated by Jack Gaist. *Journal of the Hellenic Diaspora,* vol. 5, no. 2 (summer 1978), p. 47-58.
An English translation of selected passages from a collection of short stories entitled *The time of the blissful* by the leading Cypriot prose writer. The work conveys a sense of the social atmosphere and values prevailing in the prosperous Cyprus of the period of independence 1960-74, and as such it is an important statement of social criticism directed at the complacency and self-seeking of those whom the author holds responsible for the catastrophe of 1974.

561 Refugee in my homeland: Cyprus 1974.
Rina Katselli, translated by David Bailey. Nicosia: Kyrenia Flower Show Edition, 1979. 68p.
A personal record, composed of diary entries kept from July to December 1974, registering the anguish caused by the *coup,* the Turkish invasion, war and refugee life as experienced by a woman of the picturesque city of Kyrenia. One of the most revealing sources on the human costs of the tragedy.

562 Bread and freedom.
Doros Loizou. Nicosia, 1976. xx + 135p.
A bilingual edition of the poetry of Doros Loizou, the young Cypriot activist and poet who was killed in Cyprus in August 1974. Besides a general introduction, the book also includes six prose pieces by Doros Loizou. Independently of its literary significance, this is an eloquent testimony of social and political criticism and dissent by means of which a group of progressive intellectuals attempted to warn of the coming catastrophe.

563 Slaughtered spring.
Niki Ladaki-Philippou. Nicosia, 1980. 35p.
A collection of lyric poetry inspired by the feeling of loss occasioned by the tragedy of 1974.

The Arts

General

564 **Contemporary Cyprus art.**
London: Commonwealth Institute, 1970. 42p. illus.
An illustrated catalogue of an exhibition at the Commonwealth Institute, London, in 1970. It conveys a representative impression of the state and accomplishments of Cypriot plastic arts after ten years of independent life.

565 **A. Diamantis: a retrospective exhibition of painting and drawings 1922-1978.**
London: Mall Galleries, 1979. 88p. illus.
A catalogue of a retrospective exhibition of the work of the leading 20th century Cypriot painter. It includes biographical details and appraisals of Diamantis' work. The illustrated part of the catalogue offers a panoramic overview of the development of his art from the drawings of the 1920s at the Royal College of Art to the monumental paintings of the 1960s and 1970s, including the famous 'World of Cyprus'.

Byzantine period

566 The icons of Cyprus.
D. Talbot Rice. London: Allen & Unwin, 1937. 287p. 51 plates.

A monumental work which has laid the foundations for the systematic scholarly study of the tradition of icon painting in Byzantine and post-Byzantine Cyprus. The first part of the book includes thorough chapters on the schools of later Greek icon painting, the schools of Cypriot religious painting, the character of Cypriot iconography, the techniques of Cypriot icon painting, and the evidence concerning textiles, embroidery, jewellery and heraldry as it emerges from the icons, all by David Talbot Rice. Tamara Talbot Rice contributes a chapter on the costumes of Cyprus in the Middle Ages, and Rupert Gunnis writes on the social life of mediaeval Cyprus, combatting to some extent the claims of Mas Latrie about the thoroughness of French influence and stressing the continuity of the Byzantine heritage of the island. The second part contains a detailed description of 153 pre-18th century icons which are reproduced in the plates, a list of icons not included in this publication, and indexes.

567 Ta Vyzantina mnimeia tis Kyprou. (The Byzantine monuments of Cyprus.)
G. A. Soteriou. Athens: Academy of Athens, 1935. lii + 57p. 162 plates.

Indispensable to the study of Byzantine art and archaeology in Cyprus. The first part of the work contains architectural drawings of forty-six leading Byzantine churches of the island. The second part comprises photographs of several leading Christian monuments, and of the main mosaics and frescoes of Cypriot churches of the Byzantine period dating from the 9th to the 15th century. Some attention is paid to post-Byzantine art, and the section also includes photographs of many important icons. The third part offers a photographic record of Byzantine sculpture, wood carving, metalwork and other crafts. As a whole the book offered a first codification of the range of the Byzantine artistic heritage of Cyprus, and laid the scientific foundations of systematic research in this field.

568 The painted churches of Cyprus.
Andreas Stylianou, Judith A. Stylianou. Nicosia: Research Centre, Greek Communal Chamber, 1964. viii + 171p. map. bibliog. illus.

An illustrated account of the Byzantine art of Cyprus by two of its most experienced students. It surveys two churches with mosaics (Kanakaria and Angeloktistos) and twenty-five churches with wall-paintings.

The Arts. Byzantine period

569 Cyprus Byzantine mosaics and frescoes.
Preface by A. H. S. Megaw, introduction by A. Stylianou.
New York: New York Graphic Society, in collaboration with UNESCO, 1963. 22p. bibliog. 32 plates.

A splendid album reproducing thirty-two examples of mosaics and frescoes from the leading Byzantine churches of Cyprus. Also available in French, German, Italian and Spanish.

570 Masterpieces of the Byzantine art of Cyprus.
A. Papageorghiou. Nicosia: Department of Antiquities, 1965.
v + 40p. bibliog. 56 plates. (Picture Book Series, 2).

A picture-book with a concise introduction to the Byzantine artistic heritage of Cyprus followed by plates of the most important monuments, mosaics, wall-paintings and old icons.

571 Icons of Cyprus.
A. Papageorghiou, preface by Archbishop Makarios, translated by James Hogarth. New York: Cowles Book Company [n.d.] ; Geneva: Nagel, 1970. 132p. map. bibliog. illus.

Some of the finest examples of Cypriot Byzantine icon painting (10th-15th century) are brought together in this lavish volume by the curator of ancient monuments of Cyprus. There are eighty-one magnificent colour reproductions accompanied by a historical commentary. Although the focus is on icon painting, attention is paid to mosaics and murals, and this beautiful book thus provides a survey of the greatest treasures of Byzantine art in Cyprus. The book is all the more valuable since it includes information on and plates of icons now in the Turkish-occupied territories.

572 Panayia Phorbiotissa Asinou.
A. Stylianou, J. Stylianou. Nicosia, 1973. viii + 81p. bibliog. illus.

The most recent of the studies devoted to this leading monument of Byzantine Cyprus, the book examines the architecture and wall-paintings of the church of Asinou. It identifies two main periods in the painted decoration of the church, dating from 1105-06 and 1332-33 respectively. The book contains many photographs of wall-paintings and includes the main bibliography on the subject. The text is in Greek and English.

573 The Church of Our Lady of Asinou, Cyprus: a report on the seasons of 1965 and 1966.
David C. Winfield, Ernest J. W. Hawkins. *Dumbarton Oaks Papers,* no. 21 (1967), p. 260-66. plates.

An iconographic record of the wall-paintings in one of the most important Byzantine monuments of Cyprus. The authors supervised the cleaning of these paintings.

The Arts. Byzantine period

574   **The hermitage of St. Neophytos and its wall paintings.**
Cyril Mango, Ernest J. W. Hawkins. *Dumbarton Oaks Papers*,
no. 20 (1966), p. 119-206. bibliog. plates.

A historical sketch, description and detailed study of the wall-paintings of the sanctuary of St. Neophytos in Cyprus.

575   **Report on field work in Istanbul and Cyprus, 1962-1963.**
Cyril Mango, Ernest J. W. Hawkins. *Dumbarton Oaks Papers*,
no. 18 (1964), p. 319-40. plates.

Includes a report on the monastery of St. Chrysostom Koutsovendi, surveying its history, surviving archaeological evidence and art work (p. 333-39).

576   **Middle and later Byzantine wall painting methods: a comparative study.**
David C. Winfield. *Dumbarton Oaks Papers*, no. 22 (1968),
p. 61-139. bibliog. plates.

A comparison of the method and style of wall-paintings in the churches of Asinou, Perachorio, and St. Nicholas of the Roof in Kakopetria with St. Sophia in Trebizond and other churches in Asia Minor.

577   **Byzantine architecture and decoration in Cyprus: metropolitan or provincial?**
A. H. S. Megaw. *Dumbarton Oaks Papers*, no. 28 (1974),
p. 57-88.

An examination of Cyprus's cultural ties with Constantinople, from early Christian to post-Byzantine times, through a consideration of those elements in church building and decoration which clearly reflected the influence of Constantinople as against specifically local accretions. This allows the author to appraise the quality of Byzantine art in Cyprus and to draw attention to some leading monuments, like the 12th century Church of Panayia Arakiotissa which is singled out for the outstanding achievement of the anonymous artist of its wall-paintings.

578   **The Church of the Panagia Kanakaria at Lythrankomi in Cyprus: its mosaics and frescoes.**
A. H. S. Megaw, E. J. W. Hawkins. Washington, DC: Dumbarton Oaks Center for Byzantine Studies, 1977. xx + 173p. bibliog.
143 plates.

A detailed survey of the structural history, mosaic and frescoes at the Church of Panayia Kanakaria at Lithrankomi in the Karpass peninsula. The importance of the church consists in the fact that it has preserved one of the few surviving pre-iconoclastic mosaics of the Christian East. The Kanakaria mosaic of the Virgin from the apse of the bema is reproduced in detail in the plates. The book is all the more significant given the damage to this important monument by Turkish forces in the 1974 invasion.

The Arts. Folklore

579 **The Cyprus plates: the story of David and Goliath.**
St. H. Wander. *Metropolitan Museum Journal*, vol. 8 (1973), p. 89-104.

An interpretation of the scenes of the story of David and Goliath depicted on the Lambousa silver plates, which date from the time of Emperor Heraclius.

Folklore

580 **The inner life of Cyprus.**
Demetrios Stylianou. Nicosia, 1931. 100p.

A collection of folk traditions, customs, beliefs and wisdom rendered in English. It conveys a sense of the moral culture of the traditional peasant society of Cyprus. Reprinted in *Everybody's guide to romantic Cyprus* (q.v.).

581 **Cyprus and its life: morals and customs of Cyprus, folk songs etc.**
Ismene Hadjicosta, translated by D. A. Percival. London, 1943.
48p. + 93p. of Greek text. 9 plates.

A record of the traditional customs and beliefs of the people of Cyprus. It covers customs associated with the major turning points in human life and then surveys the rituals and festivals connected with the various religious holidays, seasons and months of the year. It includes translations of traditional charms and of a folk tale. Some singular photographs depicting Cypriot life and traditions from the 19th and early 20th centuries are reproduced. Part of the material appeared in the author's article 'Some traditional customs of the people of Cyprus' (*Folklore*, vol. 55 (1944), p. 107-17).

582 **Griechische Sitten und Gebrauche auf Cypern.** (Greek mores and customs in Cyprus.)
Magda Ohnefalsch-Richter. Berlin: Dietrich Reimer, 1913.
369p. folding map. illus.

A leading source on the folk culture of Cyprus which remains an authoritative and reliable account to this day. It considers all aspects, symbolic, spiritual and material, of the traditional civilization of Cyprus, and examines the survival of ancient customs in the folk culture of modern Cyprus. It surveys the religious life, the customs associated with the major religious holidays, traditional forms of economic activity, the islanders' relations with the natural world, family life, habitation and the pattern of human settlement, the customs of hospitality, popular dress, habits and feasts, charms and superstitions. Of special importance is the description of folk arts and crafts which turns the book into an indispensable source for the study of Cypriot folk art. The value of the book is enhanced by the rich photographic documentation that illustrates its subject matter. It concludes with a consideration of the state of education and the inception of cultural change under British rule which led away from traditional civilization.

The Arts. Folklore

583 **Akritic and Homeric poetry.**
George Papacharalambous. *Kypriakai Spoudai,* vol. 27 (1963), p. 23-65.

An examination of the affinities between the Cypriot Akritic songs and Homeric poetry on the basis of textual comparisons.

584 **Cyprus embroidery.**
Angeliki G. Pieridou. Nicosia: Cyprus Research Centre, 1976. iv + 27p. 48 plates.

After an interesting historical introduction, the study examines the technique of woven and hand embroidery as well as of lace work. It glances at the traditional customs associated with the use of embroidery and concludes with some comparative observations connecting the Cypriot case with Mediterranean and Near Eastern patterns. Originally published in *Epeteris* (vol. 7 (1973-75), p. 277-303).

585 **Medical superstition in Cyprus.**
Andrew Lang. *Folklore,* vol. 11 (1900), p. 120-25.

An account of traditional folkways in coping with disease in Cyprus.

586 **The personification of plague and cholera according to the Cypriots.**
Kypros Chrysanthis. *Folklore,* vol. 56 (1945), p. 259-66.

Attempts a comparison between Greek and Cypriot personifications of the two epidemics, which are represented as dirty old women.

587 **Studien zur Volksmusik Zyperns.** (Studies on the folk music of Cyprus.)
Pieris Zarmas. Baden-Baden, GFR: Verlag Valentin Koerner, 1975. 404p. illus.

Featuring several illustrations, this is the first major musicological study of the folk music of Cyprus.

588 **A short collection of Cyprus folksongs.**
Costas D. Ioannides. *Kypriakai Spoudai,* vol. 30 (1968), p. 265-300.

A sample of Cyprus folksongs representing sixteen subject categories. The material is transcribed from tapes in the archives of the Cyprus Research Centre.

589 **Kypriakoi laikoi choroi.** (Cypriot folk dances.)
Georgios Averoph. Nicosia: Society of Cypriot Studies, 1978. 191p.

The main body of the book is made up of a transcription of the scores of the music of the folk dances of Cyprus.

The Arts. Folklore

590 **Cyprus Today.**
Vol. 16, no. 1-2 (Jan.-April 1978). bibliog.
The entire issue of this bimonthly is devoted to the folk culture of the island and contains articles on its various aspects by leading Cypriot artists and authors. A basic bibliography of Cyprus folklore is included.

Numismatics, Philately and Heraldry

591 **Catalogue of the Greek coins of Cyprus.**
George Francis Hill. London: Trustees of the British Museum, 1904. Reprinted, Bologna, Italy: Arnaldo Forni, 1964.
cxliv + 119p. 26 plates.

A catalogue of the British Museum collection of coins from the Greek city-kingdoms of ancient Cyprus, with an authoritative introduction to ancient Cypriot numismatics.

592 **Paphos: a Ptolemaic coin hoard.**
Ino Nicolaou, Otto Morkholm. Nicosia: Department of Antiquities, 1976. x + 115p. 22 plates.

A catalogue of a hoard of 1,251 Ptolemaic coins found in the House of Dionysos in Nea-Paphos in 1964.

593 **The coinage of Tiberius in Cyprus.**
Michael Grant. Melbourne, Australia: University of Melbourne Cyprus Expedition, 1957. 6p. plate. (Publication no. 1).

A study of the issue of provincial coinage in Cyprus under the reign of Tiberius.

594 **Numismatique de l'Orient latin.** (Numismatics of the Latin Orient.)
G. Schlumberger. Paris: Ernest Leroux, 1878. 504p. plates.

This monumental work on the coinage of the crusader states of the Near East includes a detailed record of the coins issued by the Lusignan kings of Cyprus (1192-1489). The section on Cyprus (p. 144-213) also covers the coinage issued under Venetian rule (1489-1570) and during the Genoese occupation of Famagusta (1373-1464). The work of one of the greatest Byzantinists, this contribution to Cyprus numismatics constitutes the definitive foundation for the study of the numismatic history of the island in the Middle Ages. Plates 6-8 reproduce the Latin coinage of Cyprus.

Numismatics, Philately and Heraldry

595 **The coins of Cyprus 1489-1571.**
Soterios Gardiakos. Chicago: Obol International, 1975. 36p.
maps. bibliog. illus.

This work concentrates on the mediaeval coins of Cyprus, which it illustrates and describes in great detail.

596 **Turkish coins in British Cyprus.**
M. Santamas. *Kypriakai Spoudai*, vol. 37 (1973), p. 163-73.

A record of Ottoman coins in circulation in Cyprus in the early years of British rule.

597 **Modern coins and notes of Cyprus.**
F. Pridmore. Nicosia: Central Bank of Cyprus, 1974. 323p.
illus. apps.

A complete illustrated record of the coinage and currency of Cyprus since 1878. The book includes a review in date order of currency measures and an exhaustive catalogue of coins and currency notes circulating in Cyprus from 1878 to the issue of the republic's currency in 1961. The appendixes comprise the pertinent documentation. Since in the 300 years of Ottoman rule no coinage was issued especially for Cyprus, this can be considered a complete guide to Cyprus numismatics in the post-mediaeval period.

598 **Numismatic Report.**
Nicosia: Cyprus Numismatic Society, 1971- . annual.

An annual publication of the Cyprus Numismatic Society. It carries articles and notes on the coinage of Cyprus in all periods of its history, including the publication of previously unpublished coins. The nine reports of the years 1971-79 (mimeographed up to 1975 and printed since the 1976 issue) constitute an important and very useful source on the coinage of Cyprus for professional numismatists and collectors.

599 **Cyprus: its postal history and postage stamps.**
Wilfrid T. F. Castle. London: Robson Lowe, 1971. rev. ed.
xii + 256p. maps. facsims. illus.

This is a unique and definitive publication on the subject, and no one can take issue with the book's preface that 'it contains almost everything that is known about the communications, postal services and stamps of Cyprus from A.D. 1324 onwards'. The book is extremely well organized and, aside from its value to philatelists, it makes pleasurable reading for the layman while revealing from an altogether different perspective the richness of such a small island.

Numismatics, Philately and Heraldry

600 **Kypriaki philoteliki etairia 1959-1979.** (Cyprus Philatelic Society 1959-1979.)
Edited by George Michaelides. Nicosia: Cyprus Philatelic Society, 1979. 143p. illus.

An illustrated album on the activities of the Cyprus Philatelic Society during its first twenty years. Among the contents are a number of articles in English on different aspects of Cyprus philately and its history.

601 **Heraldry of Cyprus.**
G. E. Jeffery. *Proceedings of the Society of Antiquaries,* vol. 32 (20 May 1920), p. 204-21. illus.

An illustrated report on surviving mediaeval heraldry in Cyprus as it could be traced in 1919.

602 **Heraldry in Cyprus.**
O. H. M. Haxthausen. *Blue Beret* (UNFICYP), nos. 22-24, 26-34, 36-38 (Sept. 1965-Jan. 1966).

A series of heraldic researches on mediaeval Cyprus by a leading Danish authority in heraldry serving with the UN Force in Cyprus. The project covers the heraldry of the Lusignan dynasty, the Palaeologues, the Order of St. John, and several Venetian coats of arms, including possibly that of Othello in number 29.

Museum Guides

603 **A guide to the Cyprus Museum.**
P. Dikaios. Nicosia: Government Printing Office, 1953. rev. ed. xx + 207p. folding maps. 36 plates.

Originally published in 1947, this is the classic guide to the exhibits of the Cyprus Museum in Nicosia by the then-curator of the museum and the only Cypriot among the founding fathers of contemporary Cypriot archaeology. The guide describes the exhibits in the museum's nine rooms, and the most important of the exhibits are reproduced in the plates.

604 **A short guide to the Cyprus Folk Art Museum.**
A. Diamantis. Nicosia: Cyprus Folk Art Museum, 1973. 18p. map. illus.

An illustrated guide to the museum by its founder and organizer. It includes a brief account of the museum's history and a description of its exhibits in the historic building of the Old Archbishopric of Cyprus. Besides photographs of some of the most valuable exhibits, it includes a map of Cyprus indicating the provenance of the exhibits.

605 **A guide to the Museum of the National Struggle: its exhibits, its national significance.**
Christodoulos Papachrysostomou. Nicosia: Museum of the National Struggle, 1978. 55p.

The work of the museum's organizer, the guide includes a brief historical introduction on the contents of its archive, which comprises documentation concerning the liberation struggle of 1955-59 and the British emergency measures to suppress it. The main part describes the collections of EOKA relics exhibited in its galleries and showcases. An essential aid to the student of this period of Cyprus's history.

606 **Cypriote antiquities in the Pierides Collection, Larnaca, Cyprus.**
Vassos Karageorghis. Athens: Ekdotike Athenon [n.d.]. 157p. illus.

An exquisitely illustrated presentation of the leading private collection of antiquities in Cyprus. The wealth and diversity of the collection serves well as an introduction to Cypriot archaeology, the main outlines of which are set forth in the introduction.

Museum Guides

607 **Handbook of the Cesnola Collection of antiquities from Cyprus.**
John L. Myres. New York: Metropolitan Museum of Art, 1914.
Reprinted, New York: Arno Press, 1974. iv + 596p. illus.

This is the definitive descriptive catalogue of the Cesnola Collection of Cypriot antiquities in the Metropolitan Museum in New York. The larger collection is broken down into special collections of pottery, sculpture, terracotta heads, small objects in stone, alabaster and Egyptian glaze, imported vases and Greek fabrics, inscriptions, terracotta figures, lamps, gold and silver ornaments, finger-rings, cylinders and oriental seal-stones, vessels of gold, silver and gilded bronze, bronzes, and objects of iron, glass, ivory, bone, shell and lead. Photographs of the most important objects illustrate the catalogue.

608 **Ancient Cyprus.**
A. C. Brown, H. W. Catling. Oxford, England: Ashmolean Museum, 1975. 85p. bibliog. illus.

An illustrated catalogue of the collection of Cypriot antiquities at the Ashmolean Museum, Oxford, which is considered the most representative outside Cyprus. The collection includes items from the neolithic to the mediaeval periods. The guide discusses the exhibits in their historical and cultural context, and includes an index of excavated material in the Ashmolean collection.

Mass Media

Dailies

609 **O Agon.** (Struggle.)
Nicosia, 1964- .
A right-wing paper. Circulation approximately 7,500.

610 **Apogevmatini.** (Afternoon.)
Nicosia, 1971- .
A popular pro-government afternoon paper. Circulation approximately 10,000.

611 **Cyprus Mail.**
Nicosia, 1945- .
An independent English-language paper. Circulation approximately 2,212.

612 **I Dilini.** (Afternoon.)
Nicosia, 1981- .
Simerini's sister evening daily. It voices the views of the DISY party and appeals to right-wing opinion.

613 **Eleftheri Kypros.** (Free Cyprus.)
Nicosia, 1977- .
A pro-government paper. Circulation approximately 6,350.

614 **I Eleftherotypia.** (Free Press.)
Nicosia, 1981- .
The daily organ of the Democratic Party (DIKO) of President Spyros Kyprianou, appealing to the broad spectrum of centrist opinion.

615 **Haravgi.** (Dawn.)
Nicosia, 1956- .
The official daily of AKEL, the communist party of Cyprus. Replaces the earlier communist paper *Neos Dimocratis* which was closed down by the British in December 1955. Circulation approximately 13,121.

616 **O Kirikas.** (Herald.)
Nicosia, 1981- .
Daily organ of the Centre Union Party, expressing right-of-centre views.

617 **Mesimvrini.** (Midday.)
Nicosia, 1980- .
An extremist right-wing opposition paper. Circulation approximately 1,000.

618 **Ta Nea.** (The News.)
Nicosia, 1969- .
The official daily of EDEK, the socialist party of Cyprus. Circulation approximately 7,000.

619 **Phileleftheros.** (Liberal.)
Nicosia, 1955- .
The authoritative medium of pro-government opinion. Circulation approximately 20,065.

620 **Simerini.** (Today's Paper.)
Nicosia, 1975- .
Extreme right-wing paper. It is the authoritative medium of the vocal anti-government Democratic Rally Party opposition. Circulation approximately 9,700.

Weeklies

621 **Alithia.** (Truth.)
Nicosia, 1951- .
A right-wing opposition paper. Circulation approximately 8,500.

622 **Ammochostos.** (Famagusta.)
Nicosia, 1975- .
A newspaper of refugee opinion. Circulation approximately 2,000.

Mass Media. Weeklies

623   **Anexartitos.** (Independent.)
      Nicosia, 1973- .
The weekly counterpart of the socialist *Ta Nea*. Circulation approximately 5,000.

624   **Cyprus Bulletin.**
      Nicosia: Public Information Office, 1964- .
A weekly report focusing mostly on developments of the Cyprus Question and cultural news. Greek, French, German, Spanish, Russian, Arabic and Turkish versions also appear. Circulation approximately 53,000.

625   **Cyprus Weekly.**
      Nicosia, 1979- .
An independent English-language paper. Circulation approximately 5,000.

626   **Demokratia.** (Democracy.)
      Nicosia, 1973- .
The weekly counterpart of *Haravgi*. Circulation approximately 10,472.

627   **Demokratiki.** (Democratic.)
      Nicosia, 1973- .
A pro-government paper. Circulation approximately 18,900.

628   **Econes.** (Images.)
      Nicosia, 1977- .
An independent weekly magazine of current events and political news with a tendency to sensationalism.

629   **I Eleftherotypia tis Defteras.** (Monday's Free Press.)
      Nicosia, 1980- .
Eleftherotypia's sister weekly, supporting the Democratic Party (DIKO). Circulation approximately 8,000.

630   **Ergatiki Phoni.** (Workers' Voice.)
      Nicosia, 1948- .
The official organ of the right-wing Cyprus Workers' Confederation (SEK). Circulation approximately 4,000.

631   **Ergatiko Vima.** (Workers' Tribune.)
      Nicosia, 1956- .
Organ of the left-wing Pancyprian Federation of Labour (PEO). Circulation approximately 9,000.

Mass Media. Turkish Cypriot press

632 **I Kypriaki.** (The Cypriot.)
Nicosia, 1981- .
Weekly organ of the Pancyprian Renewal Front (PAME), voicing left-of-centre views.

633 **Kypros.** (Cyprus.)
Nicosia, 1951- .
An independent newspaper. Circulation approximately 7,015.

634 **Satiriki.** (Satirist.)
Nicosia, 1963- .
A newspaper of satirical wit and ironic commentary on current affairs. Circulation approximately 6,500.

635 **To Vima.** (Tribune.)
Nicosia, 1981- .
Weekly organ of the New Democratic Alignment (NEDIPA), voicing right-of-centre views.

Turkish Cypriot press

636 **Birlik.** (Unity.)
Nicosia, 1980- . daily.
Mouthpiece of the Cypriot pan-Turkists, it replaced the older *Zaman* (Time) which went out of circulation. It supports the Denktash régime.

637 **Bozkurt.** (Grey Wolf.)
Nicosia, 1952- . daily.
Independent and nationalistic, moderately critical of the Turkish Cypriot régime.

638 **Demokratik Halk Gazetesi.** (Newspaper of the Democratic People.)
Nicosia, 1980- . weekly.
Organ of the Democratic People's Party of Nejat Konuk.

639 **Ekonomi.** (Economy.)
Nicosia, 1979- . weekly.
The weekly organ of the Turkish Cypriot Chamber of Commerce.

Mass Media. Periodicals

640 **Halkin Sesi.** (People's Voice.)
 Nicosia, 1941- . daily.
Controlled by the former vice-president of the republic, Dr. Fazil Kutchuk. It is critical of the current Turkish Cypriot régime, and extremely nationalist and anti-Greek in its attitudes.

641 **Isci Postasi.** (Workers' Post.)
 Nicosia, 1980- . weekly.
Mouthpiece of the pro-régime trade union Turk-Sen, its first issue called for integration with Turkey.

642 **Kurtulus.** (Liberation.)
 Nicosia, 1978- . weekly.
Official organ of the opposition Communal Liberation Party of Alpay Durduran.

643 **Olay.** (Events.)
 Nicosia, 1979- . monthly.
An independent monthly reporting mainly on political events.

644 **Soz.** (Discourse.)
 Nicosia, 1978- . weekly.
Opposes the Turkish Cypriot régime and is clearly against the incorporation of occupied Cyprus into Turkey.

645 **Yeni Duzen.** (New Order.)
 Nicosia, 1978- . weekly.
Mouthpiece of the Republican Turkish Party of Ozker Ozgur.

Periodicals

646 **Agrotis.** (Countryman.)
 Nicosia: Ministry of Agriculture and Natural Resources, 1945- . bimonthly.
Contains news and features of interest to Cypriot farmers.

647 **Apostolos Varnavas.** (Apostle Barnabas.)
 Nicosia, 1918- . bimonthly.
A bimonthly since 1956, this is the official organ of the Church of Cyprus. It publishes church news, theological treatises and articles on church history.

Mass Media. Periodicals

648   **Cyprus Today.**
Nicosia, 1963- . quarterly.
An English-language publication of cultural and general information, distributed by the Public Information Office. It usually contains brief features on various aspects of Cyprus's culture, history and politics. Prior to January 1981 it appeared as a bimonthly.

649   **Economiki Kypros.** (Economic Cyprus.)
Nicosia, 1978- . bimonthly.
A review of developments in business and economics, reflecting the views, but not an official organ, of the Cyprus Chamber of Commerce and Industry.

650   **Epeteris tou Kentrou Epistimonikon Erevnon.** (Annual of the Cyprus Research Centre.)
Nicosia: Cyprus Research Centre, 1967-68- . annual.
A massive volume of major research papers and bibliography. In 1979 a series of philosophical supplements was inaugurated, the first being *Apopseis tis typikis logikis* (Aspects of formal logic) with contributions in Greek, English and French.

651   **Geographical Chronicles.**
Nicosia: Cyprus Geographical Association, 1971- . semi-annual.
As well as articles by professional geographers, this journal contains material in all the social sciences.

652   **Karpassia.**
Nicosia, 1975- . quarterly.
A review devoted to the cause of the enclaved Cypriots of the Karpass and to the history and cultural traditions of the region. Prior to 1981 it appeared monthly.

653   **Iatriki Hirourgiki Kypros.** (Medical Surgical Cyprus.)
Nicosia: Cyprus Medical Association, 1942- . irregular.
A bilingual (Greek and English) professional journal. Prior to 1975 it appeared as *Cyprus Medical Journal*.

654   **Kypriakai Spoudai.** (Cypriot Studies.)
Nicosia: Society of Cypriot Studies, 1937- . annual.
A volume of authoritative studies on history, archaeology, religion, linguistics and folklore focusing on Cyprus. Some of the articles are in English. Occasionally it includes bibliographies and book reviews.

655   **Kypriakon Nomikon Vima.** (Cyprus Legal Tribune.)
Nicosia: Pancyprian Law Council, 1967- . bimonthly.
A legal journal.

Mass Media. Periodicals

656 Kypriakos Logos. (Cypriot Discourse.)
Nicosia, 1969- . bimonthly.
Contains mostly literary and historical features.

657 I Kypros Mas. (Our Cyprus.)
Nicosia, 1977- . quarterly.
Features news about Cyprus of interest to Cypriot emigrants, and attempts to cultivate ties and exchanges between overseas Cypriots and their native island. Published partly in English. Prior to 1981 it appeared as a bimonthly.

658 Laographiki Kypros. (Cyprus Folklore.)
Nicosia, 1971- . quarterly.
A journal of folklore studies.

659 Morphosis. (Culture.)
Nicosia, 1945- . monthly.
Devoted to commentary on education and general culture.

660 Nea Epochi. (New Epoch.)
Nicosia, 1959- . bimonthly.
Publishes literary features and essays with a progressive and critical orientation. It is the medium of expression of Cyprus's leftist intelligentsia. Prior to 1971 it appeared monthly.

661 Oikogenia kai Scholio. (Family and School.)
Nicosia, 1970- . bimonthly.
Devoted to parents' continuing education with popularized features on education, pedagogy and psychology.

662 Paidiki Chara. (Children's Joy.)
Nicosia, 1962- . monthly.
Published from September to June every school year, it is addressed to elementary school children and carries features written for children and texts by the children themselves.

663 Philologiki Kypros. (Literary Cyprus.)
Nicosia: Greek Literary Association of Cyprus, 1960- . annual.
A volume of creative writing, criticism and essays.

Mass Media. Periodicals

664 **Pnevmatiki Kypros.** (Intellectual Cyprus.)
Nicosia, 1960- . monthly.
Cyprus's literary monthly. It publishes mainly the work of conservative and established authors, and in a way has replaced the older literary magazine *Kypriaka Grammata* (Cypriot Letters) which was published from 1934-56. Both journals have emphasized and sought to cultivate the intellectual ties between Cyprus and Greece.

665 **Poleodomika Themata.** (Issues in Urban Planning.)
Nicosia: Department of Urban Planning and Housing, 1974- .
semi-annual.
Features articles on urban planning and housing.

666 **Report of the Department of Antiquities of Cyprus.**
Nicosia: Department of Antiquities, 1934-48, n.s. 1963- . annual.
Publishes fully illustrated excavation reports, articles on ancient finds and notices on acquisitions of the Cyprus Museum.

667 **Stasinos.** (Stasinus.)
Nicosia: Greek Philological Association of Cyprus, 1963- .
irregular.
Contains articles, some in English, on the classics.

668 **Ygia.** (Health.)
Nicosia: Ministry of Health, 1971- . bimonthly.
Devoted to issues in public health.

Directories

669 **Directory of the Republic of Cyprus 1962-1963.**
London: Diplomatic Press [n.d.] . 105p. illus.
An illustrated directory, carrying, besides the basic information found in a directory, a trade index and a biographical section.

670 **Cyprus directory 1968.**
A. E. Jacovides. Nicosia: the author, 1968. 385p.
A general directory to government, commerce, industry and tourism, supplemented by a classified business firms index and an economic review.

671 **Directory 1978.**
Cyprus Chamber of Commerce and Industry, compiled and edited by Kevork K. Keshishian. Nicosia: Zavallis Press, 1978. 3rd ed. 384p.
First published in 1967, this is the most comprehensive directory on Cyprus with information on the economy and a breakdown on exporters and importers. A must for businessmen.

672 **Almanac: Cyprus in 400 pages.**
Edited by Costas Yennaris. Nicosia: Target Publishers, 1980. 371p.
An illustrated survey containing comprehensive information on the government, legislature, judiciary, diplomatic missions, history, pressure groups, economy, energy, manufacture, construction, trade, agriculture, tourism, transport, education, mass media, telecommunications, health and sports in Cyprus. A special section is devoted to conditions among the Turkish Cypriots.

Bibliographies

General

673 **An attempt at a bibliography of Cyprus.**
Claude Delaval Cobham, edited by G. Jeffery. Nicosia: Government Printing Office, 1929. new ed. viii + 76p.

An updated edition of the first attempt at a bibliography of Cyprus initiated by C. D. Cobham and included in *Excerpta Cypria* (q.v.). This is an alphabetical listing of works on Cyprus in several European languages. It includes listings of official British documents and consular reports on Cyprus as well as sections on the cartography and numismatics of the island. The bibliography is limited to books and generally works of scholarly and scientific significance. In updating Cobham's material, the editor circulated the proofs of his edition to several leading European libraries for criticism and additions. The work, though far from exhaustive, constitutes a reliable guide to all the important sources on Cyprus up to the time of its publication.

674 **Kypriaki vivliographia.** (Cypriot bibliography.)
N. G. Kyriazis. Larnaca, Cyprus: the author, 1935. 343p.

This is the only compendium available which comes close to being an exhaustive bibliography of works on Cyprus as well as of works printed in Cyprus up to the time of the book's publication. The contents of the book are thematically organized in sections on political and ecclesiastical history, travel accounts, lives of the saints, linguistics, folklore and ethnology, bibliography, commerce, industry, natural history, geography and cartography, archaeology, literature, law, medicine, government publications, education and letters. It also contains a listing of published compositions by the popular rhapsodists of rural Cyprus known as *poitarides* – a subject specifically excluded from the Cobham-Jeffery bibliography. The book includes indexes of Greek and foreign authors listed. Although from the technical bibliographical point of view the work is somewhat erratic, and many citations taken out of other sources are incomplete, this remains an eminently useful and pioneering work which all future attempts at a Cypriot bibliography will only update and complete.

Bibliographies. Specialist

675 **Kypriologiki Vivliographia.** (Cypriot Bibliography.)
In: *Epeteris Kentrou Epistemonikon Erevnon* (Annual of the Cyprus Research Centre). Nicosia: Cyprus Research Centre, 1967-68- . annual.

An annual compendium of bibliographical documentation which attempts, beginning with the year 1965, to list all material written about Cyprus in every language. It is close to exhaustive as far as items published in Cyprus are concerned. The entries are arranged systematically in five broad but unequal sections: Cypriot studies; methodology of Cypriot studies; history of Cyprus (including social and economic history); literature, cultural and intellectual history (including a listing of diverse primary sources); linguistics and folklore (including material civilization). A necessary bibliographical aid to the researcher, although omissions do occur.

Specialist

676 **Kypriaki geographiki vivliographia.** (Cypriot geographical bibliography.)
G. Karouzis, A. Sophocleous. Nicosia: Cyprus Geographical Association, 1972. [viii] + 35p.

This is a thorough listing of a broad range of publications dealing with several aspects of the geography of Cyprus. Although it does suffer from serious imperfections from the technical bibliographical point of view, it provides the best and most comprehensive introduction to the literature, very broadly conceived, on the geography of the island.

677 **A German bibliography on the geography of Cyprus.**
Günter Heinritz. *Geographical Chronicles,* vol. 4, no. 7-8 (Jan.-Dec. 1975), p. 112-14.

678 **A selected French bibliography on the geography of Cyprus.**
Pierre-Yves Péchoux. *Geographical Chronicles,* vol. 7, no. 12 (July-Dec. 1977), p. 66-68.

Each of the above two contributions to the geographical bibliography of Cyprus lists works dealing with the island and published in German and French respectively.

679 **Bibliography on land tenure in Cyprus.**
G. Karouzis, P. Ioannides. Nicosia: Land Consolidation Authority, 1974. 30p.

Comprises books, reprints and articles on land tenure in Cyprus as well as the pertinent government legislation.

Bibliographies. Specialist

680 **Circum-Mediterranean peasantry: introductory bibliographies.**
Edited by Louise E. Sweet, Timothy J. O'Leary. New Haven,
Connecticut: Human Relations Area Files Press, 1969. 106p.

A comparative collection of bibliographies on Mediterranean rural societies including a section on Cyprus (p. 83).

681 **Bibliography of anthropological sources on modern Greece and Cyprus.**
Peter S. Allen, Perry A. Bialor. *Modern Greek Society: a Social Science Newsletter*, vol. 4, no. 1 (Dec. 1976), p. 6-60.

This bibliography includes a listing of works on the anthropology of Cyprus (p. 57-60).

682 **Vivliographia tis kypriakis laographias kai glossologias.**
(Bibliography of Cypriot folklore and linguistics.)
Kyriacos Hadjioannou. Nicosia: the author, 1933. 37p.

A complete listing of all sources available to the time of publication on the modern Cypriot Greek dialect and folklore. The bibliography is arranged in a thematic classification.

683 **Vivliographia kypriakou dikaiou.** (Cypriot legal bibliography.)
Konstantinos A. Aimilianides. Thessaloniki, Greece: Institute of
Public International Law and International Relations, 1974. 46p.

A comprehensive bibliography of sources on the legal history and law of Cyprus, thematically arranged in twenty-four sections. Although not purporting to be exhaustive, it lists all major works and is particularly attentive to recent professional writing on the law of Cyprus.

684 **On Greece and Cyprus: theses index in Britain (1949-1974).**
Roussos Koundouros. London: Greek Press and Information
Office, 1977. 23p.

A list of theses submitted to British universities in the post-war period and treating subjects pertinent to Greece and Cyprus.

685 **Modern Greek Society: a Social Science Newsletter.**
Providence, Rhode Island, 1973- . semi-annual.

A newsletter on research and publications pertaining to modern Greece and Cyprus in all fields of the social sciences, including history. A very useful medium of comprehensive bibliographical information with its listings of new books and articles and its specialized bibliographies.

Bibliographies. Specialist

686 **Catalogue of books on Cyprus from the library of D. N. Marangos exhibited during the Congress.**
Compiled by A. M. Lois, Costas Stephanou. Nicosia: First International Congress of Cypriot Studies, 1969. 18p.

A select list of publications about Cyprus including many valuable older editions. An indicative orientation of the range of Cypriot bibliography and of the holdings of this excellent specialized library, now of uncertain fate in occupied Famagusta.

687 **Cypern: Literaturüberblicke der griechischen Numismatik.**
(Cyprus: bibliography of Greek numismatics.)
Helga Gesche. *Jahrbuch für Numismatik und Geldgeschichte,* vol. 20 (1970), p. 161-216.

A thorough annotated survey of the bibliography on the coinage of ancient Cyprus. It is the most comprehensive guide for the professional numismaticist and the archaeologist interested in the coinage of ancient Cyprus. Of special interest is the section which records the studies of the coinage of the individual city-states of ancient Cyprus. The survey also includes studies of Cypriot coinage under Alexander and his successors, the Ptolemies and the Romans.

688 **Some Soviet works on Cyprus.**
Jacob Landau. *Middle Eastern Studies,* vol. 11, no. 3 (Oct. 1975), p. 302-05.

This survey cites the Soviet periodicals that feature new items and articles about Cyprus, and gives a capsule summary of major historical studies by Russian Soviet authors from 1878 to the present.

689 **Archival material and research facilities in the Cyprus Turkish federated state: Ottoman Empire, British Empire, Cyprus Republic.**
Mustafa Hasim Altan, James A. McHenry, Jr., Ronald C. Jennings. *International Journal of Middle Eastern Studies,* vol. 8 (1977), p. 29-42.

A descriptive account of archival material, books, newspapers and pamphlets to be found in Turkish Cypriot libraries in Cyprus.

Index

The index is a single alphabetical sequence of authors (personal and corporate), titles of publications and subjects. Index entries refer both to the main items and to other works mentioned in the notes to each item. Title entries are in italics. Numeration refers to the items as numbered.

A

A. Diamantis: a retrospective exhibition of paintings and drawings 1922-1978 565
Accommodation 73
Achaeans 118, 121
Acheson, Dean 283, 305, 307
Acheson Plan 305, 307
Across Cyprus 50
Acts of the International Archeological Symposium: the Myceneans in the eastern Mediterranean 121
Acts of the International Archeological Symposium: the relations between Cyprus and Crete, ca. 2000-500 B.C. 122
Adams, T. W. 8, 294-95, 301, 310, 324, 470
Administration
 British 208-09, 211, 224, 477, 549
 civil service 436-37, 549
 educational 539, 546-48
 Ottoman 201, 465
Administrative law 481, 483
Agee, P. 378

O Agon 609
Agricultural development 529-30
Agricultural development and co-operative marketing in Cyprus 530
Agriculture 56, 201, 219, 489-90, 508, 522, 525-28, 672, 679
 animal husbandry 522, 528, 533
 citrus fruit 507
 cooperative movement 521, 530
 crops 522, 529
 effects of rainfall 31
 exports 507-08, 518
 impact of ethnic conflict 33
 implications of EEC association 516, 518
 irrigation 532
 Middle Ages 184
 periodicals 646
 productivity 528-29
 statistics 534
Agriculture and Natural Resources, Ministry of 646
Agrotis 646
Aimilianides, K. A. 683
AKEL: the communist party of Cyprus 294-95

159

AKEL — Working People's Uplifting Party 294-96, 332, 615, 626
Akten des XI Internationales Byzantinisten Kongresses Munchen 1958 191
Alastos, D. 138, 225, 241
Alasya, H. F. 285
Alcock, A. E. 407
Alexander, G. M. 226
Ali, Ihsan 408
Alithia 621
Allen, P. S. 404, 681
Almanac: Cyprus in 400 pages 672
Alona 451-52
Altan, M. H. 689
Amathus 92
Ambelikou-Ayios Georghios 93
Ambrazeys, N. N. 20
American Expedition to Idalion, Cyprus: first preliminary reports. Seasons of 1971 and 1972 120
Ammochostos 622
Anagnostopoulos, A. 551
Anastassiades, A. G. 546
Ancient civilization of Cyprus 108
Ancient Cyprus 608
Ancient Cyprus: its art and archaeology 147
Ancient monuments of Cyprus 111
Ancient places of worship in Kypros 87
Andreou, D. 339
Andreou, P. 530
Anexartitos 623
Angeloktistos church 568
Animal husbandry 522, 528, 533
Anthias, Tefkros 559
Anthologies
 poetry 552-53, 557-58
Anthology of Cypriot poetry 553
Anthropology 150, 195, 452-56, 464, 680
 bibliographies 681
Antioch patriarchate 421
Antiquities, Department of 666
Aphrodite, Cult of 152
Aphrodite's realm 58
Apogevmatini 610
Apollo, Cult of 152
Apopseis tis typikis logikis 650
Apostolides, C. 443
Apostolos Varnavas 647
Arab raids 160-62
Arabic 418

Arakiotissa church 577
Araouzos, S. 426
Arcado-Cypriote language 95
Archaeologists 134
Archaeology 56-57, 64, 85, 87, 89-92, 108-09, 111, 128-29, 134, 147, 154, 603, 674
 archaic period 96
 Ashmolean Museum 608
 British Museum 131, 591
 Bronze Age 93-95, 102-04, 107, 114, 118, 121
 Byzantine period 115, 156, 162, 567, 575
 Cesnola Collection 86, 607
 classical period 96
 Constantia 156
 Cyprus Museum 89, 109, 112, 603, 666
 Department of Antiquities 666
 Enkomi 100
 Erimi 99
 geometric period 96
 Hellenistic period 97, 114, 123
 Idalion 120
 Karpass 88
 Khirokitia 98-99
 Kition 118-19
 mediaeval period 188
 Paphos 88
 periodicals 654, 666
 Pierides Collection 606
 religious sites 87
 Roman period 97, 114, 123
 Salamis 86, 114-17, 123, 153, 156
 Sotira 99
 Stone Age 93, 98-99, 101, 107
Archaeology of Cyprus: recent developments 128
I archaia Kypros eis tas ellinikas pigas 159
Archaic period
 architecture 96
 art 96, 130
Archiepiscopal question 426
Archimandrite Kyprianos 192
Architecture
 ancient 91, 96, 100, 114
 Byzantine 570
 churches, Byzantine 18, 567-68, 572, 577-78
 Hellenistic 97
 mediaeval 186, 189-90
 military 186, 190

monasteries 433, 575
Roman 97
Turkish Cypriot 391
Argaki 342, 454
Argyrides, P. 27
Aristides, J. 18
Armenians 195, 397-98, 472
Armenopoulos 466
Armstrong, Hamilton Fish 214
Arnold, P. 224
Arsos 92
Art 13, 17, 64
  ancient 13, 91, 96, 100, 106, 109, 112, 114, 116-17, 119, 127, 130-33, 147, 607
  Byzantine 13, 133, 434, 566-79
  calligraphy 391
  ceramics 47, 91, 96-97, 100, 119, 127, 607
  drawing 552, 565
  embroidery 47, 566, 584
  folk 13, 47, 55, 127, 582, 584, 604
  frescoes 567, 569-70, 578
  Hellenistic 97, 130
  icons 143, 566-67, 570-71
  illustrations of Nicosia 558
  jewellery 112, 566, 607
  mediaeval 189, 191
  metalwork 105, 567, 579, 607
  modern 552, 558, 564-65
  mosaics 567-71, 578
  Mycenaean 95, 100, 105-06, 110
  painting 391, 552, 565
  Roman 97, 130
  sculpture 96-97, 116-17, 119, 567 607
  textiles 47, 566, 607
  Turkish Cypriot 391
  wall-paintings 191, 434, 568, 570-74, 576-77
  wood carving 567
L'art gothique et la Renaissance en Chypre 186
Art of Cyprus 130
Ashiotis, C. A. 436
Ashmolean Museum 608
Asinou
  Panayia Phorbiotissa church 572-73, 576
Aspects of the agricultural economy of Cyprus: 1950-1967 527
Assimilation et résistance à la culture greco-romaine dans le monde ancien 154
Assizes 465
Associate status with the E.E.C. and its implications for the economy of Cyprus 516
Åström, L. 95
Åström, P. 94-95, 134
Attalides, M. A. 342, 349, 453, 456, 458
Attempt at a bibliography of Cyprus 136, 673
Authorization of appropriations for the Board for International Broadcasting and partial lifting of the Turkish arms embargo. Hearing (on S. 2230) 376
Averoph, G. 589
Aviation 508
Avraamides, A. 437
Ayia Irini 92
Ayia Phaneromene 431
Ayios Chrysostomos monastery 575
Ayios Iakovos 92
Ayios Ioannis o Lambadistis church 191
Ayios Neophytos monastery 431, 433-34, 574
Ayios Nicolaos tis Steyis church 576

B

Bailey, D. 255, 561
Baker, E. 263
Baker, Samuel White 43
Balance of payments 499
  statistics 534, 537
Balkan peoples 150
Ball, George 305, 311, 370
Banks and banking 490
  Central Bank of Cyprus 536-37
  periodicals 537
  statistics 534, 536-37
Bannerman, D. A. 81
Bannerman, W. M. 81
Barker, D. 239
Barlett, C. 305
Barston, R. P. 302
Basic issues of educational policy 548
Basil I, Emperor 160
Bater, J. H. 33
Battle of Lepanto 191a
Bayley, V. 2
Bayne, E. A. 316
Bayulken, H. 345

161

Bear, L. M. 502
Beaudoin, M. 416
Beck, H. G. 191
Beckingham, C. F. 387-89
Bell, James Bowyer 243, 333
Bellapais 24
Below the tide 260
Bennett, C. E. 413
Berengaria, Queen 170-71
Berlin, Congress of 205
Betrayal 555
Bevan, Aneurin 222
Bialor, P. A. 681
Bibliographies 136, 650, 673-75
  anthropology 681
  folklore 682
  geography 676
  history 685
  land ownership 679
  law 683
  linguistics 682
  Marangos library 686
  numismatics 687
  rural life 680
  Russian and Soviet writings 688
  social sciences 685
  theses 684
  Turkish Cypriot libraries 689
Bibliography on land tenure in Cyprus 679
Bilge, A. Suat 265, 313
Biographies 669
  Ali, Ihsan 408
  Catherine Cornaro 185
  Evgoras I, King 149
  Grivas, George 240
  Harding of Petherton, Lord 246
  Makarios, Archbishop 253, 255, 287-90
  Richard the Lionheart 171
Bird Reports 84
Birds 55, 81-84
Birds of Cyprus 81
Birlik 636
Bitsios, D. S. 303
Bitter lemons 52
Blair, J. 298
Boase, T. S. R. 189
Botany 55-56, 74-78, 220, 522
Botting, J. H. A. 442
Boustronios, George 176
Bowra, C. M. 414

Boyd, J. M. 320
Bozkurt 637
Brademas, J. 362
Braudel, F. 191a
Bread and freedom 562
Brief history of Cyprus 140
Brion, M. 185
Britain
  relations with Cyprus 281, 297-98, 308, 357, 362, 379-81, 386, 476
British Cyprus 202
British Foreign Office 212
British military bases 268, 297, 327
British Museum 131, 591
British occupation 201-06, 222
British parliamentary publications 136, 215, 222, 269-75, 379-81, 467
British rule 1, 48, 51, 210, 217, 222, 225, 234, 245-47, 250-51, 261, 268, 280, 287-89, 300
  19th century 43, 45
  administration 208-09, 211, 224, 477, 549
  coins 597
  Conservative policies 222, 249, 252
  constitutional proposals 244, 270-71
  counter-insurgency tactics 242-43, 249, 257
  diplomacy 204, 212
  economy 209, 211, 219, 261, 489-90
  education 538-40, 546
  elections 292
  ethnic relations 400-01, 409
  government 220
  history 135, 222, 276
  human rights 257
  Labour policies 226
  legislation 477
  Liberal policies 207
  Macmillan Plan 272-73
  October 1931 rising 215-17, 222
  Orthodox Church 425
  politics 209, 211, 216, 224, 245, 252, 256, 265, 292
  railway 221
  relations with Greece 212-14
  Suez crisis 249, 252
  Tripartite Conference 269
  Zurich-London agreements 222, 229, 236, 251, 261-64, 268, 274-75, 281, 304, 370, 470, 475

British university theses
  bibliographies 684
British War Office 205
Broadcasting Corporation, Cyprus 339
Bronze Age 106
  archaeology 93-95, 102-04, 107,
    114, 121
  art 130
  metalwork 105
Brown, A. C. 608
Brown, E. 396
Browne, R. V. 19
Buchholz, H.-G. 107
Bulletin 537
Bunge, F. M. 8
Burdon, D. J. 22
Burton, T. 130
Business 509-13, 674
  directories 670-71
  law 510-11
  periodicals 649
Bustron, Florio 179
Byzantine period
  Arab raids 160-62
  archaeology 115, 156, 162, 567, 575
  architecture 18, 567-68, 570, 572,
    575, 577-78
  art 13, 133, 434, 566-79
  Byzantine-Arab treaty 160
  Constantia 156
  culture 165, 577
  economy 489
  history 97, 160-66, 177
  Isaac Comnenus 166
  law 465
  population 162-63
  religion 422
  toponymy 162

C

Cadastral plans 41
Calligraphy 391
Cambridge ancient history 101-04
Cameris, C. 555
Cameron, J. 288
Camp, G. D. 359
Campbell, J. C. 341
Canada
  relations with Cyprus 357, 386
Caradon, Lord *see* Foot, Hugh
Carver, C. 246
Casdaglis, E. C. 338

Case of the missing Cypriots 449
Casson, S. 147
Castle, W. T. F. 599
Castles 56, 143
*Catalogue of books on Cyprus from
  the library of D. N. Marangos
  exhibited during the Congress*
  686
Catalogue of the Cyprus Museum 89
Catalogue of the Greek coins of Cyprus
  591
Catherine Cornaro, Queen 176
  biography 185
Catherine Cornaro, reine de Chypre
  185
Catling, H. W. 101-05, 608
*Census of population and agriculture:
  report* 450
Censuses 194, 450
Central Bank of Cyprus 536-37
Central Bank of Cyprus Annual Report
  536
Central Intelligence Agency – CIA
  378
Centre Union Party 616
Ceramics 47, 91, 96-97, 100, 119,
  127, 607
Cesnola, Alexander Palma di 86
Cesnola Collection 86, 607
Cesnola controversy 136
Cesnola, Luigi Palma di 85-86
Chacalli, G. 208
*Challenge and response in internal
  conflict: the experience in Europe
  and the Middle East: vol. 2* 242
Challenge of peace 363
Chamberlayne, T. J. 188
Chapman, E. F. 74-75
Chapman, Olive Murray 50
Charles, R. P. 150, 195
Charms 581-82
Check-list of the birds of Cyprus, 1972
  83
Child care 442
Children
  periodicals 662
*Choice and change: essays in honour of
  Lucy Mair* 403
*Chorografia e breve historia universale
  dell' isola di Cipro* 178
Chown, J. F. 509
Christianity 394
  Maronites 395-96
Christodoulides, Ch. G. 69

163

Christodoulou, Chr. 521
Christodoulou, D. 522
Christomides, K. 511
Christophides, Andreas 12, 553, 556
Christou, N. 31
Chronicle of George Boustronios 1456-1489 176
Chronique de l'île de Chypre 179
Chronologies 2, 100, 108, 143, 221, 301, 306, 315, 365-66, 370, 372, 382
Chrysanthis, Kypros 554-57, 586
Chrysomilides, G. S. 516
Chrysostomos, Abbot of Kykko 432
Church and state in Cyprus education 540
Church of the Panagia Kanakaria at Lythrankomi in Cyprus: its mosaics and frescoes 578
Church property
  Ottoman period 198
Churches 143, 429, 435
  Angeloktistos 568
  Ayios Ioannis o Lambadistis 191
  Ayios Nicolaos tis Steyis 576
  Byzantine 18, 567-69, 572-73, 576-78
  Kakopetria 18
  mediaeval 186, 188-89, 191
  Panayia Arakiotissa 577
  Panayia Kanakaria 568
  Panayia Phorbiotissa Asinou 572-73, 576
  Perachorio 576
Churches and saints of Cyprus 429
Churchill, Winston 210
Chypre d'aujourd'hui 6
Chypre: frontière ethnique et socio-culturelle du monde byzantin: rapports et co-rapports, XVe Congrès International d'Etudes Byzantines, V 165
Chypre: histoire récente et perspectives d'avenir 278
Chypre sous les Lusignans: documents chypriotes des archives du Vatican (XIVe et XVe siècles) 181
CIA – Central Intelligence Agency 378
CIA: the Pike Report 378
Circum-Mediterranean peasantry: introductory bibliographies 680
Cirilli, J.-M. 395
Citrus fruit 507, 529

Civil law 481
Civil liberties 484-85
Civil service 436-37
  examinations 549
Civilization of prehistoric Cyprus 106
Classical period
  architecture 96
  art 96, 133
Claude, I. L., Jr. 318
Clerides, Glafkos 316, 348
Climate 48, 56, 81, 84, 522
  statistics 534
Coastal regions
  Kissonerga 26
  Kyrenia 23
  Lapithos district 27
  Paphos district 26
Cobham, Claude Delaval 136-37, 196-97, 429, 673
Coinage of Tiberius in Cyprus 593
Coins 119, 136, 157, 591-98, 673
  bibliographies 687
  Cyprus Numismatic Society 598
Coins of Cyprus, 1489-1571 595
Cold war 301, 340, 342
Collenberg, W. H. Rudt de 166
Collins, J. M. 373
Commerce and Industry, Cyprus Chamber of 649, 671
Commerce and Industry, Ministry of 513
Commerce, Turkish Cypriot Chamber of 639
Committee on Turkish Affairs 392
Common birds of Cyprus: a concise, simple and fully illustrated guide 82
Commonwealth Institute 564
Communal Liberation Party 642
Communalism 343
Communications 66, 220, 672
  postal services 599
  statistics 534-35
Communism 51, 224, 297
  AKEL 294-96, 332, 615, 626
Community work 442
Le complot de Chypre 304
Comprehensive up to date Cyprus guide 70
Condit, D. M. 242
Conference on Cyprus: documents signed and initialled at Lancaster House on February 19, 1959 274
Conference on Cyprus: final statements

at the closing plenary session at Lancaster House on February 19, 1959* 275
Conference proceedings: U.S. foreign policy toward Greece and Cyprus: the clash of principle and pragmatism 340
Le conflit de Chypre 222
Le conflit de Chypre et les Cypriotes Turcs 265
Congress of Berlin 205
Constantia 156
Constitution 4, 262-63, 277-78, 286, 300, 316, 342, 346-47, 406, 467-70, 472, 474, 476, 484-86
  British proposals 244, 270-71
Constitutional and legal problems in the Republic of Cyprus 472
Constitutional crisis, 1963 232, 277-78, 300, 470, 474, 476
Constitutional proposals for Cyprus 244, 271
Constitutions of nations 468
Construction industry 672
  statistics 534
Contarini, G. Pietro 197
Contemporary Cyprus art 564
Contributions to Mediterranean sociology: Mediterranean rural communities and social change 452
Cookery books 71-72
Cooper, B. H., Jr. 242
Cooperative movement 521, 530
Copper industry, Mycenaean 105
Costume 582
  mediaeval 566
Cottrell, A. J. 294, 301, 324
Coudounaris, A. L. 211
Coufoudakis, V. 323, 340-42, 344, 350
Couloumbis, T. A. 340, 342, 344, 402
Council of Europe 337
Coup d'état, 1974 291, 299, 330-31, 364-66
  role of Greece 291, 330, 333, 371, 378
Courts
  High Court 480
  sentencing 488
  sheri 392
  Supreme Constitutional Court 479-80
  Supreme Court 480-82

Crafts 47, 96-97, 105, 112, 567, 579, 582, 584, 607
Crawshaw, N. 235
Crete, Ancient
  relations with Cyprus 122
Crime 444
  punishment 488
  statistics 534
Criminal law 481, 487
Criminal procedure in Cyprus 487
Criminality in Cyprus 444
Crisis on Cyprus: 1974. A study mission report 364
Crisis on Cyprus: 1975: one year after the invasion. A staff report 365
Crisis on Cyprus: 1976: crucial year for peace. A staff report 366
Critchley, J. 351
Crops 522, 529
Crouzet, F. 222
Crozier, B. 297
Crusades
  assizes 465
  history 167-71, 173, 177, 183
  Knights of St. John 172, 602
  Knights Templar 177
  Richard the Lionheart 170-71, 177
Crypto-Christianity 394
Cults of Aphrodite and Apollo 152
Culture 1, 4, 7, 13, 61, 68, 136, 141, 298-99, 675
  19th century 46
  Byzantine period 165, 577
  Hellenic tradition 7, 12, 140, 149, 154, 180, 208, 464
  mediaeval 180, 183
  Near Eastern influences 154
  periodicals 623, 648, 652, 659
  Turkish Cypriots 389
Currency 597
  statistics 534, 537
Current affairs
  periodicals 628, 638, 648, 657
Cypern 57
Cypria 151
Cypriot agricultural trade with the EEC: scope for assuring market access 518
Cypriot bronzework in the Mycenean world 105
Cypriot dialect 415-17, 550-51, 583
Cypriot Greek: its phonology and inflections 417
Cypriot inscribed stones 113

Cypriot Studies, Society of 654
Cypriot syllabary 125, 147, 414
Cypriot woman: rise and downfall 445
Cypriote antiquities in the Pierides Collection, Larnaca, Cyprus 606
Cypriote Question, considered from the points of history and international law 218
Cypriote shrines 431
Cypriots at table 72
Cyprus 5, 60-63, 108, 406
Cyprus 1946-68 280
Cyprus 1974: days of disaster 339
Cyprus – 1974. Hearings 370
Cyprus '74: Aphrodite's other face 338
Cyprus: a brief survey of its history and development 219
Cyprus: a country study 8
Cyprus: a handbook on the island's past and present 7
Cyprus a place of arms: power politics and ethnic conflict in the eastern Mediterranean 276
Cyprus: a portrait and an appreciation 1
Cyprus administrative law 483
Cyprus against Turkey (Aplication nos. 6780/74 and 6950/75): report of the commission 337
Cyprus Airways 508
Cyprus: an analysis of the Cypriot political discord 411
Cyprus and its constitutional and other legal problems 474
Cyprus and its life: morals and customs of Cyprus, folk songs etc. 581
Cyprus and Makarios 253
Cyprus and the War of Greek Independence 1821-1829 199
Cyprus as an issue in Greek-Turkish relations 382
Cyprus as I saw it in 1879 43
Cyprus BC: 7000 years of history 131
Cyprus between East and West 294, 301
Cyprus Broadcasting Corporation 339
Cyprus Bulletin 624
Cyprus Byzantine mosaics and frescoes 569
Cyprus challenge: a colonial island and its aspirations: reminiscences of a former editor of the Cyprus Post 224

Cyprus Chamber of Commerce and Industry 649, 671
Cyprus conflict and conciliation, 1954-1958 228
Cyprus: conflict and negotiation 1960-1980 348
Cyprus – conflict and resolution 329
Cyprus conflict and United States security interests 309
Cyprus conflict: national identity and statehood 352
Cyprus constitutionalism and crisis government 277
Cyprus Convention 204, 207
Cyprus: correspondence exchanged between the governor and Archbishop Makarios 270
Cyprus deadlock: forever or another day? 361
Cyprus demands self-determination 257
Cyprus dilemma: options for peace 315
Cyprus directory 1968 670
Cyprus economy: a case in the industrialization process 500
Cyprus-EEC association agreement 519
Cyprus embroidery 584
Cyprus Folk Art Museum 604
Cyprus: from earliest time to the present day 141
Cyprus fungi 78
Cyprus Geographical Association 651
Cyprus guerilla: Grivas, Makarios and the British 241
Cyprus: historical and descriptive from the earliest times to the present day 203
Cyprus in history: a survey of 5,000 years 138
Cyprus in international tax planning 512
Cyprus in pictures 10
Cyprus: in search of a constitution 347
Cyprus in your pocket: a practical illustrated guide book 67
Cyprus invitation 59
Cyprus: island of Aphrodite 12
Cyprus: its ancient cities, tombs and temples 85
Cyprus: its history, its present resources and future prospects 201

Cyprus: its postal history and postage stamps 599
Cyprus Law Reports 480-81
Cyprus law reports and monthly publication of judgements of the Supreme Court of Cyprus, 1956-1976 482
Cyprus Mail 284, 611
Cyprus Medical Association 653
Cyprus Medical Journal 653
Cyprus Mines Corporation 494
Cyprus Museum 89, 109, 112, 603, 666
Cyprus: nationalism and international politics 349
Cyprus Numismatic Society 598
Cyprus: past and . . . future 225
Cyprus – past and future: a personal perspective 362
Cyprus Philatelic Society 600
Cyprus Post 224
Cyprus: presented to Parliament by the secretary of state for the colonies, the secretary of state for foreign affairs and the minister of defence by command of Her Majesty July 1960 467
Cyprus problem 363a
Cyprus problem and its solution 316
Cyprus Question 230
Cyprus Question 34, 209, 226, 231, 235, 244-45, 249, 252-53, 261, 266, 276, 280, 300-02, 304, 308-11, 313, 315-16, 330-35, 341-45, 349-51, 354-56, 359, 361-62, 363a, 370-74, 378-85, 402
Acheson Plan 305, 307
British constitutional proposals 244, 270-71
British parliamentary publications 222, 269-75, 379-81
Cyprus Resettlement Project 328-29
diplomacy 227-30, 267, 303, 305, 340, 342
game theory 314
Geneva Conference, 1974 345-46
history 218, 222-23, 229-30, 276, 355
human rights 257, 337, 406, 472
humanitarian problems 364-69, 446, 448-49
intercommunal talks 299, 347, 361, 363, 474

Kyprianou-Denktash agreement, 1979 360
Macmillan Plan 272-73
Makarios-Denktash agreement, 1977 360
NATO involvement 273, 306, 356
newspapers 624
Pareto optimal analysis 314
Plaza Report 317
refugees 33, 342, 364-69, 375-77, 406, 446-47, 621
self-determination 256-58
Tripartite Conference 269
UNFICYP 318-22, 324-28
United Nations 228, 267, 283, 298-99, 306, 312, 317, 323, 336, 342, 345, 355, 357-58, 362-63, 471
   Western framework, 1978 357, 386
   Zurich-London agreements 222, 229, 236, 251, 261-64, 268, 274-75, 281, 304, 370, 470, 475
Cyprus Question: its dimensions, implications and prospects for a solution 360
Cyprus Question: the British reply to the British 258
Cyprus: reluctant republic 229
Cyprus Research Centre 588, 650, 675
Cyprus Resettlement Project 328-29
Cyprus reviewed 342
Cyprus revolt: an account of the struggle for union with Greece 235
Cyprus school history textbooks 544
Cyprus: statement of policy 272
Cyprus: suggestions for a development programme 492
Cyprus: the country and its people 3
Cyprus: the dispute and the settlement 261
Cyprus: the ideological crucible 297
Cyprus: the impact of diverse nationalism on a state 412
Cyprus: the island of Aphrodite 64
Cyprus: the law and politics of civil strife 279
Cyprus: the sweet land 13
Cyprus: the time bomb of the Mediterranean 351
Cyprus: the tragedy and the challenge 346
Cyprus: the vulnerable republic 303
Cyprus: then and now 2

167

Cyprus: Time Out 73
Cyprus Today 590, 648
Cyprus touring map 39
Cyprus Trade and Industry 513
Cyprus trees and shrubs 74-75
Cyprus under an English king in the twelfth century 170
Cyprus under British rule 208-09
Cyprus under the Turks 192
Cyprus – war and adaptation: a psychoanalytic history of two ethnic groups in conflict 410
Cyprus Weekly 625
Cyprus witness 446
Cyprus Workers' Confederation – SEK 630

D

Dams 531
Dams of Cyprus 531
'Damsel of Cyprus' 166
Dances, Folk 589
Davis, J. 403
Dawkins, R. M. 175-76, 394
Decavalles, A. 552
Delahayé, H. 430
Demetriades, C. 512
Demetriades, E.-I. 503-06
Demetriades, K. A. 462
Demetriou, N. 65
Democratic Party – DIKO 614, 629
Democratic People's Party 636
Democratic Rally Party – DISY 612, 620
Demography 32, 34, 162, 194
  Turkish Cypriots 388, 393
Demokratia 626
Demokratik Halk Gazetesi 638
Demokratiki 627
Dendias, M. 218
Denktash, Rauf 282, 286, 316, 348, 404, 636
  agreement with Kyprianou, 1979 360
  agreement with Makarios, 1977 360
Description de toute l'isle de Chypre et des roys, princes, et seigneurs, tant payens que chrétiens qui ont commandé en icelle 178
Description of the historic monuments of Cyprus: studies in the archeology and architecture of the island with illustrations from measured drawings and photographs 90
Descriptive analysis of Cypriot Maronite Arabic 418
Development of labour relations in Cyprus 437
Development of the administration of elementary education in Cyprus 546
Devia Cypria: notes of an archeological journey in Cyprus in 1888 88
Dhali
  maps 40
Diamantis, A. 565, 604
Dikaios, P. 93, 98-99, 129, 603
Dikigoropoulos, A. I. 161-62, 422
DIKO – Democratic Party 614, 629
I Dilini 612
Dimen, N. 453
Dimitri 51
Diplomacy
  16th century 196
  British 204, 212
  Cyprus Question 227-30, 267, 303, 305, 340, 342
  Greek 227-29, 303
  US 305, 340, 342
Directories 669-72
Directory 1978 671
Directory of the Republic of Cyprus 1962-1963 669
Dischler, L. 222
Discussion on Cyprus in the North Atlantic Treaty Organization 273
Disease
  superstitions 585-86
'Disloyal opposition' 291
Disraeli, Benjamin 205-07, 222
Disturbances in Cyprus in October, 1931 215
DISY – Democratic Rally Party 612, 620
Dixon, W. Hepworth 202
Dobell, W. M. 283, 354
Dr Ihsan Ali: Turkish Cypriot leader and champion of peaceful coexistence 408
Dokert, M. 8
Dolger, F. 191
Dolley, R. H. 164
Downey, G. 421
Dowries 455
Drawing 552, 565

Dreghorn, W. 23
Drooz, D. B. 335
Ducloz, C. 24
Dunard, Fr. 153
Duncan-Jones, A. 322
Durduran, Alpay 642
Durrell, Lawrence 52
Dzelepy, E. N. 304

E

Earthquakes 20
Econes 628
Economic development 284, 490-93, 496-501, 506-08
  impact on education 541
Economic geography 4, 27, 200
Economic history 177, 184, 489-90, 493-94, 675
Economic policy 302
Economics of Cyprus: a survey to 1914 489
Economiki Kypros 649
Economy 8, 299, 342, 439, 450, 490-92, 497, 504, 513, 527
  British period 209, 211, 219, 261, 490
  directories 670-72
  Five-Year Plans 493, 496-98, 506, 508
  impact of ethnic conflict 33, 495
  implications of EEC association 516
  mediaeval period 177, 184
  periodicals 649
  rural 521
  statistics 497, 534
  traditional 582
  Turkish Cypriot 393
  Turkish Cypriot, periodicals 639
Economy of Cyprus 490
EDEK — Unified Democratic Centre Union Party 618, 623
Eden, Anthony 249
Education 224, 441, 582, 672, 674
  administration 539, 546-48
  British period 538-40, 546
  economic factors 541, 545
  elementary 546
  guidance services 545
  impact of ethnic conflict 544
  impact of nationalism 540, 544
  impact of social change 545
  impact of Turkish invasion 448
  periodicals 659, 661
  political factors 541
  role of headmasters 547
  role of Orthodox Church 540
  secondary 542-43, 545, 547
  statistics 534-35
  textbooks, Greek and Turkish 544
  Turkish Cypriot 392
  villages 457
Education Advisory Committee, Parliamentary Group for World Government 544
Education in Cyprus: some theories and practices in education in the island of Cyprus since 1878 538
Education, Ministry of, Department of Higher and Secondary Education 543
Educational policy and the mission schools 540
Educational policy of the English government in Cyprus (1878-1954) 539
Edwards, I. E. S. 101-04
EEC and the Mediterranean countries 515
EEC — European Economic Community
  association agreement 514, 519
  implications of association 516-19
  relations with Cyprus 356
  trade with Cyprus 515
Effective management techniques and procedure in public examinations 548
Egge, B. 327
Ehrlich, T. 300, 471
Ekonomi 639
Elections
  British period 292
  Republic 292
Eleftheri Kypros 613
I Eleftherotypia 614, 629
I Eleftherotypia tis Defteras 629
Embroidery 47, 566
Emergency exit 248
Emigrants
  periodicals 657
Emigration 491
Emilianides, A. 466
Employment
  statistics 534
Ta en diaspora 415
Enclaved Greek Cypriots 448, 652

Encleistra and Saint Neophytos 433
Energy 672
Enkomi 92, 100
Enkomi: excavations 1948-1958 100
Enlart, C. 186-87
Enosis 51, 213, 215-18, 226, 234, 236, 243, 256, 261, 287-89, 313, 332, 403, 463
Entertainments
  periodicals 73
EOKA – National Organization of Cypriot Fighters
  British tactics 242-43, 249, 257
  EOKA-B 333, 335
  impact on civilians 259-60
  Museum of the National Struggle 605
  revolt 2, 52, 222, 227, 232-33, 235-43, 246-52, 256-57, 259-61
Epeteris tou Kentrou Epistimonikon Erevnon 650, 675
Epic poetry
  Cypria 151
Epigraphy 88, 113, 119, 123-25, 136, 155, 157-58, 188, 200, 413, 567
Erdokas, T. 447
Ergatiki Phoni 630
Ergatiko Vima 631
Erim, N. 345
Erimi 93, 99
Erkin, F. 305
Esin, E. 391
Essays on the Cyprus conflict 341
Establishment of guidance services in developing countries with special emphasis on a guidance program for the secondary schools in Cyprus 545
Ethnarchy Council of Cyprus 256
Ethnic communities
  statistics 36
Ethnic conflict 33, 232, 276, 279, 281-83, 285, 291, 297-98, 308-09, 332, 340-43, 349, 401-02, 404-05, 410-12
  impact on agriculture 33
  impact on economy 33, 495
  impact on education 544
  impact on population distribution 393
  impact on urbanization 35
  role of politics 409
  role of religion 404

Ethnic groups 55, 195, 400-01
  Armenians 195, 397-98, 472
  distribution 32, 36
  Jews 399
  land ownership 523
  Latins 398
  maps 38
  Maronites 395-96, 398, 418
  Ottoman period 195
  statistics 535
Ethnic relations 284, 401, 407-09
  19th century 199
  British period 400-01, 409
  history 400, 404
  Ottoman period 199, 409
Ethnicity in an international context: the politics of disassociation 402
Ethnography 453
Ethnology 674
Etude du dialecte chypriote moderne et médiéval 416
Euphrates valley railway 203
Europe, Council of 337
Europe, south and east: redefining the American interest. Report 371
European Commission of Human Rights 257, 337
European Economic Community – EEC
  association agreement 514, 519
  implications of association 516-19
  relations with Cyprus 356
  trade with Cyprus 515
Evcaf 392
Evdokas, T. 409
Everybody's guide to romantic Cyprus 56, 580
Evgoras I, King 149
Evgoras I von Salamis 149
Evolution of the rural land use pattern in Cyprus 522
Evreux, Bishop of 171
Evriviades, M. L. 334, 476
Evrykhou
  railway 221
Examinations
  civil service 549
Excavations in the necropolis of Salamis 115
Excerpta Cypria: materials for a history of Cyprus 136-37, 673
Exchange controls 510-11
Exhibition catalogues 131-32, 564-65

Exports 499, 505-06, 513, 671
  agricultural 507-08, 518
Expropriation and nationalization of property under the law of the Republic of Cyprus 486

F

Facing the brink: an intimate study of crisis diplomacy 305
Fairfield, R. P. 264
Fallaci, O. 353
Famagusta 146, 187, 462
  Genoese occupation 594
  maps 40
  port 462
  railway 221
  siege of, 1571 196-97
  urbanization 462
Family life 45, 71-72, 452, 456, 581-82
Fauna 56, 220
  birds 55, 81-84
  insects 80
  mites 80
  sea molluscs 79
Fawcett, J. 337
Festivals 581-82
  religious 429, 581-82
Feudal nobility and the kingdom of Jerusalem 1174-1277 173
Feudalism 170, 173, 200
Field guide to the birds of Britain and Europe 83
Finance
  periodicals 537
  statistics 534, 536-37
Fishing
  statistics 534
Five-Year Plans 493, 496-98, 506, 508
Five-year programme of economic development 496
Flinn, W. H. 219
Flora 55-56, 74-78, 220, 522
Flora of Cyprus 74
Foley, C. 232-33, 236
Folk art 13, 47, 55, 127, 582, 584
  Cyprus Folk Museum 604
Folk music 55, 587
  dances 589
  songs 588
Folk poetry 582, 674

Folk tales 581
Folklore 56, 142, 580-82, 585-86, 590, 674-75
  bibliographies 682
  periodicals 654, 658
Food 45, 62, 71-73
Foot, Hugh 11, 247-48, 287, 362
Foot, M. 252
Foot, S. 248
Ford, D. 62
Foreign policy 302, 352
Foreign policy of Turkey at the United Nations: vol. 1 312
Foreign relations 279, 301-02, 323, 343, 349, 357
  with Britain 281, 297-98, 308, 362, 379-81, 386, 476
  with Canada 357, 386
  with the EEC 356
  with France 214
  with Germany, 19th century 203
  with Greece 212-14, 226-29, 266, 268-69, 272-76, 281, 297-98, 300, 303, 330, 332-34, 350, 476
  with Israel 335
  with NATO 273, 306, 311, 356
  with Russia, 19th century 206
  with Turkey 229, 265-66, 269, 272, 274-76, 281, 297-98, 300, 305, 311-13, 332, 341, 345, 348, 360, 476
  with the United Nations 228, 267, 283, 298-99, 306, 312, 317-28, 336, 342, 345, 355, 357-58, 362-63
  with the USA 283, 297, 301, 305, 309-10, 324, 330-31, 334, 340-42, 344, 350, 356, 364-73, 375, 377-78, 385-86
  with the USSR 268
Forestry
  statistics 534
Forests 6, 56, 522
  maps 38
Forwood, W. 59
France
  relations with Cyprus 214
France de Chypre 180
Frescoes 567, 569, 578
Friedl, E. 453
Fuber, Elizabeth Chapin 167
Full circle 249
Fungi 78

G

Gaist, J. 557, 560
Gardiakos, S. 595
Gellner, E. 453
General Grivas on guerilla warfare 237
Geneva Conference, 1974 345-46
Genoese occupation
 coins 594
Geographical Association, Cyprus 651
Geographical Chronicles 651
Geographical distribution of communities in Cyprus 32
Geography 4, 90, 142, 200, 220, 453, 674
 bibliographies 676-78
 coastal regions 23, 26-27
 economic 4, 27, 200
 effects on tourism 28
 historical 90, 143, 145, 177-79, 181, 200
 human 4, 25, 27, 32, 90, 179
 Kissonerga 26
 Krasokhoria 25
 Kyrenia 23
 Lapithos district 27
 Limassol district 25
 Paphos district 26
 periodicals 651
 political 32-36, 200
Geology 19, 220, 502, 522
 coastal regions 27
 impact on topography 22
 Kyrenia mountains 21, 23-24
 Lapithos district 27
 maps 38
 Mesaoria plain 21
 Troodos mountains 21
Geology of the Bellapais-Kythrea area of the central Kyrenia range 24
Geometric period
 architecture 96
 art 96, 130
Geomorphology 21
Georgagas, D. 163
George, P. 141
Georghallides, G. S. 210-11
Georghiou, G. P. 80
Georgiades, Z. E. 545
Germany
 relations with Cyprus, 19th century 203

Gesche, H. 687
Gill, J. 424
Gillingham, J. 171
Gjerstad, E. 91-92, 96
Gladstone, William Ewart 207
Glastonbury, B. 442
Goodwin, J. C. 145
Gorges
 Panagra 23
Government
 British period 220
 directories 669-70, 672
 House of Representatives 293
 Ottoman 192
 Republic 4-5, 8, 277, 293, 300
Government publications 674
Grant, M. 593
Graves, T. 144
Gravett, G. 57
Graziani, Bishop Antonmaria 196
Great Britain and Cyprus Convention policy of 1878 204
Greece
 diplomacy 227-29, 303
 involvement in subversion 330, 333-34
 militarism 332
 relations with Cyprus 212-14, 226-29, 266, 268-69, 272-76, 281, 297-98, 300, 303, 332, 334, 476
 relations with Turkey 266, 359, 382, 384-86
 relations with the USA 342, 344, 350, 371-73, 375, 377
 role in 1974 coup 291, 330, 333, 371, 378
Greece and Cyprus, 1975. Report 372
Greece and Turkey: some military implications related to NATO and the Middle East 373
Greece, Cyprus, Mount Athos 4
Greek-American relations: a critical review 344
Greek and Latin inscriptions from Salamis 123
Greek and Roman Cyprus: art from classical through late antique times 133
Greek coins 591
Greek Cypriots 195, 274-75, 297, 335, 342
 19th century 45
 distribution 32, 36

172

enclaved villages 448, 652
missing persons 446, 449
nationalism 1, 45, 140, 211, 213,
   215-18, 224-25, 234, 256-57,
   349, 403, 411, 463
political attitudes 277
politicians 211
Greek gift: politics in a Cypriot village 454
Greek heritage of Cyprus 7
Greek Literary Association of Cyprus 663
Greek literature
   sources on Cyprus 159
Greek Philological Association of Cyprus 667
Greek secondary education of Cyprus 542
Greek War of Independence 199
Grevemeyer-Korb, V. 517
Griechische Sitten und Gebrauche auf Cypern 582
Grivas and the story of EOKA 240
Grivas, George 236-39, 241, 282, 297, 299, 325, 335
   biography 240
Grivas: portrait of a terrorist 239
Gsanger, H. 518
Guidance services, Educational 545
Guide to the Cyprus Museum 603
Guide to the Museum of the National Struggle: its exhibits, its national significance 605
Guide to the sea shells of Cyprus 79
Guidebooks 3, 6, 13, 55-67, 70
   Nicosia 14, 70
   Paphos region 16, 68-69
Gunnis, R. 143, 566
Guy de Lusignan 177

H

Hackett, J. 419
Hadjicosta, I. 581
Hadjioannou, K. P. 159, 415, 682
Hagiology 419, 429-30, 674
Hald, M. W. 493
Halkin Sesi 640
Handbook of birds of Cyprus and migrants of the Middle East 81
Handbook of Cyprus 220
Handbook of the Cesnola Collection of antiquities from Cyprus 86, 607

Haravgi 615, 626
Harbottle, M. 325, 327-28, 343
Harding of Petherton 246
Harding of Petherton, Lord 2, 245, 257, 270
   biography 246
Hare, A. P. 329
Harmanta, K. 17
Harrison, H. S. B. 60
Hartman, A. 370
Hawkins, E. J. W. 573-75, 578
Haxthausen, O. H. M. 602
Hazard, H. W. 167-69, 189-90
Headmaster in Cyprus 547
Health 672
   periodicals 668
   statistics 534
   superstitions 585-86
Health, Ministry of 668
Heinritz, G. 28, 532, 677
Hellenic tradition 7, 138, 140, 149, 154, 180, 208, 464
Hellenistic period
   archaeology 97, 114, 123
   architecture 97
   art 97, 130
   history 97
   prosopography 158
Henderson, C. 3
Henson, F. R. S. 19
Hepburn, A. C. 407
Heraclius, Emperor 579
Heraldry 566, 601-02
Hexabiblos 466
Hicks, S. M. 340, 342
High Court 480
Hill, George 135, 138, 591
Histoire de l'île de Chypre sous le règne des princes de la maison de Lusignan 177
Historic Cyprus: a guide to its towns and villages, monasteries and castles 143
Historical geography 90, 143, 145, 177-79, 181, 200
Historical topography of Kition 119
Historical toponymy of Cyprus 145
History 1-2, 5-8, 13, 48, 54-56, 61, 64, 135-43, 146, 177, 199-201, 203, 219-20, 234, 672, 674-75
   12th century 167, 170-71, 173
   13th century 167-68, 172-73
   14th century 168-69, 172, 175
   15th century 169, 175-76

173

History *contd.*
  15th century accounts 175-76
  16th century 191a
  16th century accounts 178-79, 196
  18th century accounts 197
  19th century 199
  20th century 276, 406
  Arab raids 160-62
  bibliographies 685
  British occupation 201-06, 222
  British rule 135, 207-13, 215-17, 222, 276
  Byzantine period 97, 160-66, 177
  Constantia 156
  crusades 167-73, 177, 183
  cultural 4, 180, 183, 675
  Cyprus Question 209, 218, 222-23, 229-30, 276, 355
  diplomatic 229-30
  economic 177, 184, 489-90, 493-94, 675
  enosis 234
  EOKA 233, 235
  ethnic relations 400, 404
  Greek claims to Cyprus 214
  Greek sources 159
  Greek War of Independence 199
  Hellenic tradition 138, 140, 464
  Hellenistic period 97
  Kakopetria 18
  Karavas 17
  Kyrenia 15
  Lapithos 17
  Latin church 181-83, 419, 423-24
  legal 465-66
  Lusignan period 167-70, 172-81, 184-85
  maps and mapping 144
  mediaeval period 135, 174, 182-84, 200
  Nicosia 14, 146
  Orthodox Church 419, 421-24
  Ottoman conquest 178, 191a, 196-97
  Ottoman rule 135, 177, 192-94, 197-98
  Paphos 16
  periodicals 648, 652, 654, 656
  Persians 149
  place-names 145
  political 211, 352, 674
  population 194-95
  postal services 599
  Ptolemies 114, 148, 158
  religious 420, 674
  Roman period 97
  Russian and Soviet writings 688
  Salamis 156
  social 4, 180, 183-84, 191a, 437, 444, 494, 675
  sources 136-37
  Turkish Cypriots 388-89, 393
  Vatican documents 181
  Venetian period 177-79, 183, 185, 191a, 196
History of Cyprus 135, 138
History of the cartography of Cyprus 144
History of the crusades. The art and architecture of the crusader states 189-90
History of the crusades. The fourteenth and fifteenth centuries 168-69
History of the crusades. The later crusades, 1189-1311 167
History of the Orthodox Church of Cyprus 419
Hitchens, C. 332
Hodge, B. 544
Hoffman, M. A. 464
Hogarth, G. D. 88
Hogarth, J. 571
Holmboe, J. 74
Holy royal monastery of Kykko founded with a cross 432
Home, G. 2
Honour and shame: the values of Mediterranean society 451
Hoover, J. J. 8
Hospitality 582
House of Commons. Select Committee on Cyprus 379-81
House of Dionysus 592
House of Representatives 293
Housing 441
  periodicals 665
  statistics 534
Hughes, J. 282
Human geography 4, 25, 27, 32, 90, 179
Human resources 498-99
Human rights 278, 406, 472, 484-85
  British violations 257
  European Commission of Human Rights 257, 337
  Turkish violations 337

Human rights and fundamental freedoms 484
Humanitarian problems 364-69, 446, 448-49
Humanitarian problems on Cyprus. Hearing 368
Humanitarian problems on Cyprus: part 2. Hearing 369

I

Iatrides, J. D. 344
Iatriki Hirourgiki Kypros 653
Iconoclasm 161
Icons 143, 566-67, 570-71
Icons of Cyprus 566, 571
Idalion 92, 120
Ierodiakonou, L. 230
L'île de Chypre: sa situation présente et ses souvenirs du moyen age 200
Illustrations 9-12
  archaeology 109, 111
  art, ancient 109
  art, Byzantine 569-70
  art, Mycenaean 110
  epigraphy 113
  jewellery 112
  Nicosia 558
  Turkish invasion, 1974 338-39
ILO – International Labour Organization 439-40
Impact of the European Economic Community south enlargement on Cyprus' industry: five discussion papers 517
Impartial knife: a doctor in Cyprus 259
Impartial soldier 325
Import substitution 505-06
Imports 513, 671
In an enchanted island or a winter's retreat in Cyprus 44
Inalcik, H. 193
Inan, K. 345
Income
  distribution 443
  maintenance 441
Indebtedness, Rural 521
Index to the laws of the Republic of Cyprus 478
Industrialization 500-01, 503-06, 508

Industry 219-20, 490, 494, 500, 502, 674
  directories 670, 672
  implications of EEC association 517
  periodicals 438, 513, 649
  statistics 438, 534
Inflation 499
Inheritance 455
Inner life of Cyprus 56, 580
Innocent IV, Pope 424
Inönü, Ismet 311
Les inscriptions chypriotes syllabiques: recueil critique et commenté 125
Inscriptions of Kourion 124
Insects 80
Insects and mites of Cyprus with emphasis on species of economic importance to agriculture, forestry, man and domestic animals 80
Insurance 56, 440
  statistics 534
Intercommunal talks 299, 347, 361, 363, 474
Interest rates 537
International Affairs, Royal Institute of, Information Department 261
International crises and the role of law: Cyprus 1958-1967 300
International Labour Organization – ILO 439-40
International law 218, 278, 300, 343, 471, 475-76
International regulation of civil wars 322
Interview with history 353
Investigation into matters concerning and affecting the Turkish community in Cyprus: interim report 392
Investing in the eastern Mediterranean: Greece, Egypt and Cyprus 509
Investment 507-13
Invitation 18
Ioannides, C. D. 588
Ioannides, Dimitrios 333
Ioannides, P. 679
Iorga, N. 180
Irrigation 532
  dams 531
Isaac Comnenus, Emperor of Cyprus 166
Isci Postasi 641

175

Islam 394
  role in nationalism 389
  shrines 431
Islamic law 392
Island of Cyprus: an illustrated guide and handbook 55
Island of Cyprus and union with Greece 256
Israel
  relations with Cyprus 335

J

Jacovides, A. E. 670
Jacovides, A. J. 321, 342, 360, 475
James I, King 175
Janus, King 175
Jeffery, G. 90, 170, 601, 673
Jenkins, R. J. H. 160
Jennes, D. 489
Jennings, R. C. 689
Jewellery 112, 566, 607
Jewelry in the Cyprus Museum 112
Jews 399
John II, King 175
Johnson, Lyndon 311
Jones, Hugh Lloyd 151
Jones, M. 252
Joseph, S. 404
Journey into Cyprus 54
Joyner, A. Batson 203

K

Kadritzke, N. 343
Kakopetria 18
  Ayios Nicolaos tis Steyis church 576
Kalavassos 93
Kallis, P. 482
Kalopanayiotis
  Ayios Ioannis o Lambadistis church 191
Kaminarides, J. S. 500
Kampe, D. 517
Kanakaria church 568, 578
Karageorghis, V. 106-10, 114-18, 128, 131-32, 606
Karavas 17
Karavas 17
Karouzis, G. 676, 679
Karpass 88, 448, 453, 578
  periodicals 652

Karpassia 652
Karpat, K. H. 313, 315
Katselli, Rina 15, 561
Katzer, M. L. 126
Kedourie, E. 316
Keefe, E. K. 8
Kenna, V. E. G. 95
Kennedy, Edward M. 289, 364-66
Keshishian, K. K. 14, 56, 671
Khalat-i-Sultan Tekyé 431
Khirokitia 93, 98-99
Khirokitia: final report on the excavation of a neolithic settlement in Cyprus on behalf of the Department of Antiquities 1936-1946 98
King, B. 405
Kinross, John Patrick Douglas Balfour 51
Kinship 452, 454, 456-58
Kinship and modernization in Mediterranean society 456
O Kirikas 616
Kirklar Tekyé 431
Kissinger, Henry 330, 340, 364-66
Kissonerga 26
Kitchener, H. H. 37, 144
Kition 92, 118-19
Kition: Mycenean and Phoenician discoveries in Cyprus 118
Kitromilides, P. M. 292, 340, 342-43, 402, 559
Knight, R. 255
Knights of St. John 172
  heraldry 602
Knights of St. John in Jerusalem and Cyprus c. 1050-1310 172
Knights Templar 177
Kolodny, E. Y. 393
Konteatis, C. A. C. 531
Konuk, Nejat 638
Kophinou crisis, 1967 280, 325, 476
Kopiaste: a book on Cyprus customs and cuisine 71
Kormakitis 418
Kosut, H. 280
Kouklia 399
Koumoulides, J. T. A. 199
Koundouros, R. 684
Kountoura 92
Kourion 124
Koutsovendi
  Ayios Chrysostomos monastery 575
Kranidiotis, N. 363a

176

Krasokhoria 25
Kunert, H. 527
Kurtulus 642
Kutchuk, Fazil 282, 404, 640
Kykko monastery 431-32
Kypriaka Grammata 664
Kypriakai Spoudai 654
I Kypriaki 632
Kypriaki geographiki vivliographia 676
Kypriaki philotelika etairia 1959-1979 600
Kypriaki vivliographia 674
Kypriakoi laikoi choroi 589
Kypriakon Nomikon Vima 655
Kypriakos Logos 656
Kyprianos, Archimandrite 178
Kyprianou, Spyros 258, 614
　agreement with Denktash, 1979 360
Kypros 633
I Kypros Mas 657
Kyra 93
Kyrenia 561
　history 15
　life and customs 15
　maps 40
Kyrenia: a historical study 15
Kyrenia mountains
　geography 23
　geology 21, 23-24
Kyrenia shipwreck 126
Kyriakides, S. 277
Kyriazis, N. G. 674
Kyrris, C. P. 198, 400
Kythrea 24, 92

L

Labour 56, 499
　conditions 436
　forced 448, 472
　impact of ethnic conflict 33
　legislation 436-37
　periodicals 438
　statistics 438, 534
　trade unions 629-30, 641
Labour conditions in Cyprus during the war years, 1939-1945 436
Labour movement 224
Labour relations 437
Labour Review 438

Lacrimae Nicossienses: recueil d'inscriptions funéraires la plupart françaises existant encore dans l'île de Chypre 188
Ladaki-Philippou, Niki 563
Lady's impressions of Cyprus in 1893 47
Lagoudakis, C. G. 242
Lambousa silver plates 579
Land consolidation 524, 526
Land legislation 472, 679
Land ownership 36, 43, 522-26
　bibliographies 679
　impact of ethnic conflict 33
　maps 41
Land ownership in Cyprus 523
Land use 32, 522, 527
Landau, J. 688
Lang, A. 585
Lang, Robert Hamilton 200
Language 136, 415-17
　ancient 413-14
　Arcado-Cypriote 95
　Maronite Arabic 418
　Turkish Cypriots 388
Lanitis, G. 12
Lanitis, N. C. 284, 521
Laographiki Kypros 658
Lapithos 17, 92
Larnaca 146
　maps 40
Larnaca district
　land ownership 524
Latin church
　history 181-83, 419, 423-24
　Vatican documents 181
Latins 398
Lausanne, Treaty of 266
Lauwerys, J. A. 544
Lavender, D. S. 494
Law 279, 346, 354-55, 465, 472, 477-82, 672, 674
　administrative 481, 483
　Armenians 472
　bibliographies 683
　British period 477
　business 510-11
　Byzantine 465-66
　canon 472
　civil 481, 485
　criminal 481, 487
　crusades 465

177

Law *contd.*
  forced labour 472
  human rights 472
  impact of Turkish invasion
    473-74, 476
  international 218, 278, 300, 343,
    471, 475-76
  Islamic 392
  labour 436-37
  land 472, 479
  Lusignan period 466
  mediaeval period 173
  mining 502
  Ottoman 465
  periodicals 655
  property 486
  religious bodies 486
  sentencing 488
  taxation 512
  Turkish Cypriot 392
Law Council, Pancyprian 655
Le Geyt, P. S. 254
Ledra 146
Lee, D. E. 204-05
Lee, H. 61
Lee, M. 61
Legacy of strife: Cyprus from rebellion to civil war 232
Legagneux, C. 554
Legal aspects of foreign investment in Cyprus 511
Legal history 465-66
Legal system
  role of Orthodox Church 466
Legislative Council 208
Leon VI, Emperor 164
Lepanto, Battle of 191a
Leucosia 146
Levant Company 192
Levêque, P. 153
Lewis, E. A. M. 47
Lewis, G. L. 544
Libraries
  D. N. Marangos 686
  Turkish Cypriot 689
Life and customs 1, 3, 7, 9-12, 48-52,
    55-56, 58, 71-72, 136, 298,
    580-82, 584
  19th century 42-47, 201-02
  Kyrenia 15
  mediaeval period 173, 180, 183
  Ottoman period 85, 192
  religious 429
  villages 17, 18

Lilies of the field: a book of Cyprus wild flowers 76
Limassol
  maps 40
Limassol district
  Krasokhoria 25
  land ownership 524
  villages 25
Lindros, J. 92
Linguistics 142, 674-75
  bibliographies 682
  periodicals 654
Linobambakoi sect 394
Lipertis, Dimitris 551, 559
List of publications of the Department of Statistics and Research 534
Literary Association of Cyprus, Greek 663
Literature 64, 142, 674-75
  ancient poetry 151
  folk 581-82, 674
  periodicals 656, 660, 663-64, 667
  plays 555
  poetry 550-54, 556-59, 562-63
  prose 558, 560-61
  social themes 559-63
Lithrankomi
  Panayia Kanakaria church 568, 578
Living conditions of the enclaved Greek Cypriots 448
Lloyd Jones, H. 151
Location and development of the town of Leucosia (Nicosia), Cyprus 146
Löher, F. von 203
Lois, A. M. 686
Loizides, S. 257
Loizos, P. 342, 403, 406, 453-55
Loizou, A. N. 487
Loizou, Doros 562
Luard, E. 322
Luke, Harry 1, 135, 168-69, 192, 431
Lumsden, M. 314
Lushington, F. 139
Lusignan, Etienne de 178
Lusignan period
  15th century accounts 175-76
  16th century accounts 178-79
  Catherine Cornaro 176, 185
  coins 594
  Guy de Lusignan 177
  heraldry 602
  history 167-70, 172-81, 184-85
  religion 423-24

trade 177
  Vatican documents 181
Lymbourides, A. 64
Lysi 457
Lysi: social change in a Cypriot village 457

M

McGinty, J. 19
McHenry, J. A., Jr. 689
Machlouzarides, P. 444
Mackenzie, K. 297, 299
MacLeish, K. 298
Macmillan, Harold 250-51
Macmillan Plan 272-73
Magoulias, H. J. 423
Maier, F. G. 141
Makarios: a biography 290
Makarios, Archbishop 236, 238, 241, 249, 257, 270, 277, 282, 291, 297, 299, 304, 330, 352-53, 427, 432, 496, 571
  agreement with Denktash, 1977 360
  biographies 253, 255, 287-90
  exile to Seychelles 249, 254, 257
Makarios: faith and power 287
Makarios in exile 254
Makarios: life and leadership 289
Makarios: pragmatism v. idealism 288
Makhairas, Leontios 175-76, 179
Makhairas monastery 431
Mallock, W. H. 44
Mango, C. 574-75
Mangoian, H. A. 55
Mangoian, L. 55
Manuel de céramique chypriote: 1. Problèmes historiques, vocabulaire, méthode 127
Manufacturing 500, 504-05, 672
Maps and mapping 37-38, 136, 200, 558, 673-74
  cadastral plans 41
  history 144
  land ownership 41
  street names maps 40
  tourist maps 39
Marangos, D. N.
  library 686
Maratheftis, F. S. 146
Margo 399
Marinos, C. D. 231
Marion 92

Mariti, Giovanni 197
Markides, D. 255
Markides, K. C. 291, 457, 463
Maronites 395-96, 398, 418
  language 418
Les Maronites de Chypre 395
Martinengo, Nestor 197
Mas Latrie, Louis de 135, 174, 177, 200, 566
Mas Latrie, René de 179
Masson, O. 125, 155
Masterpieces of the Byzantine art of Cyprus 570
Matthews, A. 76
Maxoudian, N. 397
Mayes, S. 253, 290, 357
Mazarakis, I. K. 446
Medical Association, Cyprus 653
Medical care 440-41
  impact of Turkish invasion 448
Medicine 674
  periodicals 653
Medieval kingdoms of Cyprus and Armenia 174
Mediterranean and the Mediterranean world in the age of Philip II 191a
Medlicot, W. N. 207
Megaw, A. H. S. 190, 569, 577-78
Megaw, E. 77
Meikle, R. D. 74, 77
Meinardus, O. F. A. 420, 435
Melamid, A. 32
Mélanges Marcel Bridel 485
Memoirs of General Grivas 236
Memoirs of Sir Ronald Storrs 217
Merlin, S. 315
Merrillees, R. S. 128
Mersinaki 92
Mesaoria plain 29-30, 457
  geology 21
Mesimvrini 617
Metalwork 105, 120, 567, 579
Meyer, A. J. 490-91
Michaelides, A. 293
Michaelides, R. Chr. 528
Michaelides, Vassilis 551, 559
Michaelidou-Nicolaou, I. 157-58
Middle Ages
  agriculture 184
  architecture 186, 189-90
  art 189, 191, 608
  coins 594-95
  costume 566
  culture 180, 183

179

Middle Ages *contd.*
  economy 489
  Famagusta 187
  heraldry 601-02
  history 135, 174, 182-83, 200
  law 173
  life and customs 173, 180, 183
  monuments 16, 90, 187-88
  Paphos 187
  relations with Near East 200
  religion 180
  society 170, 180, 183-84, 188, 566
Midgley, R. 196
Migration 458
  statistics 534
Mikes, G. 315
Militarism
  Greek 332
  Turkish 332
Military aspects of banning arms aid to Turkey. Hearing 383
Military bases
  British 268, 297, 327
  US 373
Miller, L. 279
Milliex, R. 60
Mims, A. 553
Mineral resources 29-30, 201, 220, 502
Mineral resources and mining industry of Cyprus 502
Mining 56, 220, 502
  Cyprus Mines Corporation 494
  legislation 502
Minoans 150
Minorities in history 407
Minority Rights Group 406
Missing persons 446, 449
Mites 80
Mitford, T. B. 123-24
Modern coins and notes of Cyprus 597
Modern Greek Society: a Social Science Newsletter 685
Mogabgab, T. A. H. 137
Molluscs 79
Monasteries 2, 16, 56-57, 143, 429, 435
  Ayios Chrysostomos 575
  Ayios Neophytos 431, 433-34, 574
  Kykko 431-32
  Makhairas 431
  Stavrovouni 431
  Trooditissa 43

Monastery of St. Neophytos at Paphos 434
Monasticism 419
  Byzantine period 166, 422
Montis, Costas 553, 556-57
Monuments 44, 50-51
  ancient 16, 88, 90, 111
  Christian 88, 567
  mediaeval 16, 90, 187-88
  Turkish Cypriot 391
Morkholm, O. 592
Morphosis 659
Morphou 454
  maps 40
  railway 221
Morphou region
  land ownership 524
Mosaics 567-71, 578
Moseley, L. G. 442
Moskos, C. C. 326
Mountains 6, 56, 197
  Kyrenia range 21, 23-24
  maps 38
  Troodos range 21
Mourdjis, M. 72
Muftiship 392
Museum of the National Struggle 605
Museums and collections
  Ashmolean Museum, Oxford 608
  British Museum 131, 591
  Cesnola Collection, New York 86
  Cyprus Folk Art Museum 604
  Cyprus Museum 89, 109, 112, 603, 666
  Museum of the National Struggle 605
  Pierides Collection 606
  Smithsonian Institution, Washington 132
Music, Folk 55, 587-89
Muslim-Christian conflicts: economic, political and social origins 404
My experiences in Cyprus 48
Mycenaeans 106, 121, 150
  art 95, 100, 106, 110
  copper industry 105
  metalwork 105
Mycenean art from Cyprus 110
Mylonas, G. 160
Myres, J. L. 89, 607
Myrtiotis, P. 255
Mythology 64

N

Nagel, G. 533
Nairn, T. 343
National accounts
  statistics 534
National identity 284, 349
National Organization of Cypriot
    Fighters – EOKA
  British tactics 242-43, 249, 257
  EOKA-B 333, 335
  impact on civilians 259-60
  Museum of the National Struggle
    605
  revolt 2, 52, 222, 227, 232-33,
    235-43, 246-52, 256-57, 259-61
Nationalism 284, 291, 343, 349, 411
  Greek Cypriot 1, 45, 140, 211, 213,
    215-18, 224-25, 234, 256-57,
    284, 403, 463
  impact of social change 463
  impact on education 540, 544
  Turkish Cypriot 284, 389
  villages 453
NATO and the Cyprus crisis 306
NATO – North Atlantic Treaty
    Organization 311, 373-74, 383,
    385
  relations with Cyprus 273, 306, 356
Natural resources 219, 491, 493, 499
  minerals 29-30, 201, 220, 502
  water 29-30, 492, 522, 524, 531
Navarro, C. K. 358
Ta Nea 618, 623
Nea Epochi 660
Near East
  cultural influences 154
  relations with mediaeval Cyprus 200
NEDIPA – New Democratic Alignment 635
Nedjati, Z. M. 483-84
Neokleous, G. K. 519
Neokleous, K. N. 547
Neos Dimocratis 615
*New Commonwealth and its
    constitutions* 469
New Democratic Alignment –
    NEDIPA 635
Newman, P. 139
Newspapers 136, 609-27, 629-35
  Turkish Cypriot 390, 636-38,
    640-42, 644-45
Newton, B. 417

Nicephorus II, Emperor 160
Nicocles, King 157
Nicocreon, King 114, 148
Nicolaou, I. 113, 123, 592
Nicolaou, K. 111, 119, 152
Nicosia
  guidebooks 14, 70
  history 14, 146
  in literature and art 558
  Kirklar Tekyé 431
  maps 40
  population 459-61
  railway 221
  rural-urban fringe 459-61
  siege of, 1570 179, 196-97
  social change 458
  urbanization 458-61
*Nicosia: capital of Cyprus then and
    now* 14
Nikita, E. S. 457
Nikita, H. 445
Nikovlita 92
*Norm input-output data of the main
    crops of Cyprus* 529
North Atlantic Treaty Organization –
    NATO 311, 373-74, 383, 385
  relations with Cyprus 273, 306, 356
Numismatic Report 598
Numismatics 119, 136, 157, 591-98,
    673
  bibliographies 687
  Cyprus Numismatic Society 598
Numismatiques de l'Orient Latin 594

O

O'Brien, B. J. 220
October 1931 rising 215-17, 222
Ohnefalsch-Richter, Magda 582
Ohnefalsch-Richter, Max 87, 89
Oikogenia kai Scholio 661
Olay 643
O'Leary, T. J. 680
*On Greece and Cyprus: theses index in
    Britain 1949-1974* 684
On revolt 243
*Ores tis Lefkosias stin poiesi ton
    Kyprion* 558
*Orient et Occident au Moyen Age:
    contacts et relations (XIIe-XVe s.)*
    182
Orientations 217

Ornithology 55, 81-84
Orphaned realm: journeys in Cyprus 51
Orr, C. W. J. 209
Orthodox Church 43, 143, 429, 647
  archiepiscopal question 426
  British period 425
  canon law 472
  hagiology 419, 429-30
  history 419, 421-24
  iconoclasm 161
  monasticism 166, 419, 422
  Ottoman period 198, 428
  property, Ottoman period 198
  role in education 540
  role in legal system 466
  role in politics 45, 224, 234, 256, 427-28
  sacred relics 435
  shrines 431
Osgood, R. E. 301
Osorio-Tafall, B. 322
Othello 602
Other powers: studies in the foreign policies of small states 302
Ottoman conquest 191a
  contemporary accounts 178, 196-97
Ottoman rule 85, 200-201
  18th century accounts 197
  19th century 199
  administration 201, 465
  coins 596
  economy 489
  ethnic relations 199, 409
  government 192
  Greek War of Independence 199
  history 135, 177, 192-4, 197
  law 465
  life and customs 192
  Orthodox Church 198, 428
  politics 85
  population 194-95
  religion 394
  trade 197
Our destiny 284
Our home in Cyprus 45
Ozgur, Ozker 645
Ozoran, B. R. 390

P

Paidiki Chara 662
Painted churches of Cyprus 568
Painting 391, 552, 565
Paleologues 602
Paleoskoutella 92
Pallis, A. A. 237
PAME – Pancyprian Renewal Front 632
Panagides, S. S. 495, 501
Panagra gorge
  geography 23
  geology 23
Panayia Arakiotissa church 577
Panayia Kanakaria church 568, 578
Panayia Phorbiotissa Asinou 572
Panayia Phorbiotissa church 572-73, 576
Pancyprian Federation of Labour – PEO 631
Pancyprian Law Council 655
Pancyprian Renewal Front – PAME 632
Panigyricon 430
Pantazis, Th. M. 21
Papacharalambous, G. 583
Papachristodoulou, S. 529
Papachrysostomou, C. 605
Papadopoullos, Th. 165, 194, 428
Papadopoulos, A. 18
Papadopoulos, George 333
Papageorghiou, A. 570-71
Papaiannou, Ch. 419
Papandreou, Andreas 407
Papandreou, George 407
Paphos 16
Paphos 88, 157, 187
  Ayios Neophytos monastery 431, 433-34, 574
  guidebooks 16, 68-69
  history 16
  House of Dionysus 592
  maps 40
Paphos: a Ptolemaic coin hoard 592
Paphos: a tourist guide 68
Paphos district
  Kissonerga 26
  land ownership 524
  villages 16, 26
Paris, P. 259
Park, W. 351
Parker, R. 58
Partassides, D. 339
Parthogh, L. der 339
Partition 359, 409, 411-12
Patrick, R. A. 33
Patrons and clients in Mediterranean societies 453

Pavlides, A. 339
Peace soldiers: the sociology of a United Nations military force 326
Peaceful co-existence in Cyprus under British rule (1878-1959) and after independence: an outline 400
Peacekeeping 343
  Cyprus Resettlement Project 328-29
  UNFICYP 318-22, 324-28
Peasle, A. J. 468
Péchoux, P.-Y. 25, 35, 678
Pell, C. 372
Peltenburg, E. J. 131
PEO — Pancyprian Federation of Labour 631
Perachorio church 576
Percival, D. A. 450, 581
Periodicals
  agriculture 646
  archaeology 654, 666
  banks and banking 537
  bibliography 650
  business 649
  children's 662
  culture 623, 648, 652, 659
  current affairs 628, 638, 648, 657
  economy 649
  economy, Turkish Cypriot 639
  education 659, 661
  emigrants 657
  enclaved Greek Cypriots 652
  finance 537
  folklore 654, 658
  general information 73
  geography 651
  health 668
  history 648, 652, 654, 656
  housing 665
  industry 438, 513, 649
  Karpass 652
  labour 438
  law 655
  linguistics 654
  literature 656, 660, 663-64, 667
  medicine 653
  ornithology 84
  religion 647, 654
  social sciences 651
  trade 513, 537
  Turkish Cypriot 390, 639, 643
  urban planning 655
Peristiany, J. G. 451-53, 456
Persianis, P. K. 540-41

Persians 149
Perspectives on NATO's southern flank. Report 386
Peter I, King 175
Peter II, King 175
Peterson, R. 83
Petra tou Limniti 92
Le Pétrarchisme en Chypre: poèmes d'amour en dialecte chypriote, d'après un manuscrit du XVI siècle 550
Le peuplement de Chypre dans l'antiquité 150
Phanos, T. 514
Philately 56, 599-600
  Cyprus Philatelic Society 600
Phileleftheros 619
Philia 93
Philipou, L. 16
Philological Association of Cyprus, Greek 667
Philologiki Kypros 663
Philology 142, 654, 674-75, 682
Philosophy 650
Phoenicians 118, 155
Phylactou, A. K. 68
Phylactou, T. 556
Picture book of Cyprus 11
Pierides, A. 112
Pierides Collection 606
Pierides, George Philippou 560
Pierides, Thodossis 559
Pieridou, A. G. 584
Pierre de Thomas 423
Pike, O. 378
Pikis, G. M. 487-88
Pillsbury, B. L. K. 404
Pipinelis, P. 266
Pippidi, D. M. 154
Pitsillia region 451-52
Place-names 145, 162
Plains 6
  Mesaoria 21, 29-30, 457
  Morphou 454
Planning
  Five-Year Plans 493, 496-98, 506, 508
Planning Bureau of the Republic of Cyprus, Planning Commission 499
Plays
  Chrysanthis, Kypros 555
Plaza, G. 317
Plaza Report 317

183

Pnevmatiki Kypros 664
Poems from the modern Greek 557
Poems of Cyprus: a selection from the work of Vassilis Michaelides and Dimitris Lipertis 551
Poetry
  16th century 550
  ancient 151
  Anthias, Tefkros 559
  anthologies 552-53, 557-58
  Christophides, Andreas 556
  Chrysanthis, Kypros 554, 556-57
  epic 151
  folk 582, 674
  Ladaki-Philippou, Niki 563
  Lipertis, Dimitris 551, 559
  Loizou, Doros 562
  Michaelides, Vassilis 551, 559
  Montis, Costas 556-57
  Phylactou, T. 556
  Pierides, Thodossis 559
  romanticism 559
  social themes 559, 562-63
Poleodomika Themata 655
Police 444
Polis region
  land ownership 524
Political and administrative history of Cyprus 1918-1926: with a survey of the foundations of British rule 211
Political and economic factors as the main determinants of educational policy in independent Cyprus (1960-1970) 541
Political attitudes
  Greek Cypriots 277
  Turkish Cypriots 286
Political geography 32-36, 200
Political geography and the Cyprus conflict: 1963-1971 33
Political parties
  AKEL 294-96, 332, 615, 626
  Centre Union Party 616
  DIKO 614, 629
  DISY 612, 620
  EDEK 618, 623
  NEDIPA 635
  newspapers 612, 614-16, 618, 620, 623, 626, 629, 632, 635
  PAME 632
Political parties, Turkish Cypriot
  Communal Liberation Party 642
  Democratic People's Party 636
  newspapers 638, 642, 645
  Republican Turkish Party 645
Politics 8, 51, 232-33, 235, 276, 281
  19th century 44-45
  British period 209, 211, 216, 224, 245, 252, 256, 265, 292
  history 211, 352, 674
  impact on education 541
  Ottoman period 85
  Republic 230, 277, 279, 282-83, 291-92, 297-99, 316-17, 341, 346, 349, 352, 354-55, 405
  role in ethnic conflict 409
  role of economic integration 495
  role of Orthodox Church 45, 224, 234, 256, 427-28
  Turkish Cypriot 5
  villages 51, 454
  World War II 224
Pollis, A. 343, 401
Polyviou, P. G. 342, 346-48
Poole, J. 512
Popham, M. R. 95
Population 220
  ancient times 150, 158
  Byzantine period 162-63
  censuses 194, 450
  distribution 393
  ethnic groups 32, 34, 36, 195
  maps 38
  Nicosia 459-61
  Ottoman period 194-95
  statistics 534-35
Portrait of Cyprus 9
Ports
  Famagusta 462
Post mortem report and examination of the intelligence community's performance before and during the Cyprus crisis of 1974 378
Postage stamps 56, 599-600
  Cyprus Philatelic Society 600
Postal services
  history 599
Pouilloux, J. 153-54
Poverty 225, 520
Powell, D. 12
Praktika tou Protou Diethnous Kyproloyikou Synedriou 142
Preece, R. M. 382
Prehistoric Greece and Cyprus: an archaeological handbook 107
President Makarios of Cyprus 255
Press 56, 224, 672

Pressure groups 672
Preston, R. 33
Prices
  statistics 534, 537
Pridmore, F. 597
Prisoners of war 446
Problem of Cyprus 244
Proceedings – International Symposium on Political Geography 34
Process of industrialisation in Cyprus 506
Productivity 499
  agriculture 528-29
Property
  church 198
  impact of Turkish invasion 448
  law 486
  transfer 455
Proposals for a solution of the Cyprus problem 36
Prose 558, 561
  Pierides, George Philippou 560
  social themes 560-61
Prosopography of Ptolemaic Cyprus 158
Prosopography, Ptolemaic 158
Prousis, C. M. 551
Psomiades, H. J. 281, 342
Ptolemies 114, 148, 158
  coins 592
Public Information Office 620, 648
Purcell, H. D. 5
Pusey, G. B. 63

Q

Quakers
  Cyprus Resettlement Project 328-29
Quietly men 1957: Suez + Cyprus 252

R

Radcliffe, Lord 244, 271
Railway 221
Rainfall 56, 81
  effects on agriculture 31
  maps 38
Rainfall of Cyprus 31
Ramady, M. A. 341
Rangou, E. 457
Raymond, D. 160

Recent trends in agricultural production and productivity in Cyprus 528
Recherches sur les Phéniciens à Chypre 155
Recital concerning the sweet land of Cyprus entitled 'Chronicle' 175-76
Reckitt, R. 82
Refugee in my homeland: Cyprus 1974 561
Refugees 33, 342, 364-69, 375-77, 406, 446-47, 622
Refugees of Cyprus: a representative socio-psychological study 447
Regional development 443
Les relations entre l'Orient et l'Occident au Moyen Age: études et documents 183
Relics, Sacred 435
Religion 43, 55-56, 220, 429, 431-32, 582
  ancient 87, 118, 152-53
  crypto-Christianity 394
  cults of Aphrodite and Apollo 152
  impact of Turkish invasion 448
  Maronites 395-96, 398, 418
  Middle Ages 180
  Ottoman period 394
  periodicals 647, 654
  role in ethnic conflict 404
  Turkish Cypriots 388-89
Religious bodies
  law 486
Religious festivals 429, 581-82
Religious history 419-20, 422-24, 674
Rendezvous in Cyprus 53
Report from the Select Committee on Cyprus: observations by the government 381
Report from the Select Committee on Cyprus: together with the proceedings of the committee, minutes of evidence and appendices 379
Report of the Department of Antiquities, 1940-1948 161
Report of the Department of Antiquities of Cyprus 666
Report on aspects of land tenure in Cyprus 524
Report on the archiepiscopal question 426
Report on west European communist parties 296

185

Report to the government of Cyprus on social security and related schemes 439
Report to the government of Cyprus on the development of medical care within the framework of a social security scheme 440
Reports of the Supreme Constitutional Court 479
Republic 5, 280, 287-89
  1963-64 crisis 232, 277-78, 281-83, 300, 304-05, 308, 470, 474, 476
  constitution 4, 262-63, 277-78, 286, 300, 316, 342, 346-47, 406, 467-70, 472, 474, 476, 484-86
  coup d'état, 1974 291, 299, 330-31, 333, 364-66, 371, 378
  elections 292
  government 4-5, 8, 277, 293, 300
  government, directories 669-70, 672
  Kophinou crisis, 1967 280, 325, 476
  politics 230, 277, 279, 282-83, 291-92, 297-99, 316-17, 341, 346, 349, 352, 354-55, 405
Republic of Cyprus and the events that have come to pass 285
Republican Turkish Party 645
Research for social welfare: six case studies in Cyprus 442
Revolts
  1764 197
  EOKA 2, 52, 222, 227, 232-33, 235-43, 246-52, 256-57, 259-61
  October 1931 215-17, 222
  peasant rising, 1191 170
Reynolds, S. 191a
Richard, J. 181-84
Richard the Lionheart 170, 177, 202
  biography 171
Riding the storm, 1956-1959 251
Rikhye, I. J. 327
Riley-Smith, J. 172-73
Rise and fall of the Cyprus Republic 291
Robertson, N. 128
Rocks and scenery in the Kyrenia region 23
Roman period
  archaeology 97, 114, 123
  architecture 97
  art 97, 130
  coins 593
  history 97
Rosenbaum, N. 267-68

Rossides, Z. G. 256
Royal Institute of International Affairs, Information Department 261
Rudnick, D. 356
Rudolf, J. D. 8
Rudt de Collenberg, W. H. 166
Rural development 526
Rural economy 521
Rural indebtedness and agricultural cooperation in Cyprus 521
Rural life 11, 201, 454, 520-22, 526
  bibliographies 680
  cooperative movement 521
  impact of EOKA revolt 260
  mediaeval 183-84
  poverty 520
Rural planning in Cyprus 526
Rural-urban fringe, Nicosia 459-61
Rusinow, D. I. 361
Russia
  relations with Cyprus, 19th century 206
  writings on Cyprus 688
Rustem, K. 11
Rustow, D. A. 309
Ryalis, A. 65

S

Sacopoulo, M. 6
Said, A. 402
Saint Katherine's Prison 431
St. Paul in Ephesus and the cities of Galatia and Cyprus 420
Saints 429-30, 435, 674
  Barnabas 419
  Neophytos the Recluse 430, 433
  Paul 419-20
Salamine de Chypre: histoire et archéologie, état des recherches 156
Salaminia (Cyprus): the history, treasures and antiquities of Salamis in the island of Cyprus 86
Salamis 86, 114-17, 123, 148-49, 153, 156
Salamis in Cyprus Homeric, Hellenistic and Roman 114
Salih, H. I. 411-12
Salisbury, Lord 205
Santamas, M. 596
Satiriki 634

Scala
  maps 40
Schlumberger, G. 594
Schmidt, D. 517
Scobie, W. I. 233
Sculpture 96-97, 116-17, 119, 567, 607
Sculptures from Salamis I 116
Sculptures from Salamis II 117
Sea shells 79
Second Five-Year Plan (1967-1971) 497
Secondary general education in Cyprus 543
Security, National 8
Seismic history of Cyprus 20
Seismology 20
SEK — Cyprus Workers' Confederation 630
Select Committee on Cyprus: minutes of evidence, 19 February 1976 380
Sentencing in Cyprus 488
Sergy, P. 398
Services, Public 534
Seven poems from Cyprus 556
Shaftesley, J. M. 399
Shepley, J. 353
Sheri courts 392
Shipwreck, Kyrenia 126
Shlaim, A. 515
Shopping
  periodicals 73
Short guide to the Cyprus Folk Art Museum 604
Short history of Cyprus 139
Shrines 431
Shrubs 75
Siapkaras-Pitsillides, T. 550
Sieges of Nicosia and Famagusta with a sketch of the earlier history of Cyprus 196
Simerini 612, 620
Simmons, L. 402
Sitas, A. 71
Sjoqvist, E. 92
Slaughtered spring 563
Sloan, S. R. 296
Slocum, J. L. 437
Small states in the modern world: the conditions of survival 343
Smith, A. 46
Smith, S. A. de 469
Smithsonian Institution 132

Social and economic rights under the law of the Republic of Cyprus 485
Social and historical data on population, 1570-1881 194
Social change 291, 450, 455-58, 500, 582
  impact on education 545
  impact on nationalism 463
Social change and urbanization in Cyprus: a study of Nicosia 458
Social history 437, 444, 494, 675
Social policy 498
Social sciences
  bibliographies 685
  periodicals 651
Social security 439-40
Social services 441-42
Social structure 291
  villages 452, 454
Social values
  villages 451-52
Social welfare in Cyprus 441
Society 4, 8, 291
  intercommunal cooperation 400
  mediaeval 170, 180, 183-84, 188, 191a, 566
  pressure groups 672
  statistics 450, 534
  traditional 48, 50, 451-52, 580-82
  Turkish Cypriot 265
Society of Cypriot Studies 654
Sociology 453, 460
Sofianos, C. 255
Soil 48, 522
  maps 38
Soli 92
Some relationships between geology and topography in Cyprus 22
Songs, Folk 588
Sophianos, C. 548
Sophocleous, A. 26, 676
Sophocleous, E. 73
Sophronios III, Archbishop 425
Soteriou, G. A. 567
Sotira 99
Sotira 93, 99
Soylemez, Y. 312
Soz 644
Spanos, N. S. 558
Spiteris, T. 130
Sport 220, 672
Spying 335
Spyridakis, Constantinos 140

187

Spyridakis, Costas 539, 542
Spyridakis, Konstantin 149
Stager, L. E. 120
Standard of living 51
Start in freedom 247
Stasinos 667
Statistical Abstract 534
Statistical data by ethnic group 535
Statistics 534-35
  banks and banking 534, 536-37
  economy 497
  ethnic communities 36
  ethnic groups 535
  finance 536-37
  industry 438
  labour 438
  migration 534
  prices 534, 537
  society 450
Statistics and Research, Department of 534
Status of intercommunal relationships on Cyprus 405
Statute laws of Cyprus in force on the 1st day of April, 1959 477-78
Stavrinides, Z. 352
Stavrinos, G. A. 79
Stavrou, N. A. 340
Stavrou, P. 13
Stavrovouni monastery 431
Stegenga, J. A. 318-19
Stephanou, C. 686
Stephens, R. 276
Stern, L. 330-31
Stevenson, Esmé Scott 45
Stewart, B. 48
Stewart, J. R. 93
Stone Age 106
  archaeology 93, 98-99, 101, 107
  art 130
Storrs, Ronald 215, 217, 220
Story of Cyprus Mines Corporation 494
Story of the Cyprus government railway 221
Strand, W. E. 148
Strategic position 203-04, 206, 245, 268, 276, 301, 306, 308-10, 324, 402
Stratigraphy 19
Street names maps 40
Struggle for Cyprus 233
Stubbs, W. 174
Studien zur Volksmusik Zyperns 587

Studies in the vegetation of Cyprus 74
Studies on prehistoric Cyprus 91
Studies on the Byzantine history of the 9th and 10th centuries 160
Studies presented in memory of Porphyrios Dikaios 129
Studies presented to David Moore Robinson 160
Study of the Cyprus economy 493
Stylianou, A. 17, 144, 191, 434, 568-69, 572
Stylianou, D. 56, 580
Stylianou, J. 17, 144, 434, 568, 572
Stylli 92
Subversion 335
  Greek involvement 330, 333-34
  US involvement 331, 334
Superstitions 582, 585-86
Supplementary excerpts on Cyprus or further materials for a history of Cyprus 137
Supreme Constitutional Court 479-80
Supreme Court 480-82
Surridge, B. J. 520
Survey of groundwater and mineral resources: Cyprus 29-30
Survey of international affairs 1931 216
Survey of rural life in Cyprus 520
Suspension of prohibitions against military assistance to Turkey. Hearing 374
Swedish Cyprus Expedition 91-97
Swedish Cyprus Expedition. Finds and results of the excavations in Cyprus 1927-1931 92
Swedish Cyprus Expedition: vol. 4, part 1A. The Stone Age and the early Bronze Age in Cyprus 93
Swedish Cyprus Expedition: vol. 4, part 1B. The middle Cypriote Bronze Age 94
Swedish Cyprus Expedition: vol. 4, part 1C-1D. The late Cypriote Bronze Age 95
Swedish Cyprus Expedition: vol. 4, part 2. The Cypro-geometric, Cypro-archaic and Cypro-classical periods 96
Swedish Cyprus Expedition: vol. 4, part 3. The Hellenistic and Roman periods in Cyprus 97
Sweet, L. E. 680
Swiny, S. 131

Syllabary, Cypriot 125, 147, 414
Symbiosis of the two communities 409
Symeonides, N. S. 342
Les syncrétismes dans les religions de l'antiquité 153
Szyncer, M. 155

T

Talbot Rice, D. 143, 566
Talbot Rice, T. 566
Tassos, A. 13
Tatton-Brown, V. 131
Taxation 510-11
  19th century 43
  law 512
  mining 502
Taylor, B. K. 442
Temperley, H. 206
Ténékidès, G. 278
Terrorism in Cyprus: the captured documents 238
Textbooks 544
Textiles 47, 566, 607
Theodoulou, C. 212-13
Theses
  bibliographies 684
Thin blue line: international peacekeeping and its future 327
Third emergency economic action plan 1979-1981 (summary) 499
Third Five-Year Plan (1972-1976) 498
Thomas, A. J. 343, 355
Thomas, Ann Van Wynen 343, 355
Thomas, Pierre de 423
Thompson, P. 556
Thomson, J. 42
Thorp, W. L. 492
Through Cyprus 46
Through Cyprus with the camera in the autumn of 1878 42
Thubron, C. 54
Thurston, H. 57
Tiberius, Emperor 593
Tides of fortune, 1945-1955 250
Tihony, Y. 67
Tillyrides, A. 425
Time of the blissful 560
To authorize appropriations for the Board for International Broadcasting for the fiscal year 1976; and to promote relations between the United States, Greece and Turkey to assist in the solution of the refugee problem on Cyprus, and to otherwise strengthen the North Atlantic alliance. Report: together with opposing, separate, supplemental and additional views on S. 2230 377
To promote improved relations between the United States, Greece and Turkey, to assist in the solution of the refugee problem of Cyprus, and to otherwise strengthen the North Atlantic alliance. Report: together with opposing, supplemental, dissenting, additional and separate views on S. 846 375
Tombs, Ancient 91, 100, 107, 115
Tomos K. Armenopoulou 466
Took, J. M. E. 82
Topography 90-91, 170
  geological factors 22
  Kition 119
  Nicosia 146, 188
  Paphos 16
Toponymy 145, 162
Tornaritis, C. G. 472-74, 477, 485-86
Touring Cyprus 66
Tourism 220, 491, 508, 513, 670, 672
  geographical factors 28
  statistics 534
Tourist maps 39
Towns 2, 6, 48, 56, 63, 90, 143, 202
  mediaeval period 170, 187
  Ottoman period 197
  street names maps 40
Toy, B. 53
Toynbee, Arnold J. 216
Trachonas 92
Trachonia 92
Trade 489-90, 499, 505-08
  directories 669-72
  mediaeval period 177
  Ottoman period 197
  periodicals 513, 537
  statistics 534, 537
  with the EEC 515, 517-19
Trade unions
  newspapers 630-31
  PEO 631
  SEK 630

Trade unions, Turkish Cypriot
  newspapers 641
  Turk-Sen 641
Traditional society 48, 50, 451-52,
  580-82
La tragédie Chypriote 231
Transport 66, 73, 672
  Cyprus Airways 508
  railway 221
  statistics 534
Travel guides 3, 6, 13, 55-67, 70
  Nicosia 14, 70
  Paphos region 16, 68-69
Traveler's guide to Cyprus 57
Travellers' accounts 674
  18th century 197
  19th century 42-47
  20th century 48-54
Travels in the island of Cyprus 197
Treasures in the Cyprus Museum 109
Treasures of Cyprus: an exhibition of Cypriot art 132
Treasures of Lambousa 17
Treaties 475
  Byzantine-Arab, 688 160
  Establishment, Guarantee and Alliance 229, 467, 476
  Lausanne 266
Treaties conflicting with peremptory norms of international law and the Zurich-London agreement 475
Trees 75, 522
Tremayne, P. 260
Trigonometrical survey of the island of Cyprus 37
Tripartite Conference, 1955 269
Tripartite Conference on the eastern Mediterranean and Cyprus 269
Triseliotis, J. 441
Trombetas, T. P. 315
Trooditissa monastery 43
Troodos mountains
  geology 21
  maps 38
Troulli 93
Tsiapera, M. 418, 427
Tsiknopoullos, I. P. 433
Turkey
  foreign policy 311-13, 345
  militarism 332
  relations with Cyprus 229, 265-66, 269, 272, 274-76, 281, 297-98,
  300, 305, 311-13, 332, 341, 348, 360, 476
  relations with Greece 266, 359, 382, 384-86
  relations with the USA 342, 373, 384
  US arms embargo 330, 374-77, 383
Turkey, Greece and NATO: the strained alliance. A staff report 385
Turkey's foreign policy in transition 1950-1974 313
Turkey's problems and prospects: implications for U.S. interests. Report 384
Turkish Affairs, Committee on 392
Turkish art in Cyprus 391
Turkish Cypriot Chamber of Commerce 639
Turkish Cypriot Federated State 473
Turkish Cypriots 195, 265, 274-75, 297, 342, 387, 408, 410, 412, 672
  19th century 45
  architecture 391
  art 391
  culture 388
  Cyprus Resettlement Project 328-29
  demography 388, 393
  distribution 32, 36
  economy 393, 495
  education 392
  emigration to Turkey 211
  history 388-89, 393
  language 388
  law 392
  libraries 689
  nationalism 284, 349, 389, 411
  newspapers and periodicals 390, 636-45
  political attitudes 286
  political parties 638, 642, 645
  politics 5
  religion 388-89
  social structure 265
  support of Young Turks 390
  trade unions 641
Turkish invasion, 1974 291, 313, 330-31, 336, 345-46, 348, 351, 354-56, 359, 363-72, 374, 378-82, 406, 446-49
  conditions in enclaved villages 448
  illustrations 338-39

impact on population distribution 34
impact on women 445
in literature 561, 563
legal problems 473-74, 476
violations of human rights 337
Turkish invasion of Cyprus and legal problems arising therefrom 473
Turkish newspapers and magazines published in Cyprus 1888-1915 390
Turk-Sen 641
Turner, B. S. 221
Twiss, T. 465
Tylliria region
land ownership 524

U

Ulman, H. 345
UNFICYP – United Nations Force in Cyprus 318-22, 324-28
Unified Democratic Centre Union Party – EDEK 618, 623
United Nations
Plaza Report 317
relations with Cyprus 228, 267, 283, 298-99, 306, 312, 317, 323, 342, 345, 355, 357-58, 362-63
United Nations Development Program 29-30
United Nations Force in Cyprus 318
United Nations Force in Cyprus – UNFICYP 318-22, 324-28
United Nations General Assembly 317
United Nations Monthly Chronicle 336
United Nations Security Council 317, 336, 471
Urban life 11
Urban planning
periodicals 665
Urban Planning and Housing, Department of 665
Urbanization 458-62
impact of ethnic conflict 35
US House of Representatives. Committee on International Relations (Foreign Affairs) 374-77
US House of Representatives. Select Committee on Intelligence 378
US House of Representatives. Special Subcommittee on Investigations, Committee on Foreign Affairs 373
US House of Representatives. Study Mission to Portugal, Greece, Yugoslavia, and Hungary, Committee on Foreign Affairs 371
US House of Representatives. Subcommittee on Europe and the Middle East, Committee on Foreign Affairs 384
US House of Representatives. Subcommittee on Europe, Committee on Foreign Affairs 370
U.S. intelligence agencies and activities. Hearings and proceedings: parts 1-6 378
US Library of Congress. Congressional Research Service 373
US Library of Congress. Foreign Affairs and National Defense Division, Congressional Research Service 296, 384
US military bases 373
US Senate. Committee on Armed Services 383
US Senate. Committee on Foreign Relations 372, 385-86
US Senate. Subcommittee on Health, Committee on Labor and Public Welfare 367
US Senate. Subcommittee to Investigate Problems Connected with Refugees and Escapees, Committee on the Judiciary 364-69
USA
arms embargo on Turkey 330, 374-77, 383
CIA 378
diplomacy 305, 340, 342
foreign policy 330, 340, 342, 344, 350, 367-69, 375-77, 382-83
involvement in subversion 331, 334, 378

relations with Cyprus 283, 297, 301,
    305, 309-10, 324, 330-31, 334,
    340-41, 356-57, 370, 385-86
relations with Greece 371-73, 375,
    377
relations with Turkey 345, 373, 384
study missions to Cyprus 364-66,
    371
Truman Doctrine 373
USSR
    relations with Cyprus 268
    relations with Turkey 345
    writings on Cyprus 688
Usury 521

V

Vanezis, P. N. 287-89
Vassiliou, G. 515
Vassiliou, S. 490
Vatican *Archivio Segreto* 181
Venetian period
    16th century accounts 178-79
    coins 594
    heraldry 602
    history 177-79, 183, 185, 191a, 196
Vermeule, C. 133
Verrier, A. 308
Vessberg, O. 97
Victoria, Queen 222
View from the Bronze Age: Mycenean and Phoenician discoveries at Kition 118
View from within: the role of small states and the Cyprus experience 321
Village Voice 378
Villages 6, 63, 90, 143, 429
    Alona 451-52
    Argaki 342, 454
    distribution of ethnic groups 32
    education 457
    enclaved 448
    impact of ethnic conflict 33
    impact of modernization 455-57
    Kakopetria 18
    Karavas 17
    Kissonerga 26
    Krasokhoria 25
    Lapithos 17
    life and customs 17, 18

Limassol district 25
Lysi 457
nationalism 453
Ottoman period 197
Paphos district 16, 26
politics 51, 454
property transfer 455
social structure 452, 454
social values 451-52
statistics 36
Turkish Cypriot 328-29
Villes mortes du Moyen Age 187
To Vima 635
Vital statistics 534
Vivliographia kypriakou dikaiou 683
Vivliographia tis kypriakis laographias kai glossologias 682
Voice of Cyprus: an anthology of Cypriot literature 552
Voices of stone: the history of ancient Cyprus 148
Volkan, V. D. 410
Voluntary services 442
Vouni 92
Ta Vyzantina mnimea tis Kyprou 567

W

Wade, H. W. R. 347
Wagenseil, J. 517
Wages 436
    collective bargaining 437
Wagner, W. 343
Waldheim, Kurt 363
Walker, A. 120
Wall-paintings 191, 434, 568, 570-74, 576-77
Walsh, F. R. 427
Wander, St. H. 579
Wanderer ballad 554
War prisoners 446
Ward, P. 66
Water resources 29-30, 492, 522, 524
    dams 531
    maps 38
Waterbury, J. 453
The way: Cyprus, a base for international operations 510
Weintal, E. 305
Weir, W. W. 538
Weiss, D. 517

192

Welfare 439-43
  implications of EEC association 519
  statistics 534
Western framework, 1978 357, 386
Westholm, A. 92, 97
Whitaker, D. P. 8
Who's who in Cypriote archeology:
  bibliographical and biographical
  notes 134
Who's whos
  archaeology 134
Wideson, R. 9-10
Wild flowers of Cyprus 77
Williams, Maynard Owen 49
Windsor, P. 306
Winfield, D. C. 573, 576
Wolff, R. L. 167
Women 45
  impact of Turkish invasion 445
Woodcarving 567
Working People's Uplifting Party
  — AKEL 294-96, 332, 615, 626
World hunger, health, and refugee
  problems: part 5. Human disaster
  in Cyprus, Bangladesh, Africa.
  Hearing 367
World War I 212
World War II 224, 227
  labour conditions 436
Worsley, P. 343
Wright, A. 10
Wright, G. E. 120
Wrong horse: the politics of inter-
  vention and the failure of
  American diplomacy 330

X

Xydis, A. G. 342
Xydis, S. G. 227-29, 341

Y

Yannopoulos, G. 515
Yearbook of the European Convention
  on Human Rights 337
Yeni Duzen 645
Yennaris, C. 672
Ygia 668
Yiangoullis, O. 459-61
Yiassemides, P. 527
Yon, M. 127
Young Turks 390
Younger, K. G. 325
Your guide to Cyprus 65
Your way around Paphos 69
Youth work 442

Z

Zaman 636
Zarmas, P. 587
Zevlaris, M. I. 549
Zurich-London agreements 222, 229,
  236, 251, 261-64, 268, 274-75,
  281, 304, 370, 470, 475
Die Zypernfrage 222

Map of Cyprus

This map shows the more important towns and other features mentioned in the text.

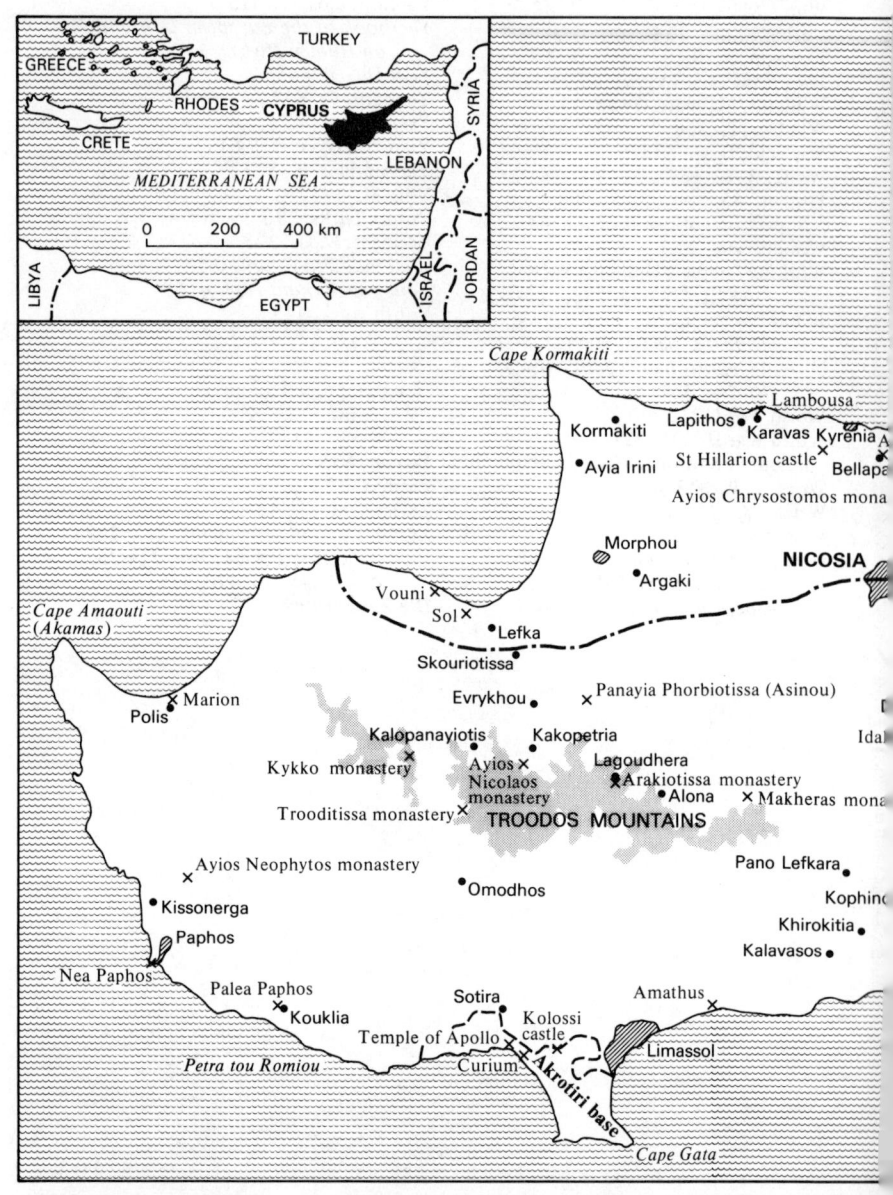

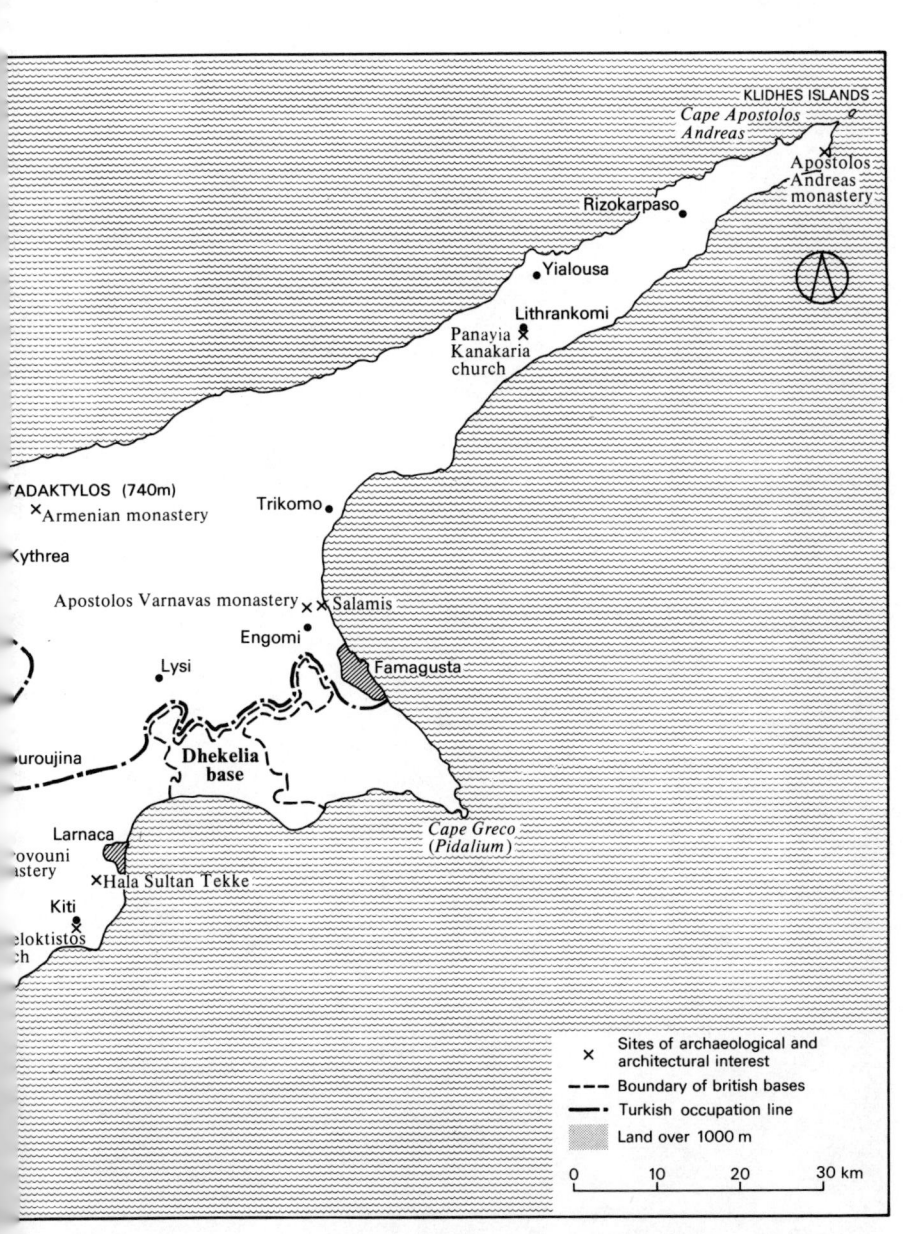

Z 3496 .K57 1982
Kitromilides, Paschalis.
Cyprus

AUG 2 1 1985